UNITS 13-18

INTER·ACTIVE Mathematics

Activities & Investigations

GLENCOE
McGraw-Hill

New York, New York   Columbus, Ohio   Mission Hills, California   Peoria, Illinois

Send all inquiries to:
Glencoe/McGraw-Hill
936 Eastwind Drive
Westerville, OH 43081

ISBN: 0-02-824487-7 (Student Resource Book)

3 4 5 6 7 8 9 10 VH/LH-P 01 00 99 98 97 96 95

To the Student:

Here is a book that will make middle school mathematics interesting and valuable for you. It is not like most other books that you have used; it doesn't have pages and pages of problems. What it does have, though, are activities, projects, and investigations that will help you become a good problem-solver. You will learn new ideas that build on what you have learned already, and you will use these ideas in solving real-life problems. At times you will learn with others in pairs and in groups and this will help you later in life when most problems are solved together. We believe that this book will create both excitement and an understanding of mathematics.

Best wishes for a successful year.

Sincerely,

David Foster

Sandie Gilliam

Kay McClain

Barney Martinez

Jack Price

Linda Dritsas

AUTHORS | INTERACTIVE MATHEMATICS

DAVID FOSTER

"The national goal is to develop mathematical power for all students. My vision for learning mathematics includes a student-oriented classroom culture, where students are taking charge of their own learning and are actively engaged in a curriculum that reflects today's world, not the mathematics of 150 years ago."

[signature: David Foster]

**Former Teaching Consultant
Middle Grades Mathematics
Renaissance
Morgan Hill, California**
Author of Units 1, 2, 5, 6, 7, 8, 10, 11, 13, 15, 16, 17, and 18

David Foster received his B.A. in mathematics from San Diego State University and has taken graduate courses in computer science at San Jose State University. He has taught mathematics and computer science for nineteen years at the middle school, high school, and college level. Mr. Foster is a founding member of the California Mathematics Project Advisory Committee and was Co-Director of the Santa Clara Valley Mathematics Project. Most recently, he has taken the position of Consulting Author for Glencoe Publishing. Mr. Foster is a member of many professional organizations including the National Council of Teachers of Mathematics and regularly conducts in-service workshops for teachers. He is also the author of a book on computer science.

SANDIE GILLIAM

"Many students only see mathematics as isolated number facts and formulas to memorize. By using this program, which incorporates the mathematics into a context of large, real-life units tied together with literature, science, and history, the middle school student can find meaning in the mathematics."

[signature: Sandie Gilliam]

**Mathematics Teacher
San Lorenzo Valley High School
Felton, California**
Co-author of Unit 14

Sandie Gilliam received her B.A. from San Jose State University and is a mentor teacher and instructor for the Monterey Bay Area Mathematics Project. She was a semi-finalist for the Presidential Award for Excellence in the Teaching of Mathematics in the state of California. Ms. Gilliam has served as a consultant for the California Department of Education and many local school districts and county offices of education. She is a member of the National Council of Teachers of Mathematics and is a frequent speaker at conferences and teacher in-service workshops. Ms. Gilliam was a writer and consultant for Glencoe's *Investigating Mathematics: An Interactive Approach.*

JACK PRICE

"This program is designed to help students become mathematically powerful as they develop problem-solving skills and self-reliance, as well as the ability to work well with others. At the same time, they will strengthen their basic skills and be exposed to new and exciting ideas in mathematics."

[signature: Jack Price]

**Co-Director, Center for Science
and Mathematics Education
California State Polytechnic
University
Pomona, California**
Author of Unit 3

Jack Price received his B.A. from Eastern Michigan University and his Doctorate in Mathematics Education from Wayne State University. Dr. Price has been active in mathematics education for over 40 years, 38 of those years at grades K through 12. In his current position, he teaches mathematics and methods courses for preservice teachers and consults with school districts on curriculum change. He is president of the National Council of Teachers of Mathematics, is a frequent speaker at professional conferences, conducts many teacher in-service workshops, and is an author of numerous mathematics instructional materials.

INTERACTIVE MATHEMATICS AUTHORS

KAY McCLAIN

"Building conceptual understanding in mathematics challenges us to re-define what it means to know and do mathematics. This program was developed to allow teachers to become facilitators of learning while students explore and investigate mathematics — strengthening their understanding and stimulating interest."

Kay McClain

**Doctoral Candidate
George Peabody College
Vanderbilt University
Nashville, Tennessee**
Author of Unit 9, Co-author of Unit 14

BARNEY MARTINEZ

"Students learn mathematics best when their teacher enables them to become actively involved in worthwhile mathematical investigations. Students should be encouraged to interact with each other. Then, through their collaborative efforts, students build their own understanding of mathematics."

Barney Martinez

**Mathematics Teacher
Jefferson High School
Daly City, California**
Co-Author of Unit 12

LINDA DRITSAS

"This program is designed to encourage students to be creative and inventive, while gaining mathematical power. Open-ended situations and investigations provide the setting that allows students to work at varying depths, while nurturing their natural curiosity to learn."

Linda Dritsas

**Mathematics Coordinator
Fresno Unified School District
Fresno, California**
Author of Unit 4, Co-author of Unit 12

Kay McClain received her B.A. from Auburn University and her Educational Specialist degree from the University of Montevallo in Montevallo, Alabama. While a teacher at Mountain Brook Middle School in Birmingham, she received the Presidential Award for Excellence in the Teaching of Mathematics in the state of Alabama. Ms. McClain is a Woodrow Wilson fellow and a member of the National Council of Teachers of Mathematics. She regularly conducts teacher in-service workshops and is a frequent speaker at local, state, and national mathematics education conferences. She is also an author of middle school mathematics instructional materials.

Barney Martinez received his B.S. in mathematics from The University of San Francisco and is an instructor of pre-service mathematics teachers at the College of Notre Dame in Belmont, California. Mr. Martinez currently serves on the Mathematics Development Team of the California Department of Education and the Pursuing Excellence Revision Advisory Committee. He is a member of the National Council of Teachers of Mathematics and is very active as a speaker and workshop leader at professional development conferences.

Linda Dritsas received her B.A. and M.A. from California State University at Fresno. She taught middle school mathematics for many years and, for two years, taught mathematics at California State University at Fresno. Ms. Dritsas has been the Central Section President of the California Mathematics Council and is a member of the National Council of Teachers of Mathematics and the Association for Supervision and Curriculum Development. She frequently conducts mathematics teacher in-service workshops and is an author of numerous mathematics instructional materials, including those for middle school students and teachers.

CONTRIBUTORS INTERACTIVE MATHEMATICS

Each of the Consultants read all 18 units while each Reviewer read one unit. The Consultants and Reviewers gave suggestions for improving the Student Resource Books, Teacher's Editions, Cooperative Group Cards, Posters, and Transparencies. The Writers wrote the Student Diversity Strategies that appear in the Teacher's Edition.

CONSULTANTS

Dr. Judith Jacobs, *Units 1-18*
Director, Center for Science
and Mathematics Education
California State
Polytechnic University
Pomona, California

Dr. Cleo M. Meek, *Units 1-18*
Mathematics Consultant,
Retired
North Carolina Dept. of
Public Instruction
Raleigh, North Carolina

Beatrice Moore-Harris,
Units 1-18
College Board Equity 2000
Site Coordinator
Fort Worth Independent
School District
Fort Worth, Texas

Deborah J. Murphy, *Units 1-18*
Mathematics Teacher
Killingsworth Jr. High School,
ABC Unified School District
Cerritos, California

Javier Solorzano, *Units 1-18*
Mathematics Teacher
South El Monte High School
South El Monte, California

WRITERS

Student Diversity
Teacher's Edition

Dr. Gilbert J. Cuevas
Professor of Mathematics
Education
University of Miami
Coral Gables, Florida

Sally C. Mayberry, *Ed.D.*
Assistant Professor
Mathematics/Science
Education
St. Thomas University
Miami, Florida

REVIEWERS

John W. Anson, *Unit 11*
Mathematics Teacher
Arroyo Seco Junior High
School
Valencia, California

Laura Beckwith, *Unit 13*
Mathematics Department
Chairperson
William James Middle School
Fort Worth, Texas

Betsy C. Blume, *Unit 6*
Vice Principal/
Director of Curriculum
Valleyview Middle School
Denville, New Jersey

James F. Bohan, *Unit 11*
Mathematics K-12 Program
Coordinator
Manheim Township School
District
Lancaster, Pennsylvania

Dr. Carol Fry Bohlin, *Unit 14*
Director, San Joaquin Valley
Mathematics Project
Associate Professor,
Mathematics Education
California State University,
Fresno
Fresno, California

David S. Bradley, *Unit 9*
Mathematics
Teacher/Department
Chairperson
Jefferson Jr. High
Kearns, Utah

Dr. Diane Briars, *Unit 9*
Mathematics Specialist
Pittsburgh City Schools
Pittsburgh, Pennsylvania

INTERACTIVE MATHEMATICS CONTRIBUTORS

Jackie Britton, *Unit 18*
Mathematics Teacher
V. W. Miller Intermediate
Pasadena, Texas

Sybil Y. Brown, *Unit 8*
Mathematics Teacher
Franklin Alternative Middle
School
Columbus, Ohio

Blanche Smith Brownley, *Unit 18*
Supervising Director of
Mathematics (Acting)
District of Columbia Public
Schools
Washington, D.C.

Bruce A. Camblin, *Unit 7*
Mathematics Teacher
Weld School District 6
Greeley, Colorado

Cleo Campbell, *Unit 15*
Coordinator of Mathematics,
K-12
Anne Arundel County
Public Schools
Annapolis, Maryland

Savas Carabases, *Unit 13*
Mathematics Supervisor
Camden City School District
Camden City, New Jersey

W. Karla Castello, *Unit 6*
Mathematics Teacher
Yerba Buena High School
San Jose, California

Diane M. Chase, *Unit 16*
Mathematics Teacher/
Department Chairperson
Pacific Jr. High School
Vancouver, Washington

Dr. Phyllis Zweig Chinn, *Unit 9*
Professor of Mathematics
Humboldt State University
Arcata, California

Nancy W. Crowther, *Unit 17*
Mathematics Teacher
Sandy Springs Middle School
Atlanta, Georgia

Regina F. Cullen, *Unit 13*
Supervisor of Mathematics
West Essex Regional Schools
North Caldwell, New Jersey

Sara J. Danielson, *Unit 17*
Mathematics Teacher
Albany Middle School
Albany, California

Lorna Denman, *Unit 10*
Mathematics Teacher
Sunny Brae Middle School
Arcata, California

Richard F. Dube, *Unit 4*
Mathematics Supervisor
Taunton High School
Taunton, Massachusetts

Mary J. Dubsky, *Unit 1*
Mathematics Curriculum
Specialist
Baltimore City Public Schools
Baltimore, Maryland

Dr. Leo Edwards, *Unit 5*
Director, Mathematics/
Science Education Center
Fayetteville State University
Fayetteville, North Carolina

Connie Fairbanks, *Unit 7*
Mathematics Teacher
South Whittier Intermediate
School
Whittier, California

Ana Marina C. Gomezgil, *Unit 15*
District Translator/Interpreter
Sweetwater Union
High School District
Chula Vista, California

Sandy R. Guerra, *Unit 9*
Mathematics Teacher
Harry H. Rogers Middle
School
San Antonio, Texas

Rick Hall, *Unit 4*
Curriculum Coordinator
San Bernardino County
Superintendent of Schools
San Bernardino, California

Carolyn Hansen, *Unit 14*
Instructional Specialist
Williamsville Central Schools
Williamsville, New York

Jenny Hembree, *Unit 8*
Mathematics Teacher
Shelby Co. East Middle
School
Shelbyville, Kentucky

Susan Hertz, *Unit 16*
Mathematics Teacher
Paul Revere Middle School
Houston, Texas

Janet L. Hollister, *Unit 5*
Mathematics Teacher
LaCumbre Middle School
Santa Barbara, California

Dorothy Nachtigall Hren, *Unit 12*
Mathematics Teacher/
Department Chairperson
Northside Middle School
Norfolk, Virginia

Grace Hutchings, *Unit 3*
Mathematics Teacher
Parkman Middle School
Woodland Hills, California

Lyle D. Jensen, *Unit 18*
Mathematics Teacher
Albright Middle School
Villa Park, Illinois

Robert R. Jones, *Unit 7*
Chief Consultant,
Mathematics, Retired
North Carolina Department
of Public Instruction
Raleigh, North Carolina

Mary Kay Karl, *Unit 3*
Mathematics Coordinator
Community Consolidated
School District 54
Schaumburg, Illinois

Janet King, *Unit 14*
Mathematics Teacher
North Gulfport Junior High
Gulfport, Mississippi

Franca Koeller, *Unit 17*
Mathematics Mentor Teacher
Arroyo Seco Junior High
School
Valencia, California

Louis La Mastro, *Unit 2*
Mathematics/Computer
Science Teacher
North Bergen High School
North Bergen, New Jersey

Patrick Lamberti, *Unit 6*
Supervisor of Mathematics
Toms River Schools
Toms River, New Jersey

Dr. Betty Larkin, *Unit 14*
Mathematics Coordinator
K-12
Lee County School District
Fort Myers, Florida

Ann Lawrence, *Unit 1*
Mathematics
Teacher/Department
Coordinator
Mountain Brook Jr. High
School
Mountain Brook, Alabama

Catherine Louise Marascalco,
Unit 3
Mathematics Teacher
Southaven Elementary
School
Southaven, Mississippi

Dr. Hannah Masterson, *Unit 10*
Mathematics Specialist
Suffolk Board of
Cooperative Education
Dix Hills, New York

Betty Monroe Nelson, *Unit 8*
Mathematics Teacher
Blackburn Middle School
Jackson, Mississippi

Dale R. Oliver, *Unit 2*
Assistant Professor of
Mathematics
Humboldt State University
Arcata, California

Carol A. Pudlin, *Unit 4*
Mathematics Teacher/
Consultant
Griffiths Middle School
Downey, California

Diane Duggento Sawyer,
Unit 15
Mathematics Chairperson
Exeter Area Junior High
Exeter, New Hampshire

Donald W. Scheuer, Jr., *Unit 12*
Mathematics Department
Chairperson
Abington Junior High
Abington, Pennsylvania

Linda S. Shippey, *Unit 8*
Mathematics Teacher
Bondy Intermediate School
Pasadena, Texas

Barbara Smith, *Unit 1*
Mathematics Supervisor,
K-12
Unionville-Chadds Ford
School District
Kennett Square, Pennsylvania

Stephanie Z. Smith, *Unit 14*
Project Assistant
University of Wisconsin-
Madison
Madison, Wisconsin

Dora M. Swart, *Unit 11*
Mathematics Teacher
W. F. West High School
Chehalis, Washington

Ciro J. Tacinelli, Sr., *Unit 8*
Curriculum Director:
Mathematics
Hamden Public Schools
Hamden, Connecticut

Kathy L. Terwelp, *Unit 12*
K-8 Mathematics Supervisor
Summit Public Schools
Summit, New Jersey

Marty Terzieff, *Unit 18*
Secondary Math Curriculum
Chairperson
Mead Junior High School
Mead, Washington

Linda L. Walker, *Unit 18*
Mathematics Teacher
Cobb Middle School
Tallahassee, Florida

CONTENTS

UNIT 13

START YOUR ENGINES

BUILDING MATH POWER

Interdisciplinary Applications

Teens In the News

Have you ever asked yourself this question:
When am I ever going to use this stuff?

Each unit begins with a *Teens in the News* feature about a successful, highly motivated teen who uses mathematics as an aid to his or her success.

UNIT 13 **Tim McCabe** of Falls Church, Virginia, is a teen who doesn't let a physical handicap keep him from accomplishing his goals.

UNIT 14 **Minnie Carachure** of Selma, California, is a teen who benefited from a series of changes in her life.

UNIT 15 **Stephen Lovett** of Reston, Virginia, started Lovett Enterprises, a car detailing service, when he was 13.

UNIT 16 **Dee Lakhani** of Staten Island, New York, is a teen who is learning about the world of high finance.

UNIT 17 **Tony Lloyd** of San Antonio, Texas, put his all into learning about math, health careers, and computers.

UNIT 18 **Jill Sheiman** of Fairfield, Connecticut, founded a cookie company called "Jill's One Smart Cookie, Inc.," at the age of 13.

Team Projects

The *Team Project* in each unit places you in a problem-solving situation that may have confronted the actual teen in *Teens in the News.*

UNIT 13 **You're in Good Company** Your team will use your knowledge of each other to form a business that best uses your strengths.

UNIT 14 **Measuring Up** Your team will do research to list units of measure and their origins.

UNIT 15 **How Slow Must You Go?** Your team will draw graphs to compare thinking distance, braking distance, and total stopping distance.

UNIT 16 **Mind Your Own Business!** Your team will form a small business and convince others that it would be a good investment.

UNIT 17 **I'm Floored!** Your team will design patterned tiles that could be used to cover a floor.

UNIT 18 **Good 'n' Fresh** Your team will determine cookie quality control factors and the best way to mail cookies to customers.

CONTENTS

UNIT 14
RUN FOR COVER
SURFACE AREA AND VOLUME

Interdisciplinary Applications

What's Different About
INTERACTIVE • MATHEMATICS?

What's a *toolkit*? What's a *menu station*? What is *assessment*? What's the purpose of a *journal* and a *portfolio*? You may not be very familiar with some of these terms. The following explanations may be helpful to you since nearly every unit contains these terms.

Mathematics Toolkit   Your math hosts are the characters in a script in which new mathematics tools are presented and explained. You are encouraged to use these tools to help solve problems and to add your own tools that you discover.

Menu Station Activity   Each Menu Station Activity is broken into five or six stations. In some Menu Station Activities, your group chooses which menu station activity to complete. In others, your group moves around the room and completes each station.

Assessment   According to the dictionary, assessment is the act of determining importance, size, or value. In school, assessment usually refers to the process of assigning grades. Here are some of the ways that assessment is continually built into your Student Resource Book.

- •Pre-Assessment Activity
- •Group Investigation
- •Individual Investigation
- •Final Assessment

•**Journals**   Journals are a perfect way to connect mathematics with your writing. In your journal, you are encouraged to summarize key topics, as well as to write about your accomplishments and frustrations.

•**Portfolios**   A portfolio is a collection of your work that you keep in a folder or bind in book form. A portfolio includes work that you have created and selected. In some cases, you will select what you think is your best work. In other cases, your teacher will select the work to be included.

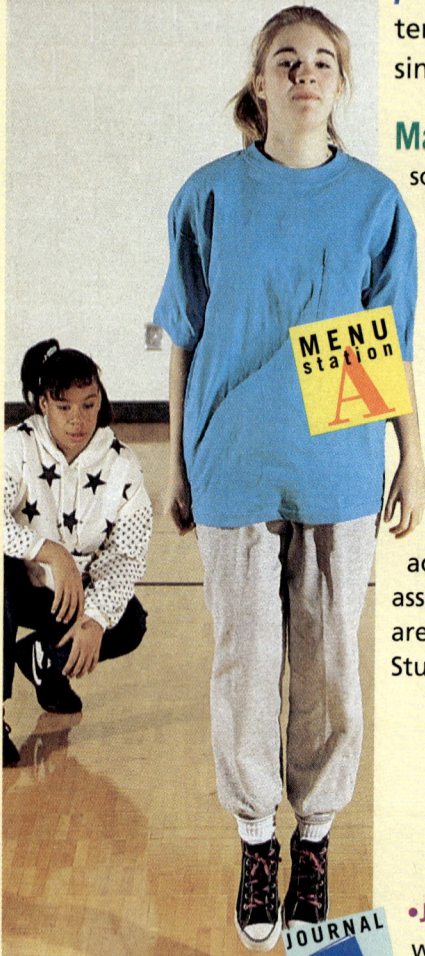

CONTENTS

UNIT 15
ON THE MOVE
GRAPHING AND FUNCTIONS

Interdisciplinary Applications

COMPUTER
investigation

NPUT DATA ENT
OAD SAVE BACK
LOPPY DISK KE
OARD MOUSE HA
RIVE DOS MEMO
RGRAMS FILES

Computer Investigations

Can you imagine what your life would be like without technology? It's truly difficult to imagine a world without computers, CDs, VCRs, calculators, and all the other wonderful electronic gadgets. The Computer Investigations in your Student Resource Book will expose you to powerful applications, many of which you will be able to use for a lifetime. The Computer Investigation Software makes it easy to complete each activity.

Unit 14 Activity Six   Cutting Corners
A **spreadsheet** is used to help determine a special relationship between the area of a square and the volume of a box.

Unit 15 Activity Eight   The Great Race
A **LOGO** program is used to allow you to race around a track, recording your time, speed, and distance traveled.

Unit 16 Activity Four   In Your Best Interest
A **BASIC** program is used to find the compound interest for an investment.

Unit 17 Activity One   Squares!
A **LOGO** program is used to help you discover relationships involving squares.

Activity Four   It's Chaos!
A **BASIC** program is used to make discoveries about fractals and chaos theory.

Activity Seven   Fractured Pictures
A **BASIC** program is used to help create a fractal according to your specifications.

Unit 18 Activity Three   The Ultimate Deli
A **BASIC** program simulates or mimics the operation of a deli. You will have the opportunity to organize the operation of the deli according to your specifications.

CONTENTS

UNIT 16

GROWING PAINS
LINEAR AND EXPONENTIAL GROWTH

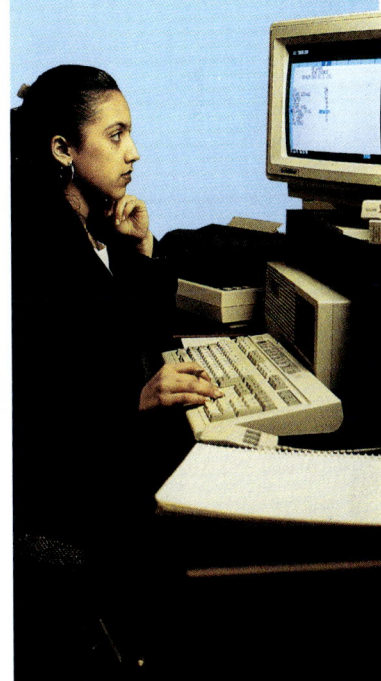

Interdisciplinary Applications

CONTENTS

UNIT 17

INFINITE WINDOWS

FRACTALS AND CHAOS THEORY

CONTENTS

UNIT 18

QUALITY CONTROL
APPLIED DATA ANALYSIS

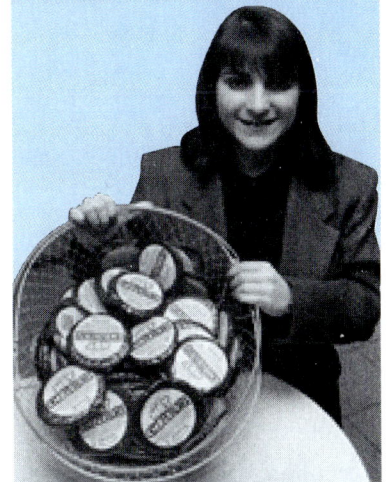

Interdisciplinary Applications

What's in the Back of Your Student Resource Book?

Have you ever wondered why all that extra material is in the back of textbooks? Have you ever used any of that stuff? In this book, the following items will be very useful to you as you work through all the activities and investigations.

PROBLEMS OF THE WEEK/EXTENDED PROBLEMS

At the end of each unit, you will find six to nine challenging Problems of the Week or Extended Problems connected to the mathematics of the unit. For example, the Problems of the Week and Extended Problems for Unit 14 are found on pages 69–74. These problems give you additional opportunities to explore the topics presented in the unit.

DATA BANK

This section, found on pages 229–261, is a group of references and resources designed to help you complete the activities and investigations or to complete an extension of an activity. One way you can think of the Data Bank is as a mini-reference library.

GLOSSARY/INDEX

The Glossary/Index on pages 262–273 contains an alphabetical listing of important words and terms. For some of the key words that you may not be familiar with, a definition is also given.

START YOUR ENGINES

Looking Ahead

In this unit, you will see how mathematics can be used to discover new methods of learning. You will experience:

▶ using manipulatives to learn new concepts

▶ working cooperatively to solve problems

▶ explaining how you solve problems through writing, speaking, and modeling

▶ learning new ways of showing what you have learned

▶ using technological tools such as calculators

Did You Ever Wonder?

What do mathematics and a "can do" attitude have to do with each other? Turn the page and see how Tim McCabe of Falls Church, Virginia, combines the two!

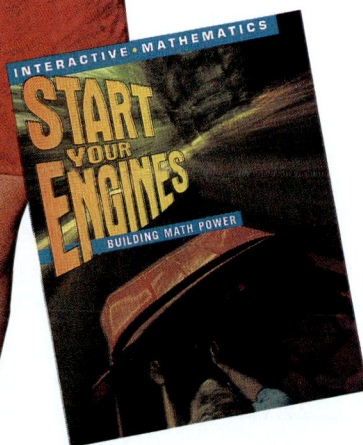

INTERACTIVE • MATHEMATICS

START YOUR ENGINES

BUILDING MATH POWER

Teens in the News

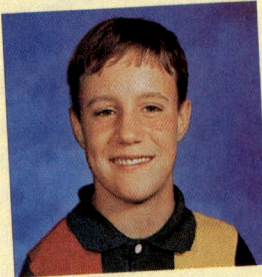

Featuring: Tim R. McCabe
Age: 14
Hometown: Falls Church, Virginia
Career Goal: Attorney or Psychiatrist
Interests: Athletics, history, travel

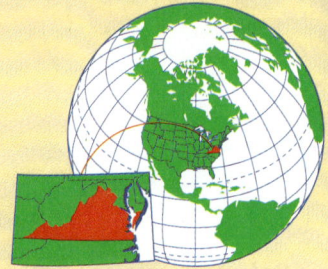

Tim R. McCabe was born without arms. Tim uses his feet to do everything! He is so flexible that he can dress himself, operate a computer, play soccer, and do almost anything other teenagers do.

Tim's school provides him with a laptop computer. He uses word processing to complete his school assignments. He is learning to use spreadsheets and databases too. Tim uses a calculator, rulers, and protractors—all with his feet —to complete his math assignments.

Tim has been playing soccer since he was about 4 years old. He expects to play on the varsity team as a sophomore at George Mason High School. Tim enjoys athletics because it gives him a chance to be with his friends and keeps him in good shape.

Like most teenagers, Tim is looking forward to driving a car. He hopes to get a special car that has the steering wheel, accelerator, and brake on the floor.

In 1991, Tim was awarded a national *Yes, I Can Award* as one of 35 exceptional youths in North America. After high school, he wants to attend college and major in pre-law or pre-med (medicine). He likes the idea of researching the "nooks and crannies" of the law to win cases. Pre-med appeals to Tim because he likes working with people. Tim's hard work and "can do" attitude will serve him well as he pursues his dreams.

Don't even think of parking here!

Fines for illegally parking in a handicapped zone

LOS ANGELES	MIAMI	MINNEAPOLIS	HOUSTON	ST. LOUIS	MANHATTAN
$330	$125*	$100	$75	$50	$50

*Fine doubles for second offense

Source: USA TODAY research

Team Project

You're in Good Company

Tim has definitely made the most of his abilities. He thinks in terms of what he *can do*, not in terms of what he *can't do*.

Imagine that you and your team members are forming a company. Your company wants to make the most of everyone's strengths. List three of your strengths.

Take some time to get to know each person in your group by discussing interests, families, goals, and so on. Then list a strength for each member of your team. Use these lists to decide what type of company you will form and to determine what company position each of you will assume. Present your company to the class.

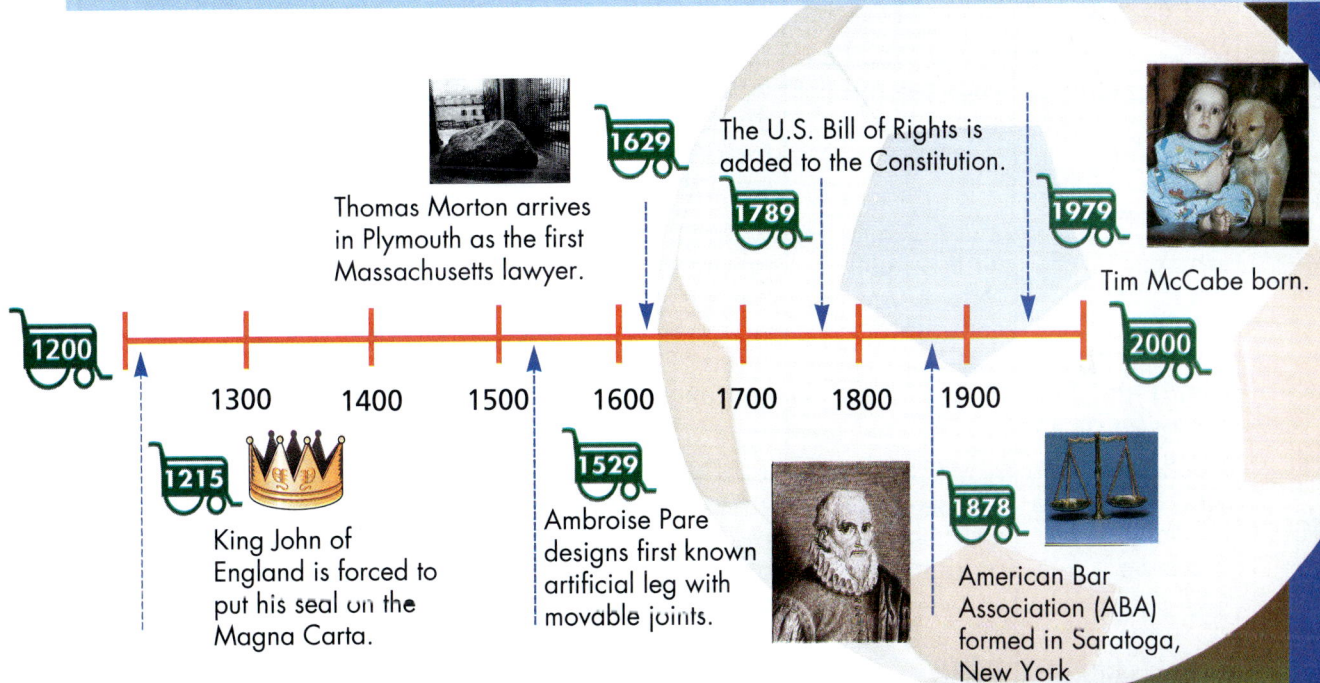

1629

The U.S. Bill of Rights is added to the Constitution.

Thomas Morton arrives in Plymouth as the first Massachusetts lawyer.

1789

1979

Tim McCabe born.

1200 | 1300 | 1400 | 1500 | 1600 | 1700 | 1800 | 1900 | **2000**

1215
King John of England is forced to put his seal on the Magna Carta.

1529
Ambroise Pare designs first known artificial leg with movable joints.

1878
American Bar Association (ABA) formed in Saratoga, New York

For more information

If you would like more information about the *Yes I Can Awards*, contact:

**Foundation for Exceptional Children
1920 Association Drive
Reston, Virginia 22091**

You can learn more about the math Tim uses by completing the activities in this unit.

Setting the Scene

TEAM BUILDERS

You Are Here

For each description below, find a person in your class or school...

whose neck has a circumference less than one foot	who can describe a *trapezoid*	who can explain the relationship between a *centimeter* and a *meter*	who can describe a pyramid	who wears a shoe size less than 6
whose palm has an area of about 80 square centimeters	who has the longest hair	who can locate an object that looks like a sphere	who can explain the difference between *perimeter* and *circumference*	whose arm is 50 centimeters long
who can explain the difference between the *radius* and the *diameter* of a circle	who is taller than 170 centimeters	whose ankle has a circumference of 20 centimeters	who can estimate the length of the chalkboard to within 5 inches	whose foot covers about 35 square inches
who can locate an object that is a *cube*	whose head has a circumference of 22 inches	who can explain the difference between a *quadrilateral* and a *parallelogram*	who can locate an object that is 20 inches long	whose arm span is more than 5 feet
whose foot is 10 inches long	who can move more than 5 feet in one step	who has a fingernail longer than 20 millimeters	who can explain the meaning of *area*	who knows how many feet are in a mile
who can explain the difference between a *cylinder* and a *cone*	who is 150 centimeters tall	whose thumb is less than 60 millimeters long	who knows how to find the area of a triangle	who has a finger less than 2 inches long

THE BEST BUY

Penny and Joshua plan to buy some blank cassettes. They discover that different stores sell the cassettes in different size packages and at different prices. The dots on the graph relate the number of cassettes per package and the cost per package at six different stores.

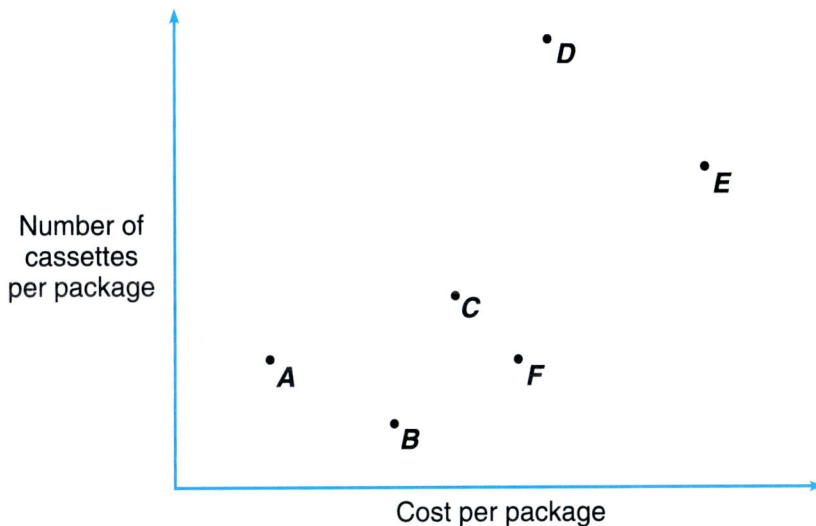

Number of
cassettes
per package

• D

• E

• C

• A

• F

• B

Cost per package

Answer each question. Explain your responses.

- Which package has the least number of cassettes?
- Which package costs the most?
- Do any of the packages cost the same? Explain.
- Do any of the packages weigh the same? Explain.
- Which package is a better deal, A or E? A or D? B or F?
- Which package is the best buy? Explain.

Sweatin' It Out

Tonya has designed a logo for the school drama club and the members of the club have decided to order t-shirts and sweatshirts with the new logo. Tonya and 24 other members each ordered one shirt. The total bill is $430. Each t-shirt costs $10, each regular sweatshirt costs $20, and each deluxe sweatshirt costs $25.

Tonya has forgotten how many deluxe sweatshirts the club members ordered, but she does know at least 6 members ordered one.

- How many deluxe sweatshirts were ordered?
- Can you find the exact number of each kind of sweatshirt ordered?
- Does the problem have more than one possible answer?
- Write a short narrative explaining your conclusions. Be sure you have answered the questions completely.

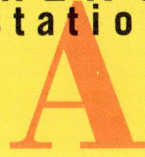

TANGRAMS AND POLYOMINOES

Tangram Designs

MENU
station
A

1 **U**se the tangram pieces to form squares.
- Can you form a square with 1 tangram piece?
- Can you form a square with 2 tangram pieces?
- Can you form a square with 3 tangram pieces?
- Can you form a square with 4 tangram pieces?
- Can you form a square with 5 tangram pieces?
- Can you form a square with 6 tangram pieces?
- Can you form a square with 7 tangram pieces?

2 **U**se the tangram pieces to form triangles.
- How many different triangles can you form with 2 tangram pieces?
- How many different triangles can you form with 3 tangram pieces?
- How many different triangles can you form with 4 tangram pieces?

3 **U**se tangram pieces to form quadrilaterals.
- Use 5 tangram pieces to form a square.
- Use 5 tangram pieces to form a rectangle that is not a square.
- Use 5 tangram pieces to form a parallelogram that is not a rectangle.
- Use 5 tangram pieces to form a trapezoid.

4 **U**se the tangram pieces to form polygons.
- Can you form a pentagon?
- Can you form a hexagon?
- Can you form an octagon?

5 **U**se your imagination to form at least 2 original designs.

MENU
station
B

Tangram Shapes

1 **S**uppose the area of the small tangram triangle is one square unit.
- What is the area of the tangram square?
- What is the area of the tangram parallelogram?
- What is the area of the large tangram triangle?

2 **U**sing the small tangram triangle as one square unit, make a figure that has an area of 10 square units.
- Describe the angles of the figure.
- Describe the other geometric characteristics of the figure.

3 **S**uppose the area of the large tangram triangle is one square unit. Make a figure that has an area of $2\frac{1}{2}$ square units.
- Describe the geometric characteristics of the figure.
- Compare this figure with the figure you made in Exercise 2.

4 **M**ake a triangle, a square, and a trapezoid so that each figure has the same area as the others.

Tangram Angles

1 **D**escribe the angles of each tangram piece.
- How many of the angles are acute angles?
- How many of the angles are right angles?
- How many of the angles are obtuse angles?

2 **U**se the tangram pieces to form figures with exactly 2 acute angles and 2 obtuse angles.
- Can you form such a figure with 2 tangram pieces?
- Can you form such a figure with 3 tangram pieces?
- Can you form such a figure with 4 tangram pieces?
- Can you form such a figure with 5 tangram pieces?
- Can you form such a figure with 6 tangram pieces?
- Can you form such a figure with 7 tangram pieces?

3 **U**se the tangram pieces to form a figure with exactly 1 acute angle, 2 right angles, and 1 obtuse angle. Draw the figure and describe its other geometric characteristics.

4 **U**se the tangram pieces to form a figure with exactly 3 right angles and 2 obtuse angles. Draw the figure and describe its other geometric characteristics.

5 **C**over the figure on Blackline Master 13-2B using all the tangram pieces. Do not cover the black region. Draw your solution. Describe how you solved the puzzle.

Polyominoes

This activity will use one-square-inch tiles. These tiles *can* be placed side by side, so that they share one edge; however, they *cannot* be placed diagonally, so that they share only a vertex.

This placement is acceptable.

This placement is not acceptable.

The shapes that are made when you place the tiles side by side are called **polyominoes**. Each polyomino can be named by the number of tiles used. If there are two tiles, the shape is called a *domino*. Three tiles are called *triominoes*, four tiles are called *tetrominoes*, and six tiles are called *hexominoes*.

1 How many dominoes are there?

2 How many triominoes are there?

3 How many tetrominoes are there?

4 If you were working with hexominoes, how would you be sure that you had found all of the possible shapes?

5 What strategy did you use to be sure you found all of the shapes that are possible? What discoveries, observations, surprises, or generalizations did you find as a result of this exploration?

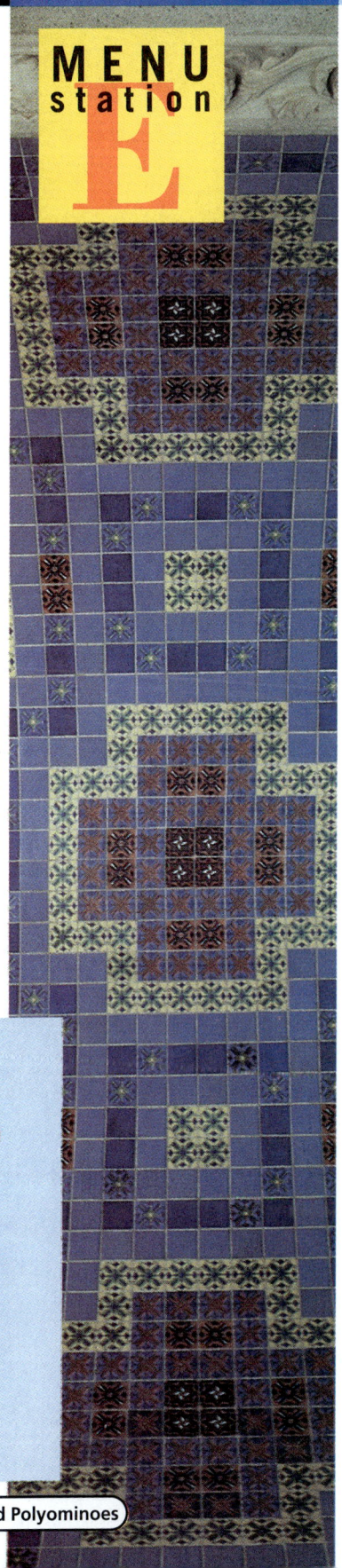

Pentominoes

This activity will use one-square-inch tiles. These tiles *can* be placed side by side, so that they share one edge; however, they *cannot* be placed diagonally, so that they share only a vertex.

This placement is acceptable.

This placement is not acceptable.

The shapes that are made when you place the tiles side by side are called **polyominoes**. Each polyomino can be named by the number of tiles used. If there are five tiles, the shape is called a *pentomino*.

1 How many pentominoes are there?

2 Use one-inch square tiles to form all the pentominoes that you have discovered. Can you arrange 5 tiles in ways other than the pentominoes in Exercise 1? Explain your answer.

3 Each member of your group should write a description of how to form one of the pentominoes with the tiles. Place the descriptions in a container. Then each member should choose a different description and see if he or she can match the correct pentomino with the description.

4 Continue picking descriptions and matching them with the pentominoes. Discuss which descriptions are confusing and which descriptions are specific. How could you clarify the confusing descriptions?

Do You Have a Clue?

The information your group needs to solve a problem has been put on clue cards. Each member of your group will have a different piece of information, so your entire group will have to cooperate to solve the problem.

Each group will receive an envelope with six clue cards in it. There will be enough cards so that each member of your group will receive at least one. When the clues are distributed, you may look only at your own card. You may tell others what your clue is, but you may not show your card to anyone else.

Your task is to work together to solve a problem. After you have solved the problem, write a one-page report that includes answers to the following questions.

- What worked well in your group?
- How did your group decide on a process for solving the problem?
- Was there more than one solution to the problem? Why or why not?

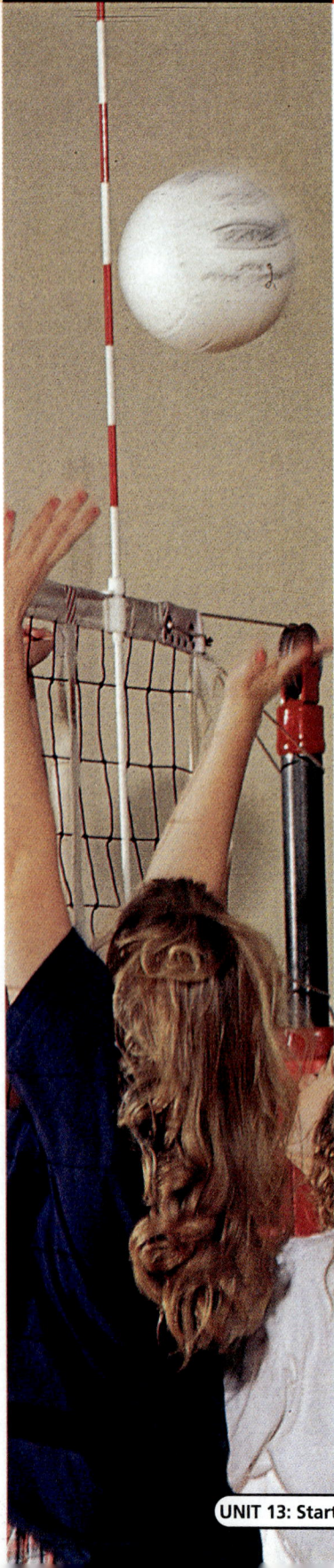

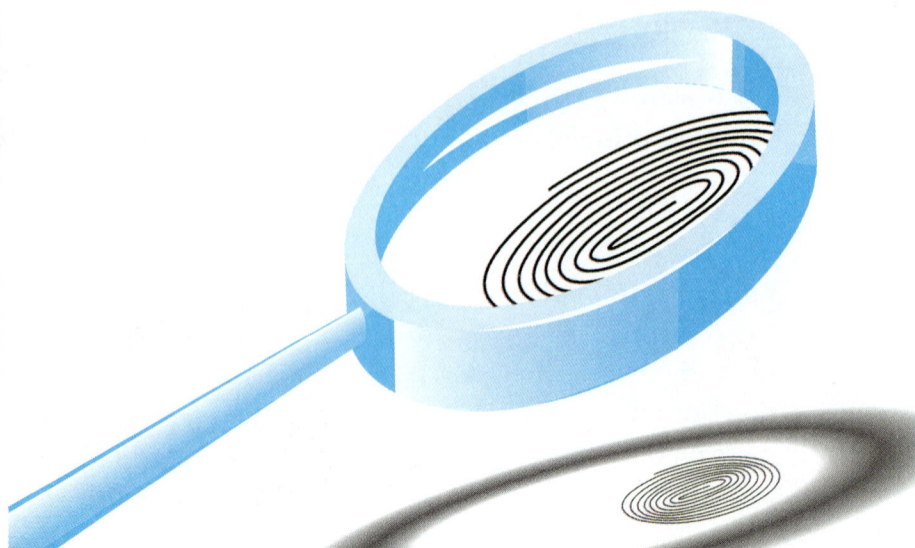

All Tied Up

This activity will help you to experience mathematics through movement. Here's what you do.

1. Get into groups of between 6 and 10 students. Join hands to make a circle.

2. Each member of your group should move toward the center of the circle until he or she is standing shoulder to shoulder with another member of the group. Then drop hands.

3. Now try to rejoin hands with two people in the circle according to the following rules.

   - A person may not join hands with another person that has been directly to their immediate left or right.

   - You must join hands with two different people. That is, two people may not join both of their hands together.

4. When everyone has rejoined hands according to the rules, try to untangle yourselves. All members of your group must continue holding hands throughout the entire untangling process.

5. Repeat the process several times to see if the outcome is always the same.

When you have successfully untangled yourselves several times, write a one-page narrative describing the process. Here are some questions you may want to answer.

- What do untangled formations look like?
- Do all group sizes untangle in the same way or with the same result?
- Can you predict beforehand what will occur? Why or why not?
- Can you justify your findings? Explain.

Switching Places

You will use the playing board below to play this game. Place three markers of the same color on the squares labeled A and three markers of a different color on the squares labeled B.

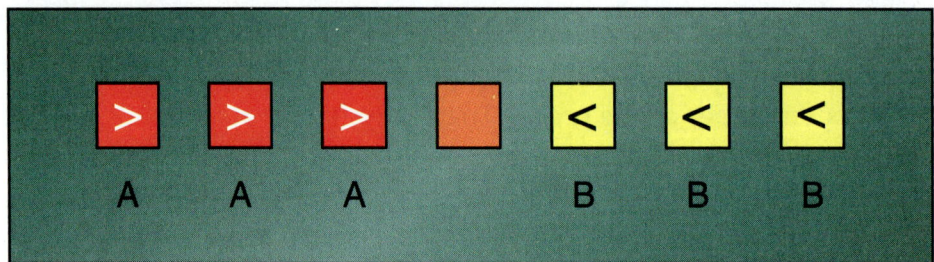

The goal of this game is to move all the markers on the A side to the B side and all of the markers on the B side to the A side. In other words, you want to switch the markers. To play this game, you will need to keep in mind the following rules.

- The markers on the right must always move to the left.
- The markers on the left must always move to the right.
- A marker can move into an empty space next to it.
- A marker can jump one marker of the other color if it lands on an empty space. The marker must start and end on a space next to the marker being jumped.
- A marker *cannot* jump a marker of the same color.
- One marker is moved at a time.
- No two markers can be on the same space at the same time.

Suppose three markers of one color were placed on the A side of the playing board and three markers of another color were placed on the B side of the board.

- How many moves would it take to get all of the markers on the A side over to the B side and all of the markers on the B side over to the A side?
- What would be the least number of moves necessary?
- How do you know that you have the least number of moves possible?

Design a recording sheet to keep track of your strategies and your findings. Be sure that it is clear and complete.

Write a one-page report detailing your findings. Make sure that you answer the following questions.

- What would happen if there were more markers on each side?
- What if there were a different number of markers on each side, like four on one side and five on the other side? Does your solution still work?

Hit the Target

Let's play a number game.

1. Name five 2-digit numbers.
2. Select one of the five numbers as the target.
3. Use the other four numbers in some combination, using any operations you choose (+, −, ×, or ÷), to write an expression that equals the target number. You can only use each of the four numbers once.

For example, say your numbers are 18, 27, 29, 33, and 36 and you want to make 33. Your expression could be 36 ÷ (27 − 18) + 29.

$$36 ÷ (27 − 18) + 29 = 36 ÷ 9 + 29$$
$$= 4 + 29$$
$$= 33$$

Develop at least five *Hit the Target* problems.

Extension

Select a significant year, like the year in which you were born, or a historical year like 1776. Then create the numbers 1 through 50 using each of the digits in that year exactly once.

For example, say you chose the year 1961. Here's how to get started.

$$9 − 6 − 1 − 1 = 1 \qquad (9 − 6) × 1 × 1 = 3$$
$$9 − 6 − 1 × 1 = 2 \qquad 9 − 6 + 1 × 1 = 4$$

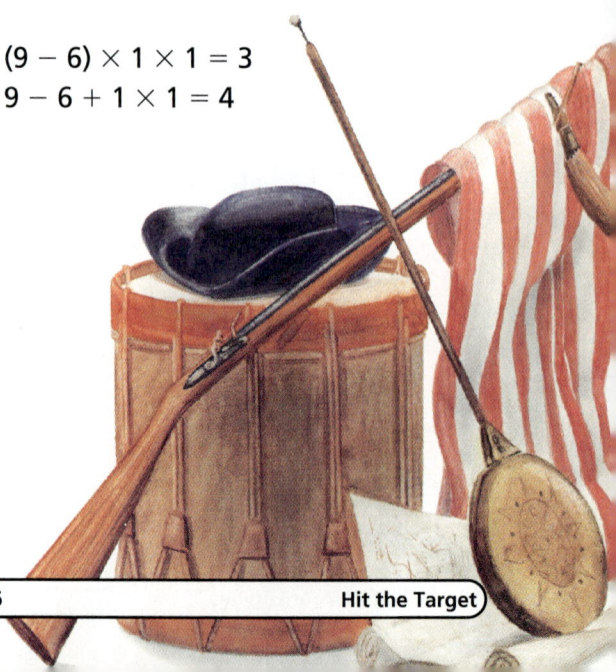

Sequences

A sequence is a list of numbers, called *terms*, that are in a specific order. Examine the sequences below. Determine the rule that will help you extend each sequence and list the next three numbers in the sequence.

a. 96, 48, 24, 12, 6, ...

b. 0, 3, 8, 15, 24, ...

c. $\frac{1}{3}$, $\frac{3}{4}$, 1, $\frac{7}{6}$, $\frac{9}{7}$, ...

d. 2, 5, 11, 23, 47, ...

Could there be more than one rule for extending the sequences? Give an example of a situation where this could be the case. Explain how you arrived at your conclusions.

A Frozen Treat

John Venn (1834–1923) was an English logician who used diagrams to help solve problems. Overlapping circles indicate sets that share some of the same elements. These diagrams, like the one shown at the right, are called **Venn diagrams**.

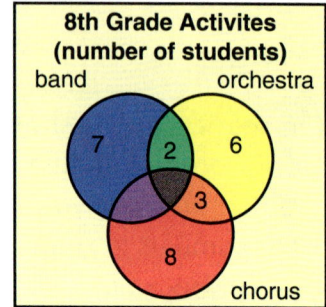

8th Grade Activites (number of students)

band / orchestra / chorus

7 2 6 3 8

Jared conducted a survey in his homeroom about the kinds of frozen yogurt that his friends like. His results are shown in the table below.

Student	Preference
Jared	vanilla, chocolate, strawberry
Jorge	chocolate, strawberry
Keisha	chocolate
Carmen	chocolate, vanilla
Meagan	vanilla, strawberry
Lu-Chan	vanilla
Brittany	chocolate
Nate	strawberry, vanilla
Chad	none (He's allergic to milk.)
Ichiko	strawberry

Make a Venn diagram of the students' preferences.

Make another Venn diagram. You will need to conduct a survey to gather data for your diagram. Here are some topics to choose from.

- pets
- favorite radio stations
- favorite pizza toppings
- favorite types of music
- favorite TV shows
- favorite video games

You may want to limit the choices to two, three, or four items.

Spring Fashions

Andy designs clothes. He is designing some new slacks and shirts for next spring, but he has lost track of how many of each type of garment he has already completed.

- An assistant counts the plaid slacks. There are 11 plaid slacks.
- Andy knows that he has completed a total of 32 shirts. Some of the shirts are plaid, some are striped, and the rest are a solid color.
- Andy also knows that he has completed a total of 27 slacks. The slacks are either plaid or a solid color.
- Andy and his assistant remember that 17 of the garments are plaid.
- Nineteen of the garments are a solid color.

Can Andy and his assistant determine how many of each type of garment he has completed? Organize the data in this problem. If possible, determine how many plaid shirts, striped shirts, solid-color shirts, plaid slacks, and solid-color slacks Andy has completed. Explain your reasoning.

International Festival

Your school is planning an international festival. Students with ties to other countries are asked to display items from the countries, and the French, Spanish, and German clubs are planning to sell food. Your group is in charge of arranging the cafeteria for the festival.

The rectangular cafeteria is 40 feet by 45 feet. Large doors for entering and exiting the cafeteria are along one of the sides that measures 40 feet. The school has tables that are $6\frac{1}{2}$ feet by $2\frac{1}{2}$ feet. You should allow a minimum of 4 feet between each table to allow for the movement of visitors.

The following is a list of clubs and students who want space at the festival.

- Each club wants 35 square feet to sell their food.
- Miwa Yamaguchi wants 25 square feet to display items from her native country Japan.
- Niki Marsico wants 20 square feet to display items from her grandfather's native country Italy.
- Ton Pham wants 20 square feet to display items from his parent's native country Vietnam.
- Rosa Garcia wants 40 square feet to display items from her native country Mexico.
- Kholic Hamilton wants 30 square feet to display items from his mother's native country Kenya.
- Ali Reda wants 35 square feet to display items from his native country Syria.

Prepare an oral presentation about how you would arrange the tables, the clubs, and the exhibitors. Include in your presentation your strategies, assumptions, and conclusions.

Collect 'Em All

The baseball cards of six of the all-time greatest baseball players are being reissued and put into bubble gum packages. Each package has Babe Ruth, Lou Gehrig, Ty Cobb, Ted Williams, Joe DiMaggio, or Willie Mays. The cards have been distributed randomly, but evenly.

How many of the gum packages would you have to buy in order to collect the complete set of player cards? Be sure to explain your thinking completely. How might the information you have learned from this investigation help you in other decision-making situations?

GAME OF THE CENTURY

BABE RUTH
AMERICAN LEAGUE – RIGHT FIELD   1933

TED Williams
BOSTON RED SOX OUTFIELD

LOU GEHRIG

Lou Gehrig says.

TRIPLE CROWN WI

HORSE

The game of HORSE is played with a basketball and a hoop. When two players play this game, one player shoots the basketball from any place on the court. If he or she makes the shot, the other player must shoot the ball from the same location. If the second player misses the shot, he or she gets a letter in the words *HORSE*.

If the second player makes the shot, the first player picks any location and attempts another shot. The game continues in this fashion until the first player misses a shot. At this time, the roles of the players switch. The second player picks the location of the shot and attempts to make the shot, and then, assuming the shot is made, the other player must duplicate the shot or receive a letter.

Nick and Amy are playing the game of HORSE. They are both 50% shooters. In other words, for any given shot, Nick and Amy are as likely to make the shot as to miss it. At this point in the game, Nick has three letters and Amy has one letter. Amy is the lead shooter. Estimate the probability that Amy will win the game.

Make a plan for solving this problem. Carry out your plan recording all information as you work. Explain each step and your conclusion.

Music, Music, Music

The music department at Kennedy Middle School is planning a fall production. Scheduling the order of the performance is a problem since many students are in more than one performing group.

- There are a total of 159 students who are performing.
- Two students are in all three performing groups: the chorale, the band, and the orchestra.

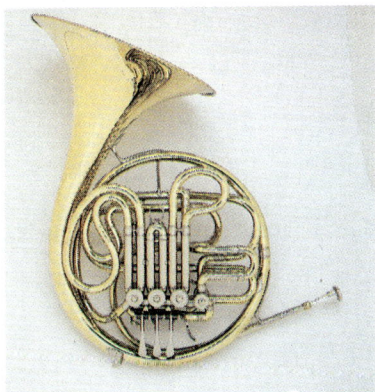

- The chorale has 55 members.
- The band has 84 members.
- One third of the band members also sing in the chorale.
- One fifth of the chorale members also play in the orchestra.
- Five students play in both the band and the orchestra, but not in the chorale.

How many students are in each group? How many are only in the chorale? only in the band? only in the orchestra? How many are in both the chorale and the band? the band and the orchestra? the orchestra and the chorale? Explain your reasoning. Try to justify your conclusion in at least two ways.

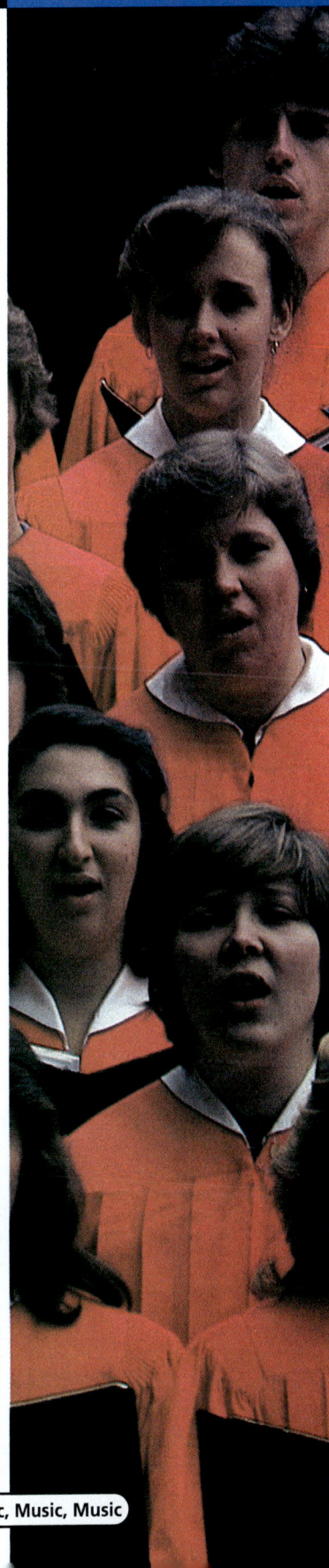

Not On the Lines

You will use the game board your teacher has provided to play this game.

Place a red marker in each of the boxes labeled 1 and 2. Place a yellow marker in each of the boxes labeled 9 and 10. Your task is to get the two markers on the left to exchange places with the two markers on the right. Here are the rules.

- You can move a marker one at a time, as far as you wish, along the lines. You may not stop on the lines, only at the boxes.
- At the end of any move, the markers from opposite sides may not lie on the same straight line.

Work with a partner if you wish. See if you can find the shortest, most efficient solution. How will you know if you have found it? Record your strategies, what works and what doesn't work, and any solutions you may reach.

Who's Who?

Five friends who attended Camp Wilderness when they were teenagers have come together for a reunion. The friends are Carlos, Doug, Masato, Alyssa, and Heidi. Their occupations are teacher, scientist, electrician, veterinarian, and park ranger, but not necessarily in that order. As the friends sat around the campfire remembering old times, they decided to take turns telling old camp stories.

Use the clues to determine each person's occupation, the order of the stories, and who told each story.

- The park ranger told a story that made Masato and Heidi laugh.

- While listening to the story about the great chief, the teacher and Carlos were bothered by mosquitoes. However, the veterinarian was too interested in hearing the story to notice the mosquitoes.

- The park ranger and Carlos had not remembered the story that the electrician told.

- The teacher listened to the story about the old trapper and the next story about the sly fox, while Doug planned the tale that would follow these two stories.

- Alyssa, Masato, and the veterinarian were not interested in the third story about why the eagle soars.

- Being a professional scientist, Carlos told a story about his favorite animal.

- As Alyssa completed the last story about the resident ghost of the lodge, she noticed that everyone except the electrician had fallen asleep.

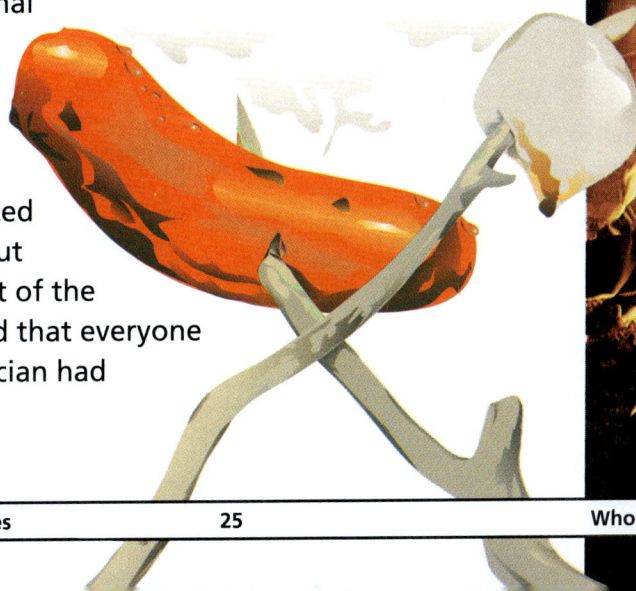

Selection and Reflection

- Describe one thing you learned from working in a cooperative group in this unit.

- Describe one thing you learned by working with manipulatives in this unit.

- What was your favorite activity in this unit? Gather together the papers or the work you did in your favorite activity. Explain what the activity was about and why you liked it.

- Was there anything you studied in this unit that you still feel you don't understand? Explain.

The Problem

Teresa is taking a vacation in Mexico. She goes to a souvenir shop to buy souvenirs for her family and friends back home. The souvenirs she likes best are the brightly painted clay pots for $10.00 each, the beaded necklaces for $3.00 each, and the pencils with "Mexico" printed on them for $0.50 each. If she wants to spend exactly $100.00 and buy at least one of each type of souvenir, how many of each item should she buy?

South of the Border

Extension Suppose the pots were $7.00 and the pencils were $0.25. How many of each item should she buy then?

Rep-Tiles

The Problem

Certain polygons, such as the ones shown below, can be fitted together to form the same shape in a larger size. Solomon Golomb, a mathematics and engineering professor at the University of Southern California, discovered a large class of these polygons and called them *Rep-Tiles*.

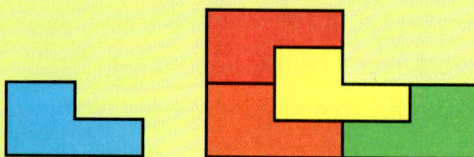

Using the trapezoid at the right, create a Rep-Tile of this trapezoid.

Extension Using the polygon at the right, create a Rep-Tile of this polygon.

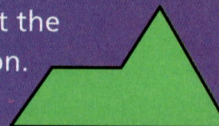

The Problem

Four married couples hike together in the Smoky Mountains every spring. The men's names are Ken, Ernesto, Charles, and Dan. The women's names are Carmen, Eva, Dawn, and Kate. Use the following clues to determine who is married to whom.

1. Dawn is Ken's sister.
2. Kate has two brothers, but her husband is an only child.
3. Dan was the best man at Dawn's wedding.
4. The names of Carmen and her husband both begin with the same initial.

Carmen is married to Charles; Eva is married to Ken; Dawn is married to Ernesto; Kate is married to Dan.

Take a Hike!

Winning Combinations

1234567890
1234567890
1234567890
1234567890

The Problem

The number puzzle below is similar to a word search puzzle. The goal of this puzzle is to find and circle as many number combinations as you can find that, when linked together with operation symbols like +, −, ×, ÷, and =, will form a correct mathematical equation. Three of these number combinations have already been circled for you. Find at least five more.

15	5	10	42	14	66
7	6	9	3	56	38
3	7	42	10 + 18 = 28		
63	5	49	2	31	20
7	13	12	32	43	4
1	9 × (3 + 6) = 81				5

(9 = ... ÷ ... 63)

The Problem

Figure A contains 3 rectangles.

Figure B contains 9 rectangles.

Figure C contains 18 rectangles.

How many rectangles are there in Figure D?

Ⓐ
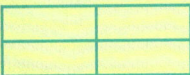

Ⓑ

Ⓒ
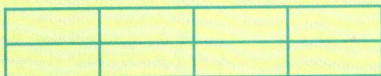

Ⓓ
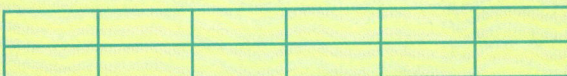

Ⓔ

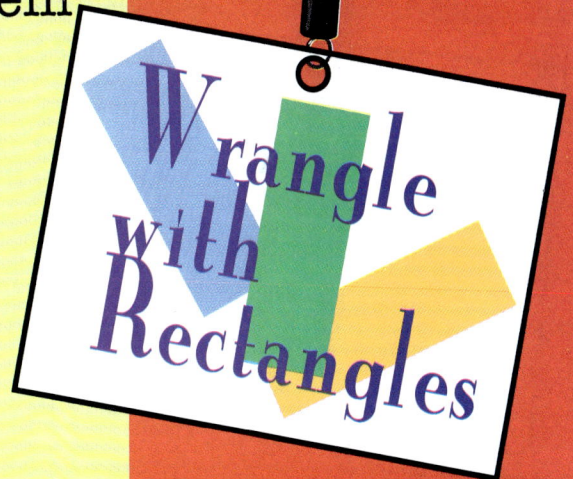

Extension How many rectangles are there in Figure E?

CHOSEN AT RANDOM

The Problem

Yuji has 2 red pens, 3 blue pens, 1 black pen, and 4 green pens in his desk drawer. All of the pens are the same size and shape. Suppose he opens the drawer and grabs a pen without looking. In other words, he chooses the pen at random and each outcome is equally likely. What is the probability that the pen chosen is blue? $\frac{3}{10}$

RUN FOR COVER

INTERACTIVE MATHEMATICS

RUN FOR COVER

SURFACE AREA AND VOLUME

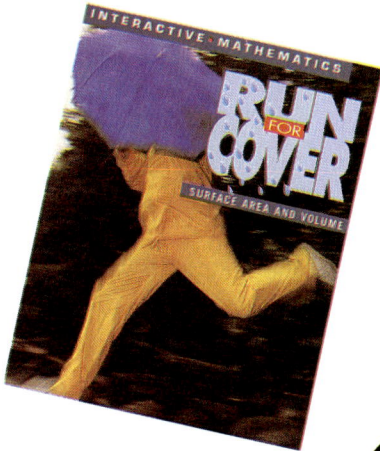

Looking Ahead

In this unit, you will see how mathematics can be used to answer questions about surface area and volume. You will experience:

▶ discovering formulas for the area of geometric figures

▶ finding the volume of solid figures

▶ exploring surface area by building a parachute

▶ examining the relationship between surface area and volume in objects of varying shape and size

Did You Ever Wonder?

What do mathematics and changing relationships have to do with each other? Turn the page and see how Minnie Carachure of Selma, California, combines the two!

Teens in the News

Featuring: Minerva "Minnie" Carachure
Age: 18
Hometown: Selma, California
Career Goal: Civil engineering and politics
Interests: Working with people

Minerva "Minnie" Carachure grew up in a family of six children. When Minnie was barely ten years old, her mother died. Minnie's father tried to raise the children by himself. However, in 1989, Minnie and her brothers and sisters were placed in foster homes. Since then, Minnie has been in ten foster homes!

All of these changes were hard on Minnie. She was very angry with the world. Minnie's anger and the choices she made got her expelled from high school her freshman year.

Minnie was moved to a foster home in Selma, California, where she entered Selma High School. She met two friends at Selma High who helped her change her life. Her friends didn't believe in peer pressure. They told Minnie that every choice she made was hers and hers alone.

Now Minnie chooses to spend her time in fun, productive activities. She was elected Student Body President her senior year. She belongs to the Mathematics, Engineering, and Science Achievement Club and serves as a math tutor and peer counselor to other teens. As a member of Students for the Ethical Treatment of Animals, Minnie helps out at the local animal shelter. She even finds time to work as a grocery store cashier.

The one thing that has been constant in Minnie's life is *change*. Minnie has decided that *good change* is a wonderful thing!

Market of the Future

Breakdown of U.S. children age 14 and under

1993 56,824,000

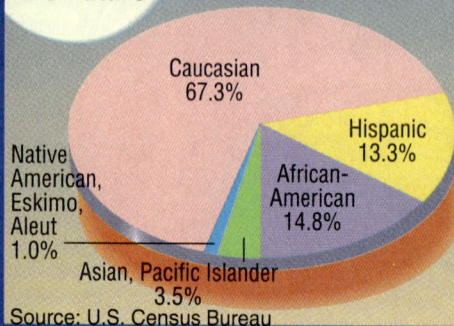

- Caucasian 67.3%
- Hispanic 13.3%
- African-American 14.8%
- Native American, Eskimo, Aleut 1.0%
- Asian, Pacific Islander 3.5%

2010 60,463,000

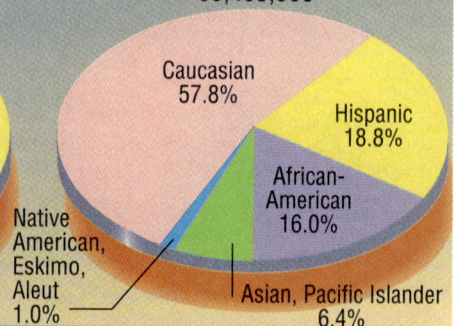

- Caucasian 57.8%
- Hispanic 18.8%
- African-American 16.0%
- Native American, Eskimo, Aleut 1.0%
- Asian, Pacific Islander 6.4%

Source: U.S. Census Bureau

Team Project

Measure Up

As a member of the Future Farmers of America, Minnie found out that she lives in the raisin capital of the world. Hundreds of acres of land in Selma, California produce thousands of bushels of raisins.

An *acre* is a unit of measure of land area equal to 43,560 square feet. A *bushel* is a unit of measure of capacity equal to 8 gallons. Do research and compile a list of units of area and capacity in the metric and customary systems. Try to find how the units were named and when they were first used.

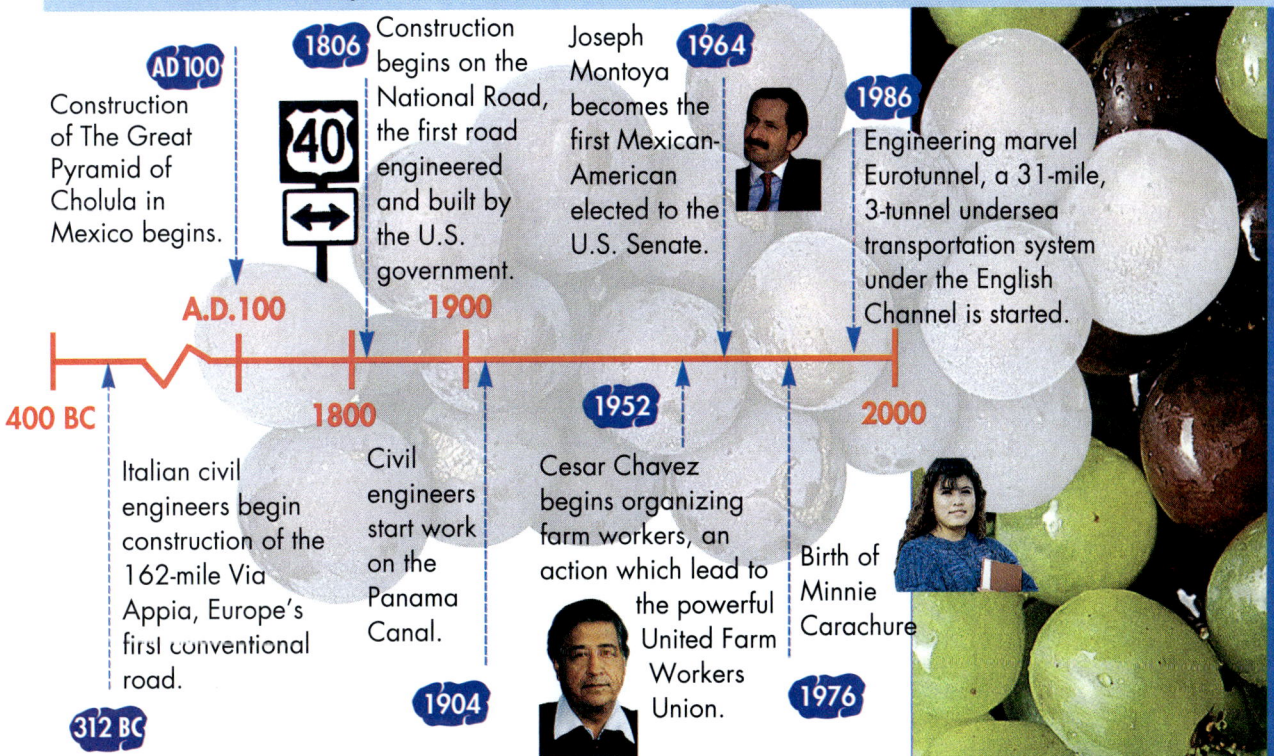

AD 100
Construction of The Great Pyramid of Cholula in Mexico begins.

1806
Construction begins on the National Road, the first road engineered and built by the U.S. government.

40
US

Joseph Montoya becomes the first Mexican-American elected to the U.S. Senate. **1964**

1986
Engineering marvel Eurotunnel, a 31-mile, 3-tunnel undersea transportation system under the English Channel is started.

A.D.100 — 1900

400 BC — 1800 — 2000

312 BC
Italian civil engineers begin construction of the 162-mile Via Appia, Europe's first conventional road.

Civil engineers start work on the Panama Canal. **1904**

1952
Cesar Chavez begins organizing farm workers, an action which lead to the powerful United Farm Workers Union.

Birth of Minnie Carachure **1976**

For more information

If you would like more information about scholarship possibilities, contact:

**National Hispanic Scholarship Fund
P.O. Box 728
Novato, California 94948**

You can learn more about the math Minnie uses by completing the following activities in this unit.

Setting the Scene

MATHEMATICS TOOLKIT

Many professions require the use of tools. This mathematical toolkit includes tools you may find useful as you study this unit.

You may remember reading the book James and the Giant Peach by Roald Dahl. It is about a boy named James who was sent to live with his two aunts after his parents were killed. In the story, a tiny old man appears to James and gives him a bag of small, magic, green things about which he says, "Whoever they meet first, be it bug, insect, animal, or tree,...will be the one who gets the full power of their magic!" By accident, James drops the bag near a peach tree and, as a result, a peach receives the full power of the magic green things. Take time to read this toolkit and remember the questions that are asked and answered by the characters.

Narrator: Nigel, Carmelita, Moon, and Simone are students at Great Plains Middle School. They have just read the book James and the Giant Peach to a group of 4th graders at the nearby elementary school. They are discussing some of the mathematical curiosities of the book with their math teacher, Mr. Hernandez.

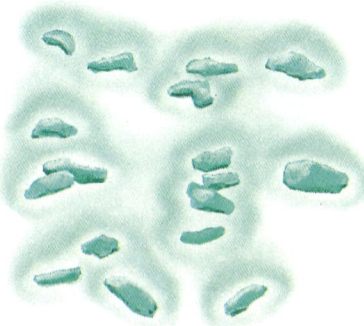

Mr. Hernandez: What kinds of things did you discover while reading James and the Giant Peach to the children?

Nigel: I don't know if I made any discoveries, but I did have some questions.

Mr. Hernandez: What kinds of questions?

Nigel: Well, for example, in Chapter 6, when James' aunts were looking at the peach they said, "The thing really *is* growing! It's nearly twice as big already!" Did they mean twice as much to eat, twice the diameter, or twice the surface area?

Carmelita: Well, I think it means that there was twice as much to eat. That's the same as twice the diameter, isn't it?

Moon: I don't know, Carmelita. Isn't the diameter the distance across the peach through the center, Mr. H?

Mr. Hernandez: Yes, it is.

Moon: Well, if you doubled the diameter, you would double the distance around the peach. So that means there would be twice the surface area.

Simone: I don't think that's right either, Moon.

You're trying to use a circle to describe something that is close to a sphere in shape. A sphere is a 3-dimensional object. I don't think the rules work that way.

Mr. Hernandez: That's a good point, Simone. Sometimes questions like this don't have one right answer. They might have meant twice as much to eat or twice the diameter. Only the author knows what he meant. While we're on the subject, Simone, what did you find interesting about the story?

Simone: In Chapter 7, it says that James—well, let me read it: "He could see the peach swelling larger and larger as clearly as if it were a balloon being blown up. In half a minute, it was the size of a melon!" I was wondering how many times its size it would have to grow for it to be the size of a melon. I mean, how many peaches would fit inside a melon?

Carmelita: That depends on what kind of melon it was. The volume of a cantaloupe is different from the volume of a watermelon.

Moon: I found something in Chapter 7, too. It says, "Soon it was the size of a small car, and reached halfway to the ground." Then a little later, it says, "Bigger and bigger grew the peach, bigger and bigger and bigger. Then at last, when it had become nearly as tall as the tree that it was growing on, as tall and wide, in fact, as a small house, the bottom part of it gently touched the ground—and there it rested." Okay. How tall was the tree? How big could the peach have been? I mean, this stuff is unbelievable!

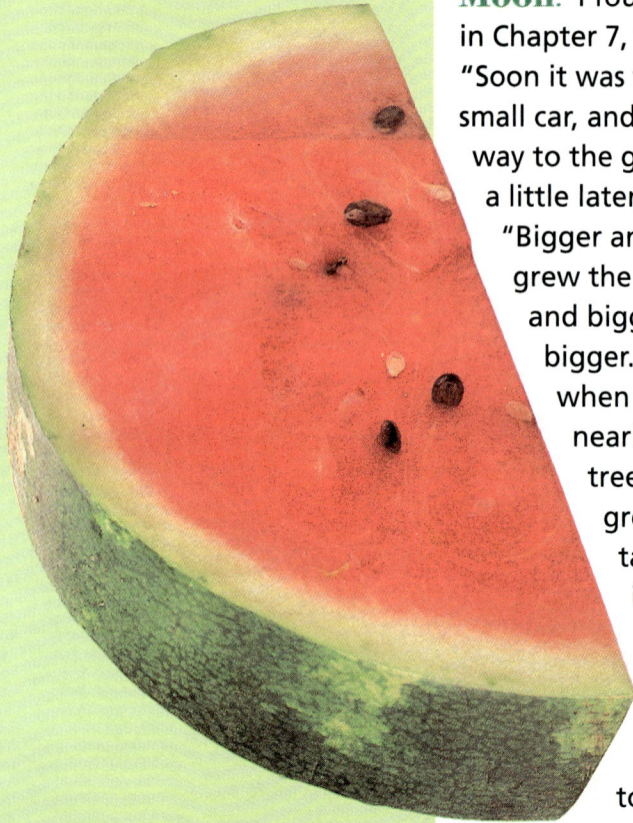

Mr. Hernandez: What does volume have to do with it, Carmelita?

Carmelita: Volume describes the size of the inside of something. We could find the volume of a melon, and then divide it by the volume of a peach to find out how many peaches would fit inside a melon.

Mr. Hernandez: Good thinking! What about you, Moon? Did you have questions about the story?

Mr. Hernandez: Don't forget, Moon, that this book is fiction.

Moon: I know that, Mr. H. But how big *could* the peach have been?

Mr. Hernandez: Well, how big is a small car? And how big is a small house?

These are the kinds of questions you would need to answer in order to know how big the peach was.

Simone: What kinds of measurements would we use?

Nigel: I think we would need to know the surface areas of a small car and a small house.

Carmelita: But Nigel, the surface area wouldn't help. That only tells us how much material would be needed to say, paint the car or the house. I think we need to know the area. That would tell us how much of the ground it covered.

Moon: But what do we care about the ground it covered? We are comparing the sizes of the peach, a small car, and a small house, right? I think we need to know the volume of all three.

Mr. Hernandez: Okay, you guys. Why don't you work together to figure it out?

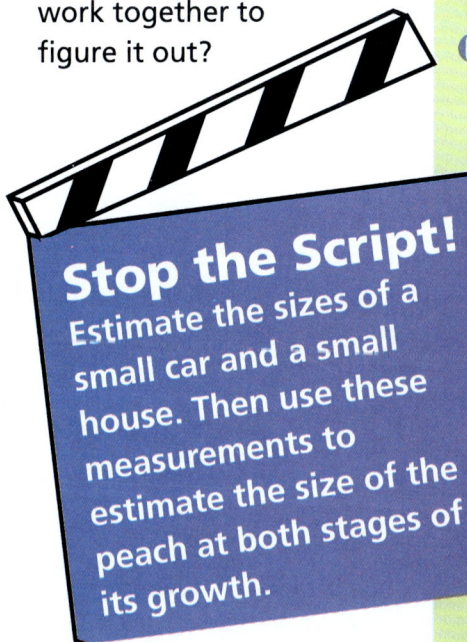

Stop the Script!
Estimate the sizes of a small car and a small house. Then use these measurements to estimate the size of the peach at both stages of its growth.

Narrator: The next day, the students report their findings to Mr. Hernandez.

Mr. Hernandez: So, what did you find out?

Moon: We found out that volume was the best measurement to use to describe the size of the peach—just like I said! The volume of a small car turned out to be about 6 cubic meters and the volume of a small house turned out to be about 370 cubic meters. That would be a huge peach!

Carmelita: Well, Moon, since you know so much, I've got a question for you. In Chapter 16, I read a part that really stumped me. You try and figure it out.

Moon: Okay, shoot.

Carmelita: It's talking about what happened after the centipede chewed through the peach stem and the peach started rolling down the hill. "The peach was now only a hundred yards away from the cliff—now fifty—now twenty—now ten—now five—and when it reached the edge of the cliff it seemed to leap up into the sky and hang there suspended for a few seconds, still turning over and over in the air... Then it began to fall... Down... Down... Down... SMACK! It hit the water with a colossal splash and sank like a stone. But a few seconds later, up it came again, and this time, up it stayed, floating serenely upon the surface of the water." How is that possible? Shouldn't the peach have sunk? Was it because it was magic?

Moon: Well,...uh...I'm not sure.

Mr. Hernandez: For tonight's homework...

All: (moans and groans)

Mr. Hernandez: ...I'd like you to do a little research on something called Archimedes' principle. That's spelled A-R-C-H-I-M-E-D-E-S, but it's pronounced Ark-uh-meed-ees. Write a one-page report about this principle for tomorrow's class. Have a nice day!

Narrator: The next day, the students discuss their reports in class.

Mr. Hernandez: Nigel, what did you find out?

Nigel: Well, Archimedes was a Greek philosopher who lived in the third century B.C. His principle says that the buoyant force on an object in a fluid is equal to the weight of the fluid displaced by the object.

Mr. Hernandez: Does anybody else know why the peach didn't sink?

Simone: Maybe it was wearing a life jacket! (laughter)

Mr. Hernandez: You're not too far off, Simone. What makes a person float when they're wearing a life jacket?

Simone: Oh, I don't know. I was only kidding!

Carmelita: Doesn't it have something to do with weight? I mean, a rock will sink, but those pool toys that you blow up won't.

Nigel: That's right! Maybe whatever it is just has to be heavy enough.

Moon: I don't know. After all, a person is pretty heavy, but some people can float.

Carmelita: I found the same information. But what does that mean?

Simone: I know! My mom explained it to me. It means that an object will float when it displaces enough fluid to equal its weight.

In other words, if the density of the object is greater than the fluid it's in, the object will sink. If not, it will float.

Mr. Hernandez: So how does that answer your question, Carmelita?

Carmelita: Now I know that the density of the peach was not as great as the density of the water that the peach was in. That means that the peach weighed less than an equal amount of water. So, it floated.

Mr. Hernandez: Excellent reasoning, Carmelita. Well, I guess everyone else has chosen a part of the

book to discuss, so let me tell you the part of *James and the Giant Peach* that I found the most interesting. It's in Chapter 18. Poor old Earthworm was worried that they would all starve. "'If this peach is not going to sink,' the Earthworm was saying, 'and if we are not going to be drowned, then every one of us is going to starve to death instead.

Do you realize that we haven't had a thing to eat since yesterday morning?' ...James took a deep, slow breath. 'Can't you realize,' he said patiently,' that we have enough food here to last us for weeks and weeks?'" I like this part because I *love* peaches! How long do you think it would take James, eating normal-sized meals, to eat the peach, assuming that, by this time, the peach was the size of a small house?

Stop the Script!
Estimate the number of normal-sized meals that you could eat from the peach.

Simone: Since we already found that the volume of a small house was about 370 cubic meters, we can find the volume of a normal-sized meal and divide that into the volume of the house. Isn't that right, Mr. Hernandez?

Mr. Hernandez: That's one way to go about it, Simone.

Nigel: I think a normal-sized meal is about the size of a square dinner plate measuring, oh, about 25 centimeters on a side. If the food is say, 3 centimeters high, the volume of that meal would be 1,875 cubic centimeters. But how many cubic meters is that?

Moon: Boy, is this complicated!

Mr. Hernandez: Not really, Moon. Remember that 1 cubic meter = 100 centimeters × 100 centimeters × 100 centimeters. Take a look at this model.

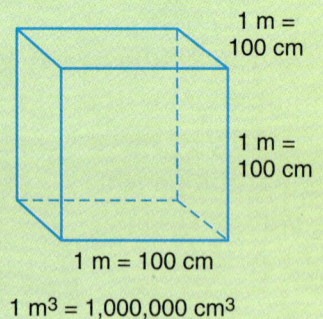

1 m = 100 cm
1 m = 100 cm
1 m = 100 cm
$1 m^3 = 1,000,000 cm^3$

Moon: Oh yeah! I'd forgotten about that. 1 cubic meter = 1,000,000 cubic centimeters. Therefore, 1,875 cubic centimeters = 1,875 ÷ 1,000,000 or 0.001875 cubic meter.

Carmelita: So that means James could eat 370 ÷ 0.001875 normal-sized meals of peach. When I punch that into my calculator, I get 197,333.33. That's a lot of meals!

Mr. Hernandez: Don't forget, class, that the pit takes up a significant amount of space.

Simone: I don't know, Mr. Hernandez. Say we ignore the pit for a minute. If James ate three meals a day, that's about 180 *years* worth of meals! Even if we consider the pit, he'd still have—what—100 years worth of meals?

Nigel: You know, I love peaches too. But I think that would be one peach pie too many!

This concludes the Mathematics Toolkit. It included many mathematical tools for you to use throughout the unit. As you work through this unit, you should use these tools to help you solve problems. You may want to explain how to use these mathematical tools in your journal. Or you may want to create a toolkit notebook to add mathematical tools you discover throughout this unit.

May I Take Your Order?

The **surface area** of an object is the number of square units needed to cover the object. The **volume** of an object is the number of cubic units needed to fill the interior space of the object.

Cut out the models on Blackline Masters 14-PA and 14-PB. Fold and tape them together to form rectangular prisms, cubes, and cylinders.

Using the materials your teacher has provided, arrange the models in order from least to greatest surface area. Then arrange the models from least to greatest volume.

When your group is finished, write down as many conclusions as you can draw from your experiment.

Make a poster that reflects what you have learned. Be prepared to explain your technique for ordering the models.

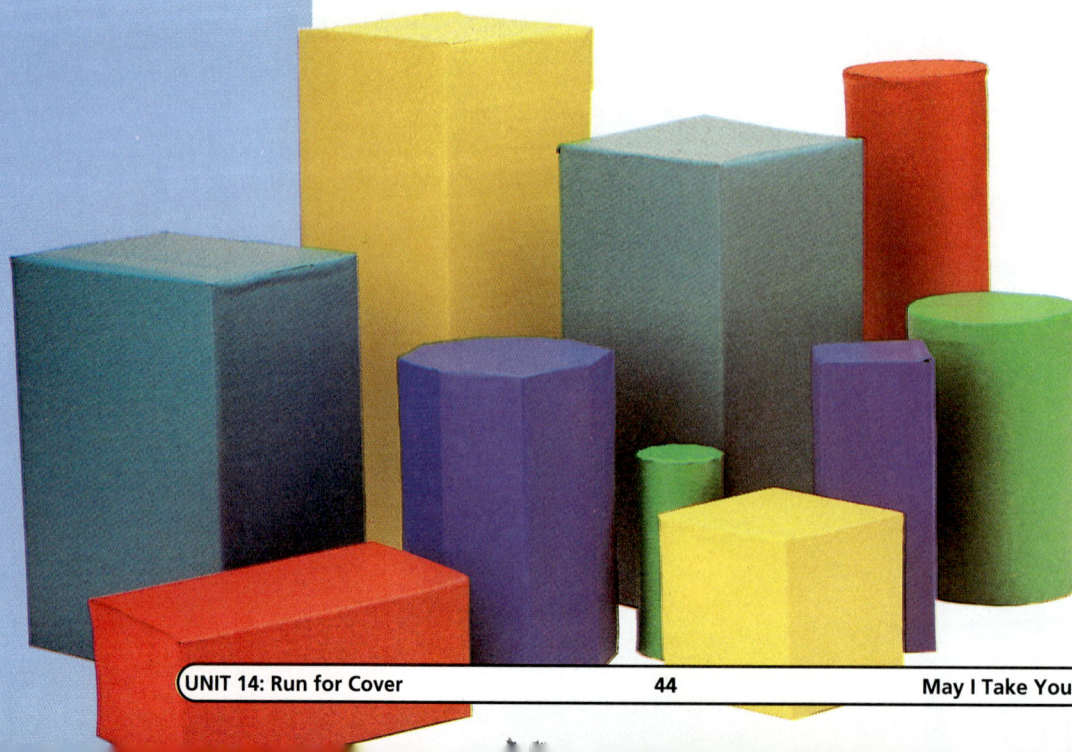

In This Area,...

You can find the areas of certain figures by looking at examples and then finding a pattern.

The rectangles below have areas measuring 24 square units and 35 square units.

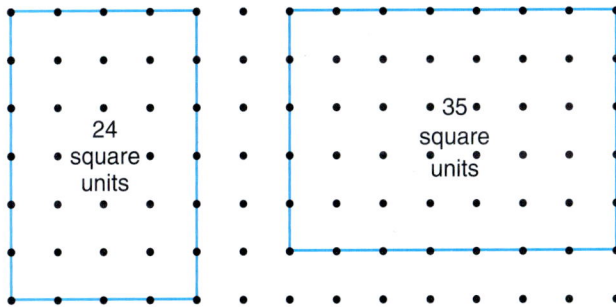

Can you determine a method for finding the area of a rectangle?

Work with your group to determine methods for finding the areas of rectangles, right triangles, acute triangles, obtuse triangles, parallelograms, and trapezoids. Then write a one-page report explaining how to find the areas of these figures.

You can use the methods for finding area that you developed in this activity to find the surface areas of 3-dimensional objects. How much area do you need to cover to paint the barn shown below? Assume that there are four windows on two sides of the barn and a pair of doors and one window on each end of the barn. Be sure to consider the surface areas of all doors and windows. Then write a one-page analysis that describes your method.

30 ft

30 ft

20 ft

40 ft

20 ft

40 ft

3 ft

3 ft

60 ft

120 ft

Cast Your Net

How Many Nets?

1 Using a cube and some construction paper, design and cut out all of the different possible nets that will completely cover (but not overlap) the cube. Share your nets within your group. Then glue or tape your nets to a sheet of posterboard.

2 Find a strategy for finding all of the patterns for the nets to cover the cube.

3 How many 1-centimeter cubes would fill your cube?

4 The number of centimeter cubes that would fill the cube is the volume of the cube. Find a method that you could use to calculate the volume. Explain your method.

5 Summarize your findings in writing.

MENU station B

Fill the Nets

1 **C**hoose a container from the ones you brought in. Then design and cut out all of the different possible nets that will completely cover (but not overlap) the solid.

2 **F**ind a strategy for finding all of the patterns for the nets to cover the solid, without using trial and error.

3 **H**ow many 1-centimeter cubes would fill each container?

4 **T**he number of centimeter cubes that would fill each solid is the volume of the solid. Find a method that you could use to calculate the volume. Explain your method.

5 **S**ummarize your findings in writing.

Upstairs, Downstairs

Use construction paper to design one net to cover each solid shown below. Then find the surface area and volume of each solid figure.

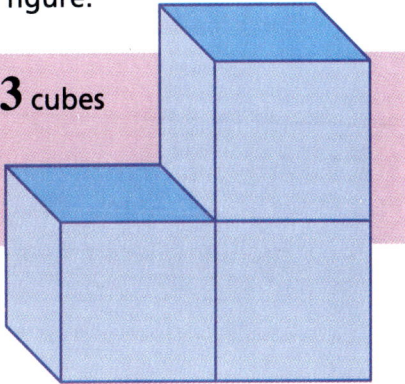

1 **3** cubes

2 **4** cubes

3 **S**ummarize your findings in writing.

MENU station D

Prisms

You can use other measures to determine the size of a container.

1 Choose a container from the ones you brought in. Using the measuring tools and your container, estimate how many of each measuring tool the container will hold.

2 Sketch your container on a sheet of paper. Use a centimeter ruler to measure each side and write these measurements on your sketch.

3 Find the volume of your container in cubic centimeters.

4 Use the measuring tool to fill your container. Then find the conversion factor of your measuring tool. For example:

1 (my measuring tool) = _____ cubic centimeters

5 Use this conversion factor to verify the volume you found in #3.

6 Summarize your findings in writing.

Cylinders

MENU station E

You can use other measures to determine the size of a container.

1 Choose a container from the ones you brought in. Using the measuring tools and your container, estimate how many of each measuring tool the container will hold.

2 Sketch your container on a sheet of paper. Use a centimeter ruler to measure the cylinder and write these measurements on your sketch.

3 Find the volume of your container in cubic centimeters.

4 Use the measuring tool to fill your container. Then find the conversion factor of your measuring tool. For example:

1 (my measuring tool) = _____ cubic centimeters

5 Use this conversion factor to verify the volume you found in #3.

6 Summarize your findings in writing.

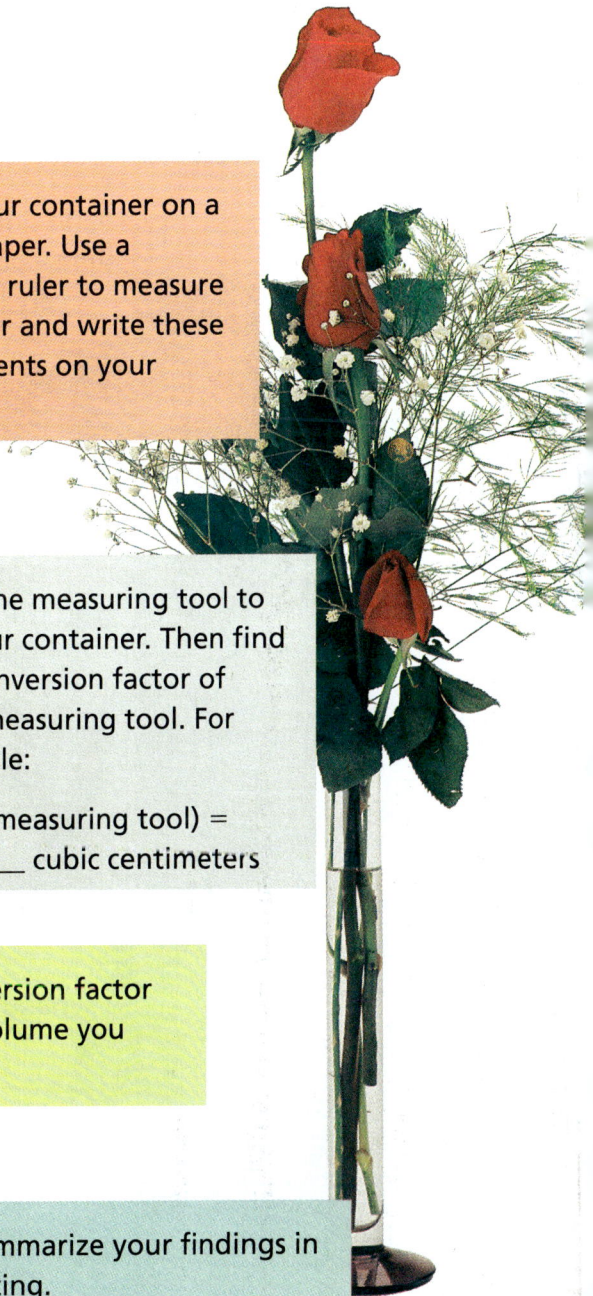

JUST HANGIN' AROUND

The United States Armed Services are in need of new parachutes. They are looking for a parachute that has good hang time—that is, it stays in the air for a relatively long time—but doesn't cost much money. Both of these factors are very important. They are asking your company to submit a parachute for testing. The government contract will be awarded to the company with the greatest hang time for the money.

Your task is to construct a parachute with the materials provided. At the end of the designated time, you will be asked to submit your parachute for an official test flight. (You should test your parachute yourselves first.) You will not be able to use any additional materials, but you can cut the ones you have been provided (except for the paper clip).

It is very important that you remember that both hang time and surface area will be considered. The government is looking for the best combination; that is, the longest hang time and the least surface area.

Keep a record of the steps you follow while constructing your parachute. Explain how you arrived at your parachute size and shape.

Float On

1. Fill a graduated cylinder with water so that it won't overflow when you add a cube. Write down the amount of water in the cylinder.
2. Place the cube in the water. What happened? Why do you think it happened?
3. With the tip of a pencil, make sure that the cube is submerged, but very little of the pencil is. Write down the measure of the water level. How much different is this measure? Why is this measure different?
4. Draw conclusions based on your experiment. Verify your conclusions by using two other different-sized cubes.
5. Find an irregularly-shaped object either inside or outside the classroom and find its volume by using this method.

After verifying your conclusions, write a summary of your experiment. Be sure that your summary answers the following questions.
- Given a container of water, what will be the effect of putting a cube into the water?
- Does the size of the cube affect anything?
- How could a container of water be used to find the volume of a cube?

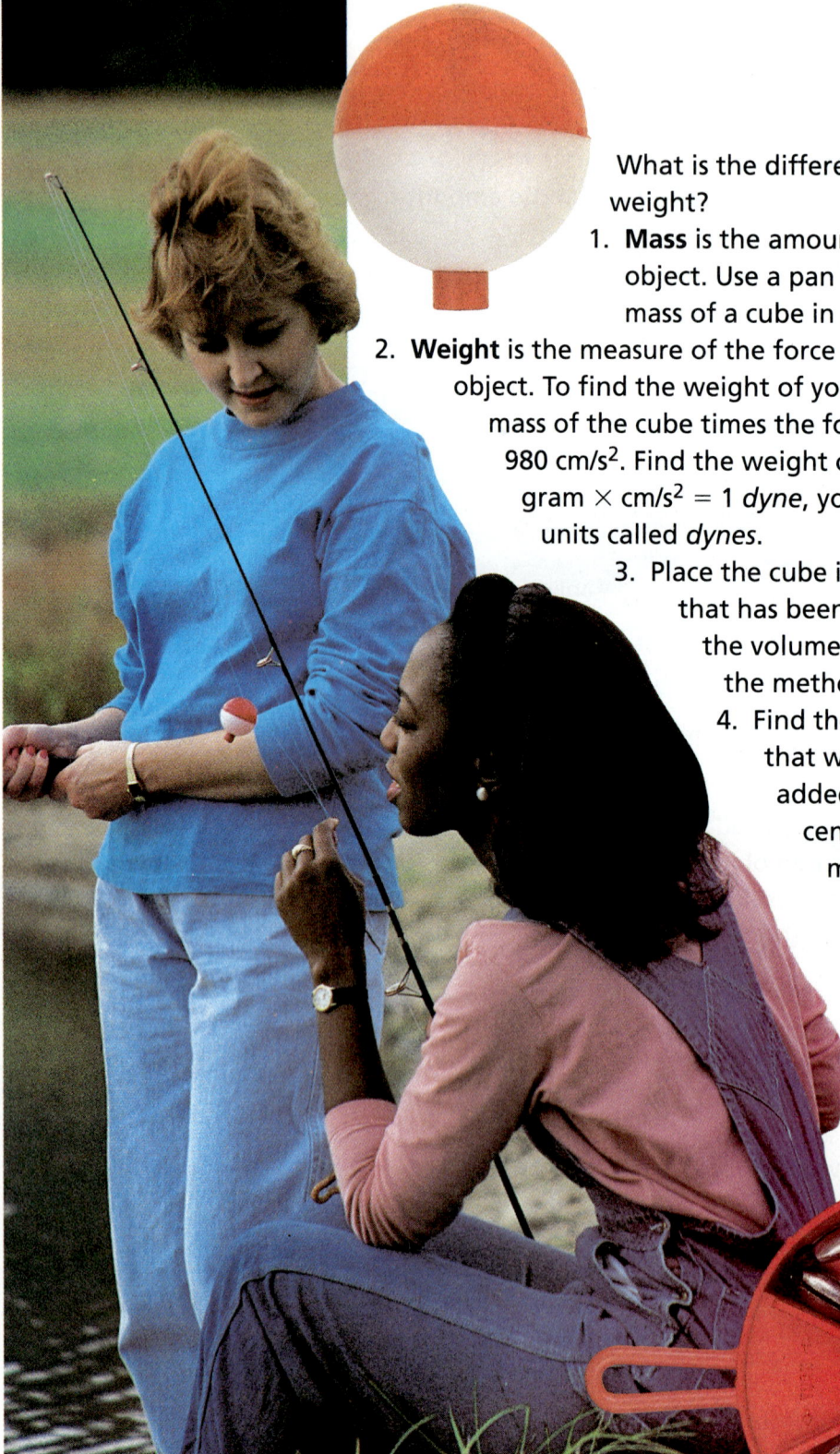

What is the difference between mass and weight?

1. **Mass** is the amount of matter in an object. Use a pan balance to find the mass of a cube in grams.

2. **Weight** is the measure of the force of gravity acting on an object. To find the weight of your cube, multiply the mass of the cube times the force of gravity, which is 980 cm/s². Find the weight of your cube. Since 1 gram $\times$ cm/s² = 1 *dyne*, your answer should be in units called *dynes*.

3. Place the cube in a graduated cylinder that has been filled with water. Find the volume of the cube. Explain the method you used.

4. Find the volume of the water that was displaced when you added the cube. Every cubic centimeter of water has a mass of 1 gram. Use this information to find the weight of the water that was displaced (in dynes).

5. Compare your answers in parts 2 and 4.

Why do some things float and others sink? Find an object that will sink in water.

1. Use the pan balance to find the mass of the object.

2. Calculate the weight of the object.

3. Fill a container with water. Add the object and calculate the amount of water that is displaced when the object is submerged.

4. Find the weight of the displaced water.

5. Compare your answers in parts 2 and 4.

6. How do you predict whether an object will float or sink? Explain your reasoning.

7. Find an object. Use mathematics to predict whether it will float or sink. Then test your conclusion.

Archimedes' Principle

In the third century B.C., Archimedes, a Greek philosopher, proposed an explanation for why objects float or sink. Archimedes' principle states that the buoyant force on an object in a fluid is equal to the weight of the fluid displaced by the object.

That means that an object will float when it displaces enough fluid to equal its weight. A life jacket is lightweight compared to water since it displaces much more water than it weighs. Therefore, you float more easily.

If the density of an object is greater than the fluid it is in, the object will sink. If the density of an object is less than the density of the fluid, the object will float. What happens if their densities are exactly equal?

Submarines pump water into and out of chambers in order to regulate the depth at which they operate. How does Archimedes' principle apply to this situation?

Cool It!

The Social Club at Great Plains Middle School has planned a picnic. They want to take along an ice chest filled with soft drinks. Carmelita has offered to get an ice chest and fill it with drinks and ice. Moon asks her if she will use cubes of ice or one block of ice. Carmelita responds that she hasn't really thought about it.

Nigel says that the block will take up more space. Simone argues that it will take the same space. Moon says that the block is better. Who is correct?

Carmelita has room in her ice chest for a block of ice that is 10 inches by 10 inches by 10 inches and she will still have plenty of room for soft drinks. But remember, she could fill the same space with ice cubes.

Help the students keep cool! Decide if they should take the block of ice or the ice cubes, which each measure 1 inch by 1 inch by 1 inch. Write a statement that reflects your opinion and be prepared to defend it to your classmates.

You may use cubes to help you visualize the problem. A drawing may also be helpful.

Extend the problem by answering the following. If you had a block of ice measuring 10 inches by 10 inches by 10 inches, how could you cut it to maintain the volume, but increase the original surface area by one third?

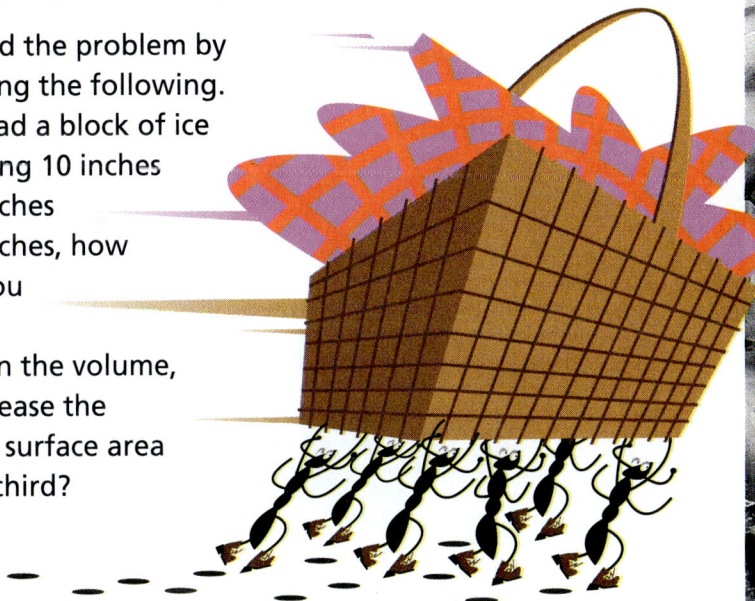

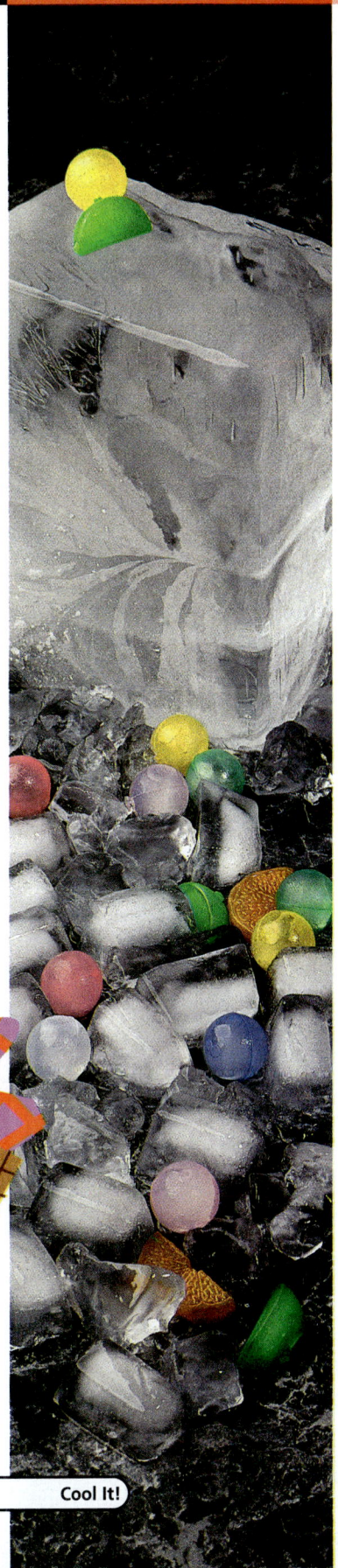

Paint the Cube Red

Masaki has a cube that is 4 inches long on each side. He paints the cube red and then cuts the cube into smaller cubes that measure 1 inch on each side.

- How many of the smaller cubes does Masaki now have?

  - How many of the smaller cubes have exactly three sides painted red?

  - How many of the smaller cubes have exactly two sides painted red?

  - How many of the smaller cubes have exactly one side painted red?

    - How many of the smaller cubes have no sides painted red?

    - How could Masaki paint the original cube so that he would have exactly 27 cubes with exactly one side painted red?

Cutting Corners

The Choc Full Chocolate Company is designing boxes to be used in selling their candies. The company is in the process of trying to determine which size would be best. One of the employees has suggested that they take a piece of cardboard 20 centimeters wide by 20 centimeters long, cut off the corners, fold it up, and make a box. The manager thought this was a great idea and sent an order to the local box company.

The box company was faced with a dilemma—they didn't know how much to cut off each corner. When they called Choc Full, the manager replied, "We don't want to cut corners! Make a box that will hold the most candy!"

You are an employee of the box company. You have been assigned the task of determining the dimensions of the box for the Choc Full Chocolate Company. Use the paper, scissors, and tape that have been provided to experiment with the boxes.

After you have determined a solution to the box problem, tape your box to the chart paper and list the dimensions. Be prepared to discuss how you determined the size and shape of your box in class.

Debriefing Guide

- What are the dimensions of the box with the greatest volume?
- How did you arrive at that conclusion?
- Would this be the best box? Why or why not?
- What other factors would you need to consider in making your decision?
- What factors would the Choc Full Chocolate Company need to consider in selecting the best box?
- Would the box with the greatest volume necessarily hold the most candies? Why or why not?
- What conclusions can you draw?

Using a Spreadsheet

COMPUTER investigation

Many companies use computer programs to help run their businesses more efficiently. One application program that is often used is called a **spreadsheet**. A spreadsheet is a computer program that is specially designed to create charts by doing many calculations. Let's investigate how a spreadsheet could be used to solve the box problem for The Choc Full Chocolate Company.

The sample headings below could be used in the spreadsheet program.

Length of Side of Square Cut Off	Length of Box	Width of Box	Height of Box	Volume of Box

Suppose we tell the computer the length of the side of the square that we will remove from each of the four corners of the cardboard. Let's investigate how we might tell the computer to calculate each of the numbers in the remaining columns. Examine the chart below.

Length of Side of Square Cut Off	Length of Box	Width of Box	Height of Box	Volume of Box
1 cm	18 cm	18 cm	1 cm	324 cm^3
2 cm	16 cm	16 cm	2 cm	512 cm^3
3 cm	14 cm	14 cm	3 cm	588 cm^3

Do you see a pattern developing? Use this pattern to write a formula to calculate a value for each column. Write a statement to explain the process you used.

IT'S A GAS!

Your company distributes gasoline to local gas stations and service stations. You have tankers that haul the gasoline and fill the buried storage tanks at each station. In the past several months, your company has been delivering gas to about fifty new dealers. Unfortunately, they are not familiar with your company and have been calling to complain about being cheated. One station owner said that the level in his tank dropped one fourth of the way and he had not used one fourth of the supposed volume.

Your customer service office tried to explain that since the tanks are cylinders and are buried on their side, a one-fourth drop in the level does not correspond to the usage of one fourth of the gasoline. As a result, station managers are requesting that they receive a stick that has been calibrated to indicate exactly how much gas remains in the tank at any one time.

Your research and development team has been asked to investigate the problem. Upper management would like for you to develop a stick that can be used to indicate what percentage of the tank is full. You want to be able to place the stick in the tank, read where the gasoline registers on the stick, and then determine how much gas remains in the tank. Remember, the tank is resting on its side. You should attack the problem assuming that the diameter of the tank is 1 meter and that the tank is 3 meters long.

Research this problem and be prepared to present a solution at the next board meeting. In addition to developing the stick, prepare a detailed report as to how you arrived at your solution.

Debriefing Guide

- What factors did you have to consider in marking your stick?
- Are your markings evenly spaced on the stick? Why or why not?
- What is the relationship between the marks on the stick and the volume in the tank?
- Would your stick work for any cylinder? Why or why not?
- Is there another size cylinder for which your stick would work?
- Would you have to dig out the same volume of dirt to bury the tank standing upright?
- How would the stick be different if the tank were standing upright?
- Which research and development team made the best recommendation? Why?

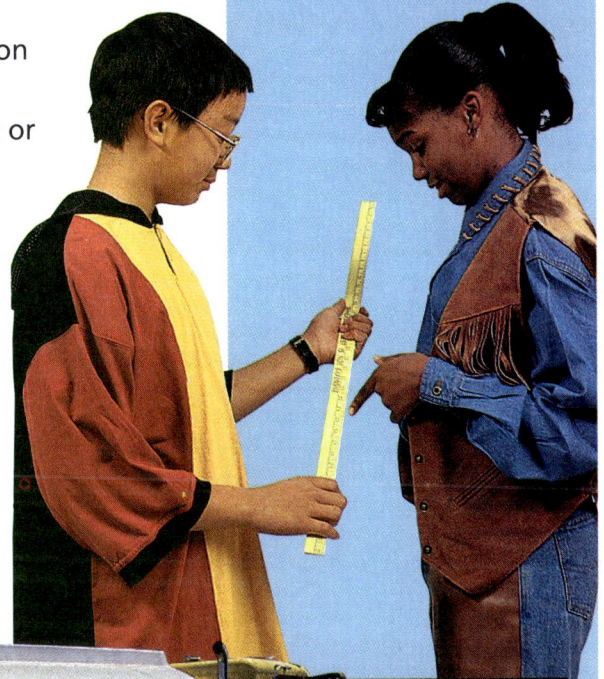

Protecting the Environment

Have you ever thought about all that is involved in getting gasoline into an automobile? When you look at a gas station or service station, you never see the storage tanks. That's because they are buried underground. Recently, the Environmental Protection Agency (EPA) found that many of these underground storage tanks are letting the gasoline seep out. As a result, some stations are having to have the tanks dug up and replaced with new ones. This expense is putting many small stations out of business. Has this happened in your area? How can you find out?

Contact a local gas or service station and find out the following.
- How has the EPA's ruling affected their station?
- How do they determine if a tank is leaking?
- What is the hazard if the tank is leaking?
- What is involved in replacing leaking tanks?
- Do they use a calibrated stick to determine how much gas remains in their tanks?

Write a one-page narrative describing the problem and its effect on the station you researched.

Can the Idea

America's soft drink companies have been trying to establish good public relations by using aluminum cans and encouraging people to recycle them. It has been brought to their attention, however, that if they were truly interested in best utilizing America's resources, they would restructure the soft drink can.

Unbelievable! Could it be possible to make a more efficient soda can? The soft drink companies of America have decided to hire an outside agency to investigate this and present their findings.

Your company has been asked to investigate the soft drink can problem. The soft drink companies want to know if the current can is really the most efficient way to package their soft drinks. Your company's task is to investigate the relationship between the surface area of the can and its volume. You want to know if it would be possible to make a cylinder that uses less aluminum, but holds the same volume of soda.

After your company has investigated the problem, your task, as the executive vice-president, is to present your company's findings in the form of a report that includes a recommendation based on the findings.

Debriefing Guide

- What is the surface area of the can?
- What is the volume of the can?
- Were you able to design a better can? If so, what are its dimensions?
- What other factors need to be taken into consideration before changing the can size?
- What conclusions can you draw?

What Size Can?

Have you ever thought about the different-sized cans in which items are packaged? Do you think that the size of the can is always the most efficient?

Find three items in your home that are in cans. Calculate the volume and surface area of each can.

Select one of the cans and redesign it so that the same contents are contained in a can with the same volume, but less surface area.

Which has the greater impact on volume, an increase in the height of the can or an increase in the radius of the base?

What factors do you think manufacturers consider when designing packaging for their products?

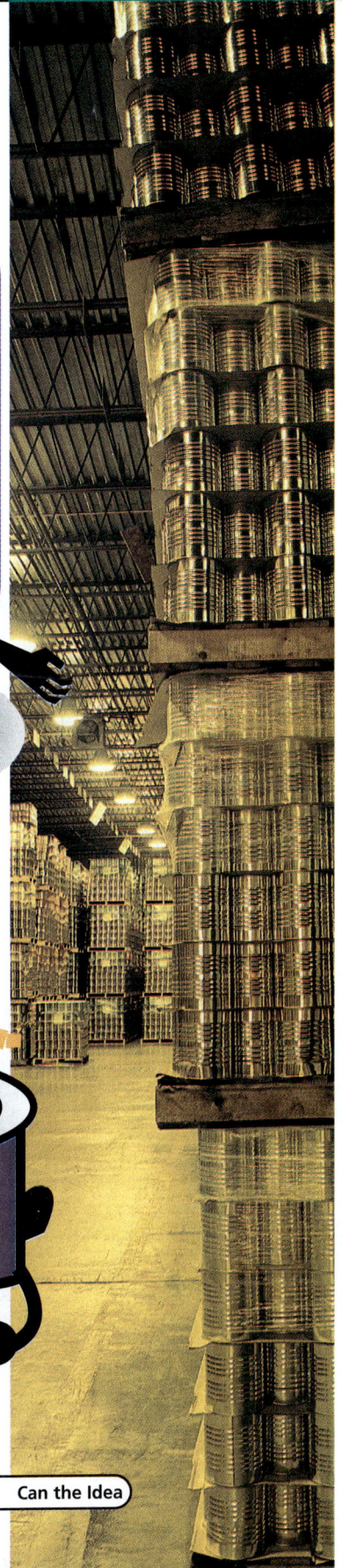

SELECTION AND REFLECTION

What have you learned about surface area and volume while studying this unit? What was your favorite activity in this unit? Gather together the papers or the work you did in your favorite activity. Explain what the activity was about and why you liked it. Was there anything you studied in this unit that you still feel you don't understand? Was there anything you didn't study in this unit that you wish you had?

The Problem

Mr. Jackson owns a plot of land in the shape of a trapezoid, as shown below. He plans to give half of the land to his son, Ben, as a wedding present. Where should the boundary line be placed so that Mr. Jackson and Ben get equal-sized plots?

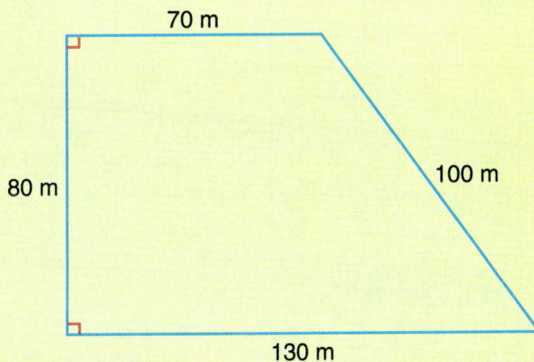

THE GREAT DIVIDE

70 m

80 m

100 m

130 m

Fold or Be Fooled

The Problem

Five squares were used to form each of the pentominoes shown below. Which of these figures can be folded into an open-top box? (Only fold on the dashed lines.)

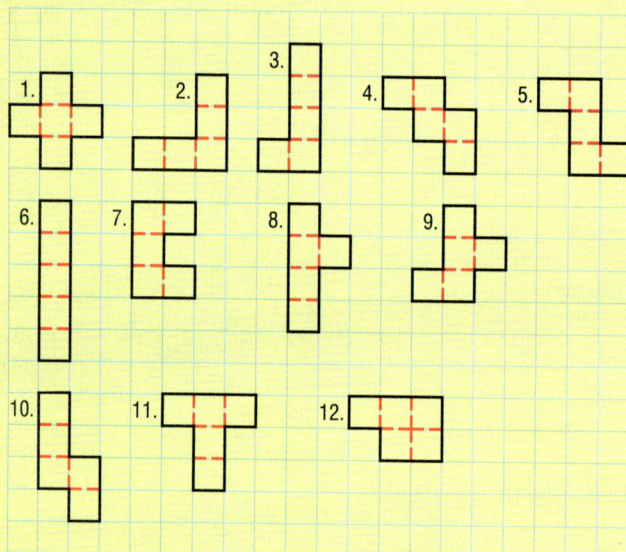

1.
2.
3.
4.
5.
6.
7.
8.
9.
10.
11.
12.

The Problem

Imagine that there are five rectangles where the measure of the length and width of each rectangle is a whole number from 1 to 10, and that you can only use each number once. Now imagine that these five rectangles can be fit together to form a square, with no spaces between the rectangles. Draw a sketch of this square, showing how each rectangle fits.

A Tight Fit

Don't Be So Dense

The Problem

In physics class, Mike accidently drops a sugar cube into the graduated cylinder shown below. If the sugar cube is $\frac{1}{2}$ inch on a side and has a mass of 3.2 grams, where would it end up in the graduated cylinder? (Assume that the sugar cube will not dissolve.)

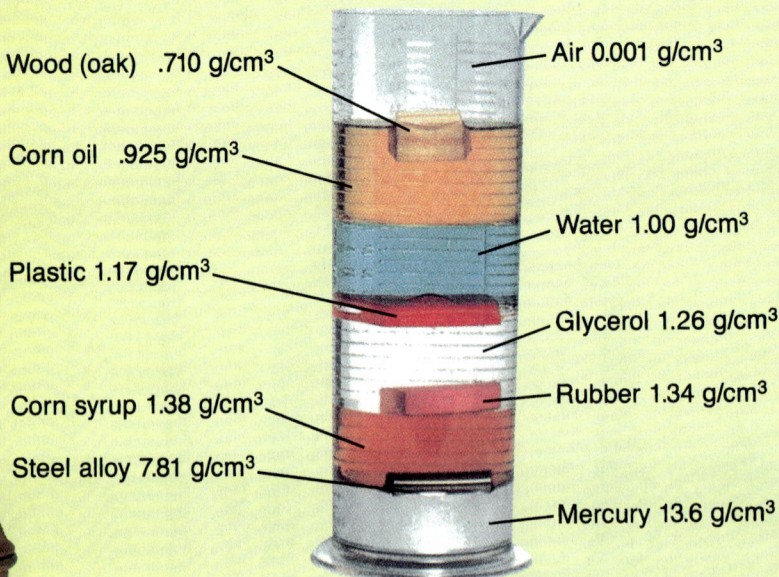

Wood (oak) .710 g/cm³

Corn oil .925 g/cm³

Plastic 1.17 g/cm³

Corn syrup 1.38 g/cm³

Steel alloy 7.81 g/cm³

Air 0.001 g/cm³

Water 1.00 g/cm³

Glycerol 1.26 g/cm³

Rubber 1.34 g/cm³

Mercury 13.6 g/cm³

Extension Use the Densities of Common Materials table in the Data Bank to find out where ethanol, blood, and copper would fall in the graduated cylinder shown above.

The Problem

Each square below is 6 units long on a side. Find the area of the circle inscribed in the first square and the sum of the areas of the circles inscribed in the other two squares. Which square contains the greatest area covered by circles? What is that area?

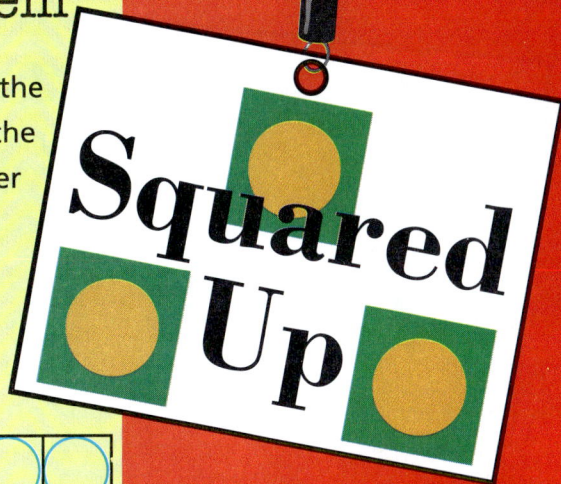

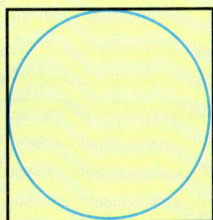

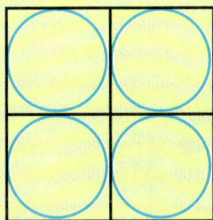

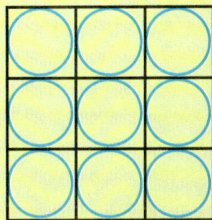

Squared Up

Extension Predict the sum of the areas of the circles inscribed in the squares below.

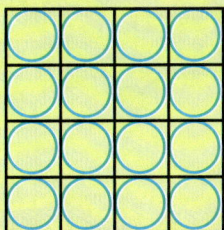

Is It Magic?

The Problem

José goes to a friend's birthday party where a magician is putting on a show. The magician holds up a Greek cross like the one shown below and says, "For my next trick, I will change this cross into a square with two straight cuts." José politely responds, "That's not magic—I can do that, too!" and proceeds to change the Greek cross into a square by dividing the cross into four pieces with two straight cuts. How did José do it?

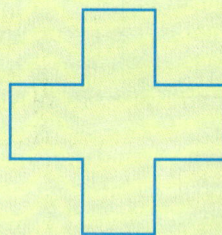

ON THE MOVE

INTERACTIVE • MATHEMATICS

on the move
GRAPHING AND FUNCTIONS

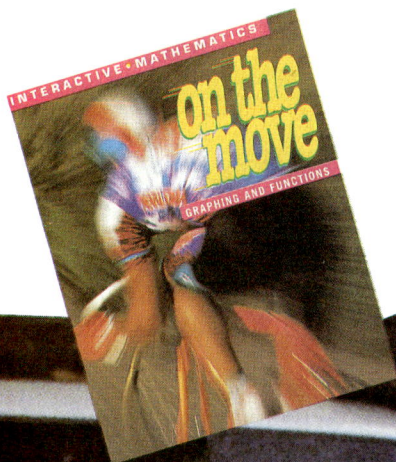

Looking Ahead

In this unit, you will see how mathematics can be used to answer questions about motion and change. You will experience:

▶ using graphs and maps to communicate information

▶ recording data and constructing graphs of the data

▶ determining speed and distance

▶ determining acceleration and deceleration

▶ analyzing data using graphs

Did You Ever Wonder?

What do mathematics and cars have to do with each other? Turn the page to see how Stephen Lovett of Reston, Virginia, combines the two.

JAN Virginia
BIO-744

Teens in the News

Featuring: Stephen A. Lovett
Age: 17
Hometown: Reston, Virginia
Career Goal: Chief Executive Officer of Chrysler Corporation
Interests: Water sports, community service projects

Several years ago while Stephen Lovett was mowing a neighbor's grass, he noticed that their car was really dirty. He offered to wash and wax it. Stephen really got carried away, and before he knew it, he had completely cleaned and detailed the car!

Word quickly got around the neighborhood about what a great job Stephen had done on the car. Neighbors started calling Stephen and asking him to clean their cars. So, at age 13, Stephen started Lovett Enterprises. He specializes in providing detailing services, such as thorough vacuuming of carpets and cloth upholstery, glass cleaning, and wheel and tire cleaning at a fraction of the cost that professional car detailers charge.

Business grew, and Stephen created a franchise agreement. He supplies four other teens with all the materials and supplies that they need to do car detailing. These teens agree to operate under the name Lovett Enterprises. In return, each teen pays Stephen a percentage of the business he or she conducts each month.

Stephen uses a computer and a software program to do all of the accounting for Lovett Enterprises. He keeps track of the money he earns and the money his franchises earn.

Stephen pays a lot of attention to his customers. He sends every customer a thank-you note and he leaves candy in their car when they come to pick it up. At Lovett Enterprises, the difference really is in the details!

SUM OF THE PARTS

Retail price: $9,845
Cost of all parts purchased separately: $38,652

Buying a car piece by piece would cost considerably more than buying the assembled car. Consider the 1990 Ford Escort LX.

Team Project

How Slow Must You Go?

Original Speed (mph)	Thinking Distance (ft)	Braking Distance (ft)	Total Stopping Distance (ft)
15	16	12	28
25	27	34	61
35	38	67	105
45	49	111	160
55	60	165	225

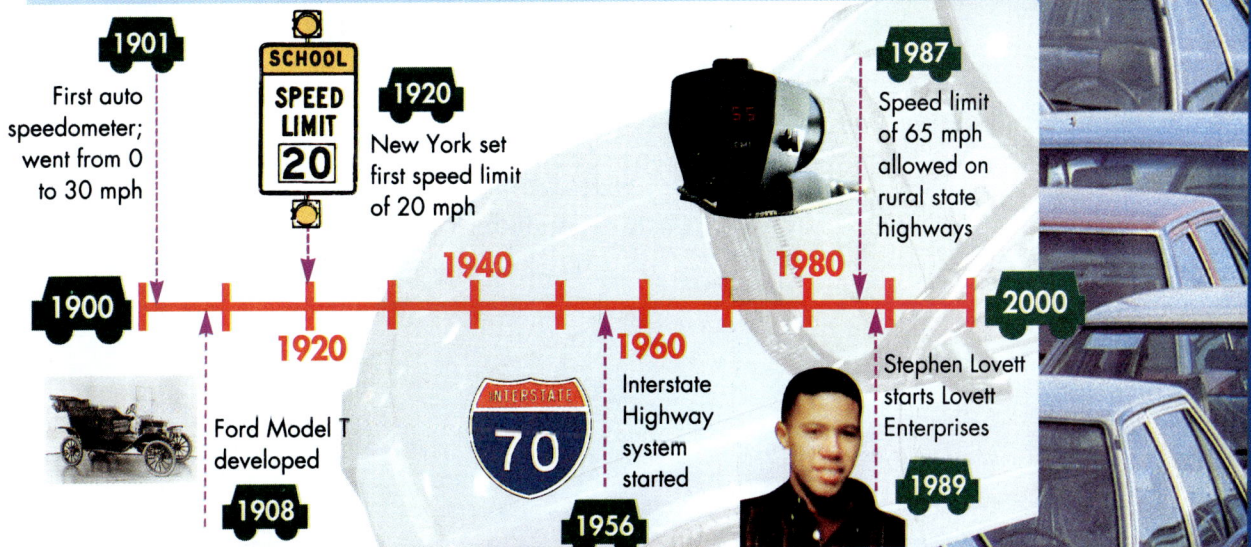

Stephen can make a car shine like a dime. But no one can make a car stop on a dime. The *total stopping distance* depends on the speed of the car, the thinking distance, and the braking distance.

Find out what is meant by *thinking distance* and *braking distance*. Use the information in the chart to make three graphs comparing the thinking distance, braking distance, and total stopping distance with its original speed. Use your graphs to predict the total stopping distance for a car going 65 miles per hour. The State Highway Patrol recommends that for every 10 mph of speed you keep one car length between you and the car in front of you. Does that seem reasonable? Explain why or why not.

1901
First auto speedometer; went from 0 to 30 mph

SCHOOL SPEED LIMIT 20

1920
New York set first speed limit of 20 mph

1987
Speed limit of 65 mph allowed on rural state highways

1900 — 1920 — 1940 — 1960 — 1980 — 2000

1920
Ford Model T developed
1908

INTERSTATE 70

1960
Interstate Highway system started
1956

Stephen Lovett starts Lovett Enterprises
1989

For more information

If you would like more information about starting your own business, contact:

FUTURE BUSINESS LEADERS OF AMERICA
1908 Association Drive
Reston, Virginia 22091

You can learn more about the math Stephen uses in his business by completing the activities in this unit.

Setting the Scene

MATHEMATICS TOOLKIT

Many professions require the use of tools. This mathematics toolkit includes tools you may find useful as you study this unit. At times you may feel lost or not know where to begin when presented with a problem situation. You should take time to review this toolkit to see how the characters in the script used mathematics to solve their problem.

Narrator: Hector, Amber, and Mi-Ling are friends having lunch at their middle school. It's the first day back after the winter break.

Hector: So what kinds of presents did you guys get over the holidays?

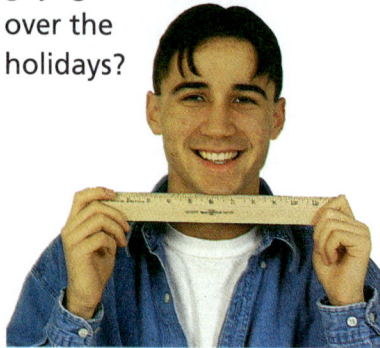

Mi-Ling: I got some new outfits. In fact, I'm wearing one now. How do you like it?

Amber: You look great!

Hector: Simply stunning, darling. How about giving us a fashion show?

Mi-Ling: Okay, get real. So what did *you* get, Hector? A roll of quarters for the arcade?

Hector: Hey, lay off. So, I like to play video games, okay? I like the action and the speed.

Amber: That reminds me. My little brother Ryan got one of those Speed Track sets for Christmas. You know, those miniature cars that race around the track.

Hector: Yeah. On TV, they say those cars are "faster than real life."

Mi-Ling: Are you serious? Something that small can't travel that fast, can it? I don't think, those little cars can go faster than a regular car.

Amber: I don't know. When you see those little cars shoot around that track, they sure look fast. How can you tell?

Hector: I think it's just a gimmick. You know, just to get you to buy it.

Mi-Ling: They can't do that. Aren't there, like, truth in advertising laws?

Amber: I don't know, but I'll bet there's a way to find out.

Hector: Yeah! Maybe we can sue them for false advertising and make a million bucks!

Amber: You watch way too much TV, Hector. Anyway, how can we do this?

Mi-Ling: Well, tell us about the set.

Amber: Okay. The track is set up in an oval shape. At each end, there are three curved pieces. The sides of the track are made of straight pieces. The track is designed for two cars. In each straightaway, the cars cross over and change position. Let me draw you a picture.

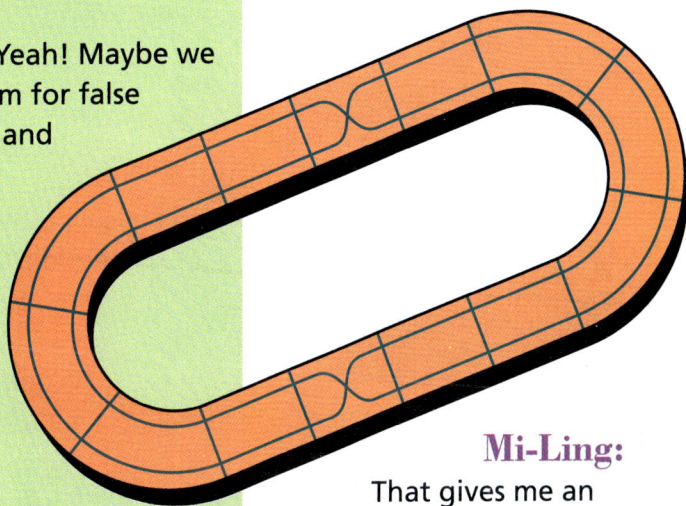

Mi-Ling: That gives me an idea. I think I know how to figure out how fast the cars really go. Can we come over to your house after school and "test drive" my idea?

Amber: Very funny. Sure, that would be cool.

Hector: Maybe we'll be able to write to one of those consumer shows and tell them about our case. We could be famous!

Stop the Script! Determine how you could find the speed of the miniature cars.

Narrator: The friends meet at Amber's house after school.

Amber: Okay, so here it is. I asked Ryan if we could use it, and he said okay, but I had to give him a dollar!

Hector: Hey, this is pretty cool! Almost as cool as video games, but not quite. So, Mi-Ling, what's this hot idea?

Mi-Ling: Okay. We can find the speed by timing the cars as they go around the track.

Amber: That's it? Won't that just give us their time in seconds?

Hector: Yeah. We need to know the speed in miles per hour, not seconds.

Mi-Ling: I know. We can calculate speed by dividing the distance by the time. But first, we need to convert seconds to minutes and minutes to hours. We'll just use a calculator.

Hector: I don't get it— you're gonna have to show me.

Mi-Ling: I have a stopwatch. Hector, you start the cars.

Hector: Okay.

Mi-Ling: Amber, you take the stopwatch and time the car for exactly one lap around the track. Start the watch when the car is here and then stop it when the car comes back to the same exact place on the track. We'll do this at least four or five times.

Narrator: They timed the miniature car five times as it went around the track. The car's times are shown below.

Lap	Time (seconds)
1	4.18
2	3.21
3	3.20
4	3.18
5	3.22

Hector: Now that we've got these times, how do we find an average time?

Amber: Well, it looks like I messed up timing the first one and three of them are almost the same. Why don't we use 3.21 seconds as the average time?

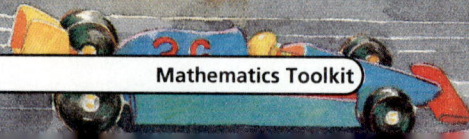

Mi-Ling: That makes sense. Okay, now let's convert the number of seconds to hours.

Amber: Wait a minute—3.21 seconds isn't even close to an hour!

Mi-Ling: Right. We need to find out what part of an hour it is. We can do that by first changing the number of seconds to parts of a minute. So, divide 3.21 by 60, since there are 60 seconds in a minute.

Amber: I get 0.053508.

Mi-Ling: That's 0.053508 *minutes*.

Hector: Hey, I get it. Now we need to turn this minute number into parts of an hour. So we divide again by 60.

Amber: Because there are 60 minutes in an hour?

Hector: Yeah. 0.053508 divided by 60 is 0.0008918 *hours*.

Amber: Okay, we've got the time in parts of an hour, but what about the speed?

Mi-Ling: You can find the speed by finding the distance the car traveled and dividing by the time. You know, miles per hour means miles divided by hours. Like if you drove 100 miles and it took 2 hours, how fast did you go?

Hector: That's easy—50 miles an hour. You just divide 100 by 2.

Amber: So how are we going to find the distance?

Hector: Well, just look at the track. There are four straight pieces on each side and three curved pieces at each end. If we measure the two kinds of pieces, then we can find the total distance.

Mi-Ling: That works great for the straight track, but what about the curves?

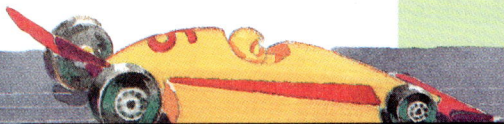

Amber: I think I know how to measure the curve. If you put the two ends together, you get a circle. You can find the distance around a circle, or the **circumference**, by multiplying the distance across the circle, called the **diameter**, by 3.14. Don't you guys remember this stuff?

Hector: Oh, yeah. We learned that stuff last year in math class. Okay, a straight piece is about 7 inches long. So, 7 inches times 8 straight pieces of track is 56 inches.

Amber: Okay. For the curves, I can measure across the race track from the center of one straightaway to the center of the other. I get $18\frac{3}{4}$ inches.

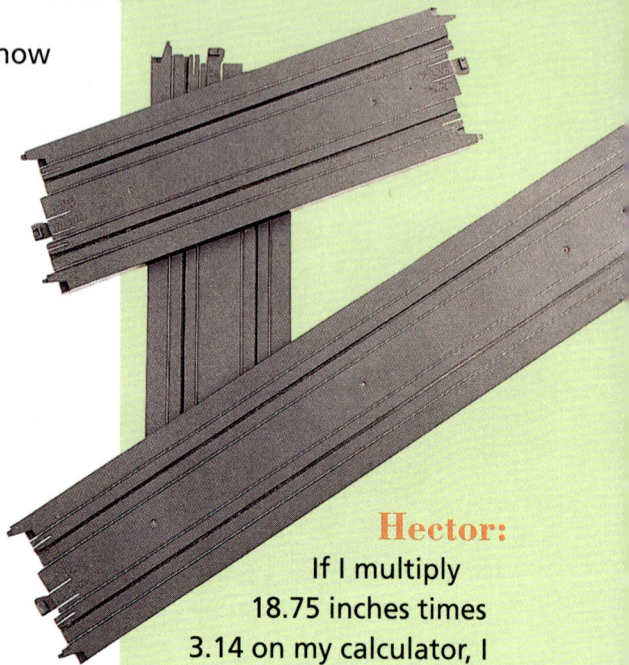

Hector: If I multiply 18.75 inches times 3.14 on my calculator, I get...58.875 inches. So the total track is $56 + 58.875$ or...114.875 inches long.

Mi-Ling: Now we need to convert 114.875 inches to miles. Let's start by rounding 114.875 to 115. That will make our calculations a little easier.

Amber: We can do the same thing with inches that we did with seconds. We'll need to convert 115 inches to feet, and then to miles.

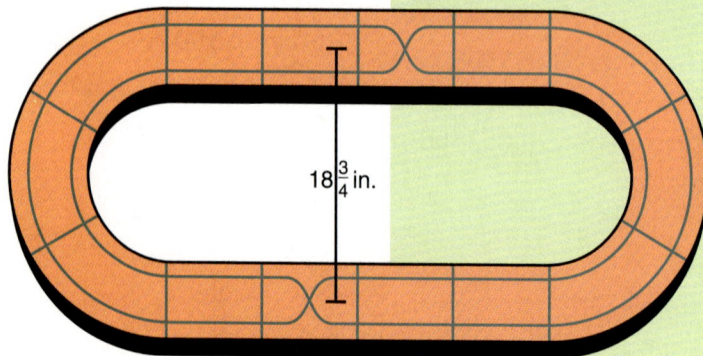

$18\frac{3}{4}$ in.

Mi-Ling: You're right. There are 12 inches in a foot and 5,280 feet in a mile.

Amber: So we divide 115 by 12 inches and get 9.583333 feet.

Hector: Now divide 9.583333 by 5,280. What did you get?

Amber: 0.001815 miles.

Hector: Hey, wait a minute. That's so small! Does this really work?

Amber: Sure! Remember that we also got a small number for the time. It was 0.0008918 hours.

Mi-Ling: Since speed is distance divided by time, let's divide 0.001815 miles by 0.0008918 hours.

Amber: I get 2.0352. Wow, the car only goes about 2 miles an hour!

Hector: What a ripoff! Two miles an hour is top speed for a real-life car. NOT!

Amber: Let's write to that consumer show.

Hector: Yeah, we'll be famous.

Mi-Ling: Hey, this was pretty cool.

This concludes the Mathematics Toolkit. It included many mathematical tools for you to use throughout the unit. As you work through this unit, you should use these tools to help you solve problems. You may want to explain how to use these mathematical tools in your journal. Or you may want to create a toolkit notebook and add the mathematical tools you discover throughout this unit.

On the Road

A class from Pleasanton Middle School went on a field trip to the Monterey Bay Aquarium on Cannery Row in Monterey, California. The map and graph below illustrate the bus trip from Pleasanton to Monterey.

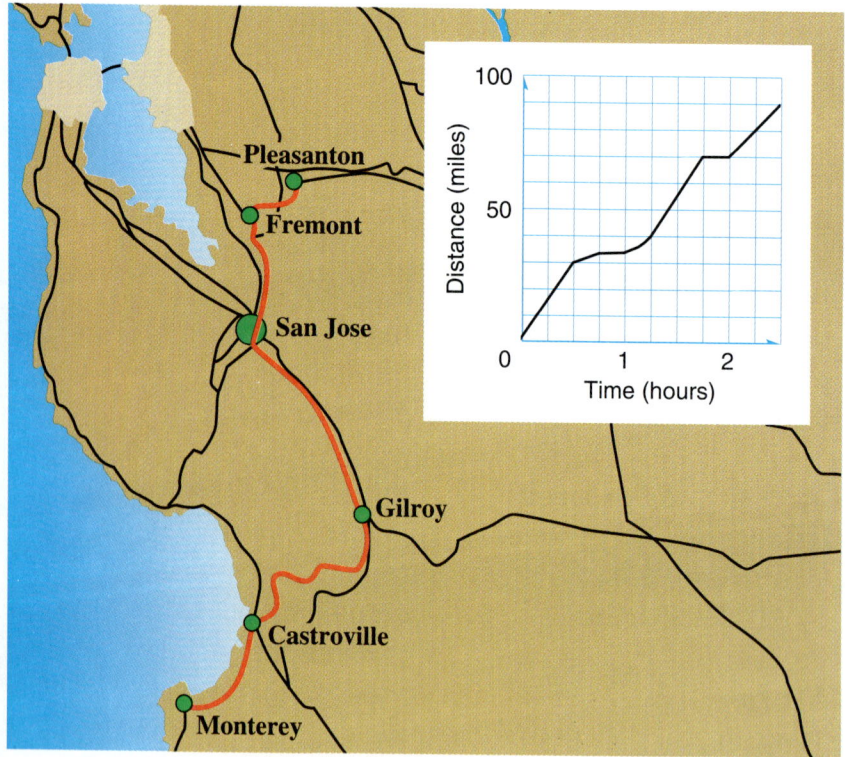

Describe the trip, making use of the graph and the map. It will be easier if you describe the trip in sections. Be sure to include the speed of the bus in your description. Be prepared to present your findings to the class.

THE OLYMPIAD

One-Legged Hop Race

In this activity, each person in the group will race against time. Choose one person to be the starter and another person to be the timer.

1 Measure out a course of six meters. Use masking tape to make a starting and a finish line.

2 At the starter's signal, one member of the group hops on one leg over the six-meter course.

3 Record the time that it took the person to hop the length of the course.

4 Repeat the race, rotating the positions of starter and timer, until each member of the group has raced.

5 Construct a graph of your group's performance. Let one axis represent the distance and let the other axis represent the time in which each racer finishes. Plot a point on the graph showing the time and distance for each racer. Then draw a separate line from the origin to each point. Label each line with the racer's name.

MENU
station
B

TWO-LEGGED HOP RACE

In this activity, each person in the group will race for distance. Choose one person to be the spotter and another person to be the timer.

1 **U**se masking tape to make a starting line.

2 **A**t the timer's signal, one member of the group hops on two legs as far as he or she can go in six seconds. The timer calls out the seconds as they pass ("1, 2, 3,...").

3 **T**he spotter locates where the racer was when the timer yelled "6." The distance the racer was from the starting line is measured and recorded.

4 **R**epeat the race, rotating the positions of spotter and timer, until each member of the group has raced.

5 **C**onstruct a graph of your group's performance. Let one axis represent the distance and let the other axis represent the time in which each racer finishes. Plot a point on the graph showing the time and distance for each racer. Then draw a separate line from the origin to each point. Label each line with the racer's name.

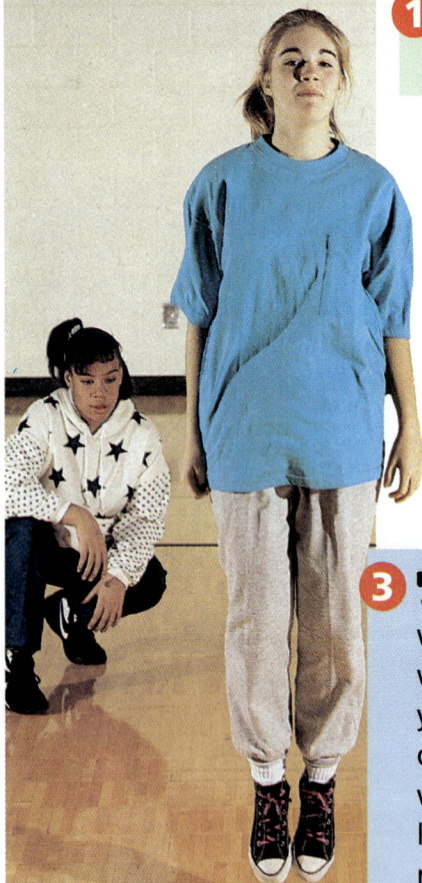

Relay Race

In this activity, the members of the group will run a relay race. Choose one person to be the timer.

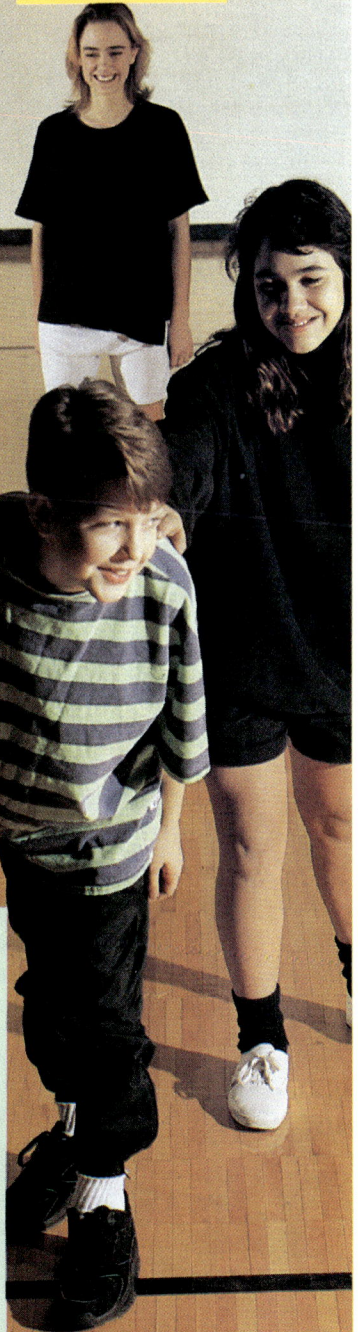

1 Use masking tape to make a starting line. Five meters from the starting line, make a second line. Five meters from the second line, make a third line. Five meters from the third line, make a finish line.

2 Set up a relay race with three racers, with a racer on each line. On the timer's signal, the first racer begins by walking heel-toe, heel-toe. The timer calls out the seconds as they pass ("1, 2, 3,..."). When the first racer reaches and tags the second racer, the first racer listens for his or her time. The same thing happens with each racer. The timer stops the watch when the third racer crosses the finish line.

3 All three times are recorded.

4 Run the relay again, this time with another person as the timer.

5 Construct a graph of your group's two races on the same set of axes. Let one axis represent the distance and let the other axis represent the time in which each racer finishes. Plot a point on the graph showing the time and distance for each racer. Then draw lines from the origin to the first racer's time, from the first racer's time to the second racer's time, and from the second racer's time to the third racer's time. You may want to use different colors for the two races.

MENU station

D

SHUTTLE RACE

In this activity, each member of the group will run a shuttle race. Choose one person to be the timer and another to be the recorder.

1 Use masking tape to make a starting line. Five meters from the starting line, make a second line.

2 In this shuttle race, the racers race back and forth four times between the two marks, ending at the starting line. On the timer's signal, the racer walks *forward* heel-toe, heel-toe. On the way back, the racer walks *backward* heel-toe, heel-toe. Then the process is repeated. The timer calls out the seconds as they pass ("1, 2, 3,...").

3 The recorder notes the times that the racer touches each line and crosses the finish line. Thus, four times should be recorded for each race.

5 Construct a graph of each racer's performance. Let one axis represent the distance and let the other axis represent the times at which each racer touched each line. Plot a point on the graph for each of the four times. Then draw a line from the origin to the first point, from the first point to the second, from the second to the third, and from the third to the fourth.

4 Repeat the race, rotating the positions of timer and recorder, until each member of the group has raced.

MEDLEY RACE

In this activity, the members of the group will run a medley race. A medley race requires a number of different types of racing styles. Choose one person to be the timer.

1 **U**se masking tape to make a starting line. Five meters from the starting line, make a second line; eight meters from the second line, make a third line; ten meters from the third line, make a finish line.

2 **S**et up a relay race with three racers, with a racer on each line. On the timer's signal, the first racer begins by hopping on one foot. The timer calls out the seconds as they pass ("1, 2, 3,..."). When the first racer reaches and tags the second racer, the first racer listens for his or her time. When tagged by the first racer, the second racer begins walking heel-toe, heel-toe and listens for his or her time. When tagged by the second racer, the third racer begins hopping on two feet.

3 **A**ll three times are recorded.

4 **R**un the relay again, this time with another person as the timer.

5 **C**onstruct a graph of your group's two races on the same set of axes. Let one axis represent the distance and let the other axis represent the time in which each racer finishes. Plot a point on the graph showing the time and distance for each racer. Then draw lines from the origin to the first racer's time, from the first racer's time to the second racer's time, and from the second racer's time to the third racer's time. You may want to use different colors for the two races.

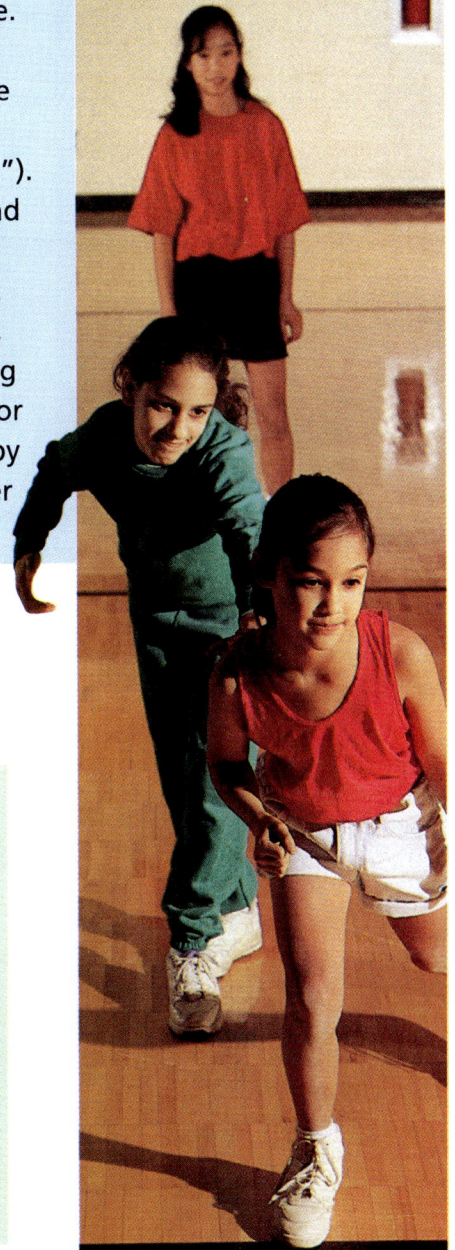

Once Upon a Time ...

Each graph below shows the distance an object moves over a certain time period. Interpret each graph and create a story for each that explains the movement of the object.

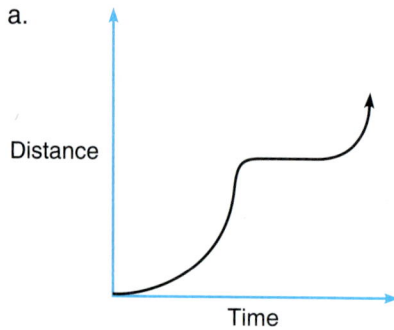

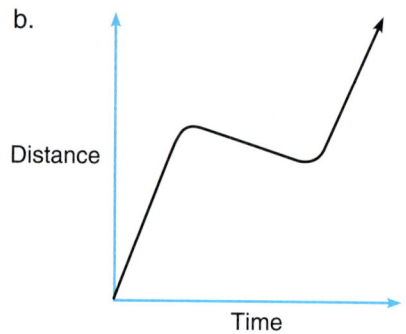

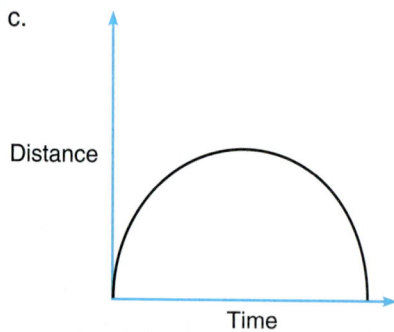

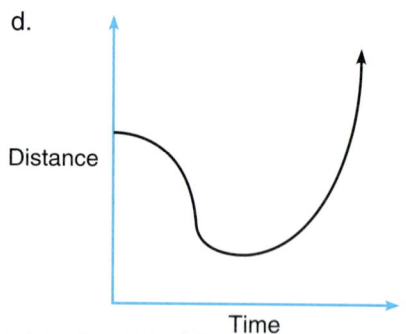

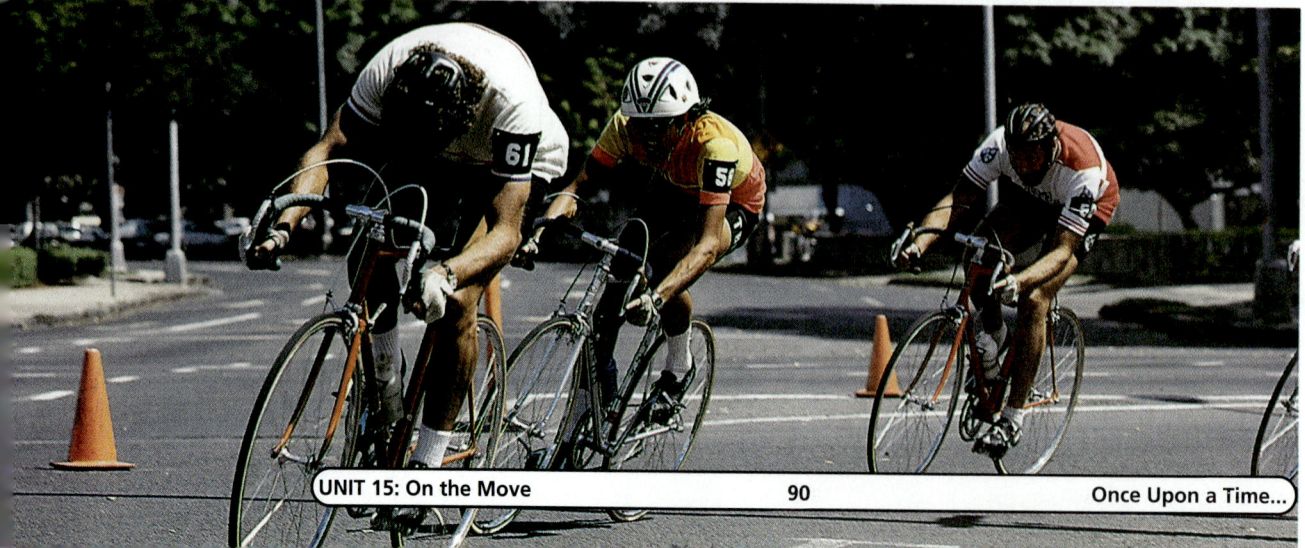

a.

Distance

Time

b.

Distance

Time

c.

Distance

Time

d.

Distance

Time

A Day at the Races

The graph below illustrates a six-furlong horse race involving four horses. The names of the horses are shown on the graph. Imagine that you are the race announcer. Describe the race as you would announce it at a race track. Be sure to write exactly what you would say as the announcer.

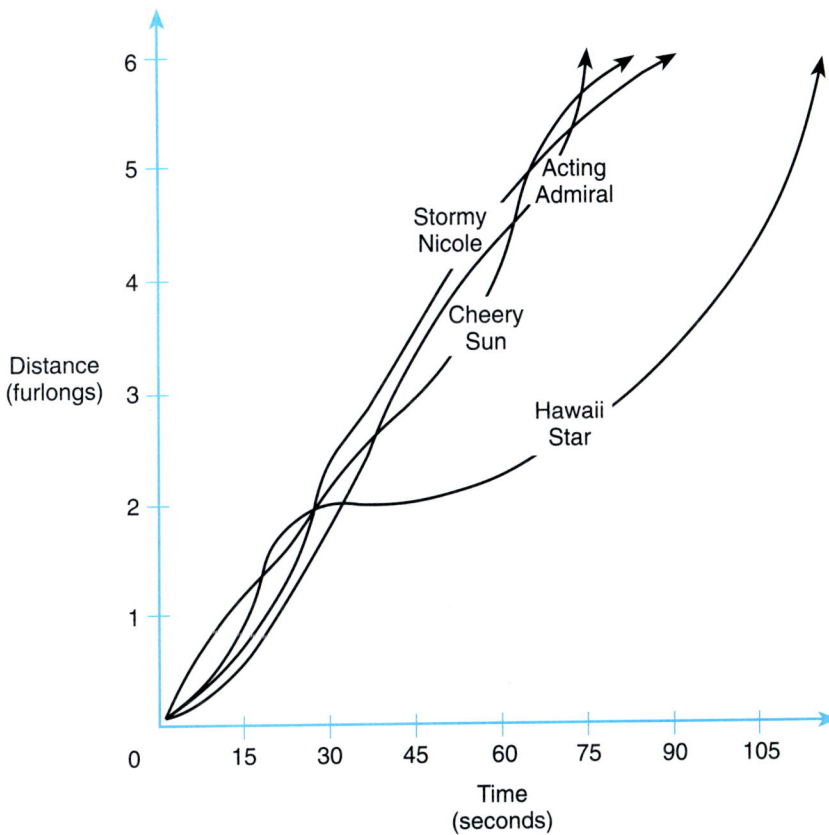

Distance (furlongs)

Acting Admiral

Stormy Nicole

Cheery Sun

Hawaii Star

Time (seconds)

3-2-1 BLAST OFF!

You are a NASA engineer at Mission Control. Your job is to analyze the launch of a space shuttle. From your analysis, adjustments can be made for future shuttle missions. Your analysis will take the form of an oral presentation to your supervisors on the speed and **acceleration**, or the rate of change in speed, of the space shuttle during the launch.

In order to do your analysis, you will use data from the launch of a space shuttle. This data is provided in the Data Bank. Use the data to sketch a graph or series of graphs that describe the flight. Calculate the average speed of the shuttle and illustrate intervals of acceleration and speed on your graph(s).

Plan and give an oral group presentation. Use poster board to display your graphs, illustrations, charts, or other findings. Explain the characteristics of the launch and how they are illustrated through the graphs that you drew.

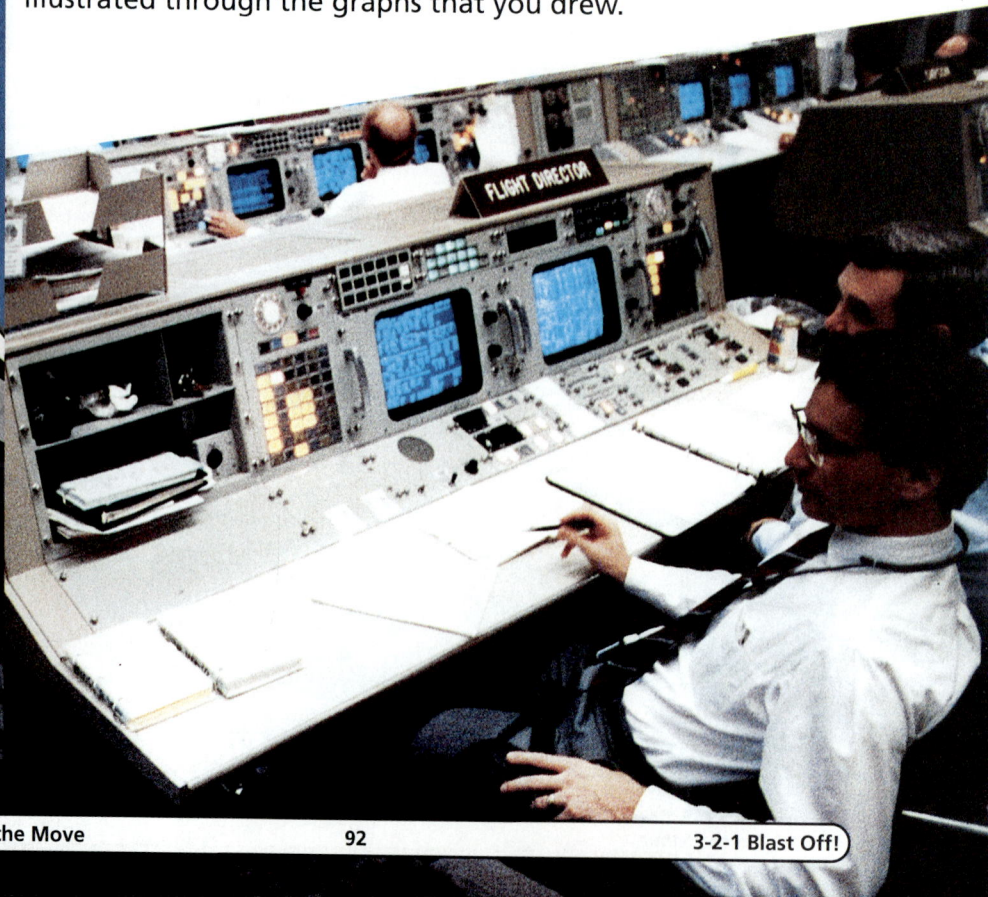

The Speeding Ticket

You are a highway patrol officer, seated on a motorcycle, on a curvy section of Highway 1. The posted speed limit is 45 miles per hour (mph) on this stretch of highway. You are monitoring traffic with a radar gun. The first exit is 3.6 miles up the road. Your radar picks up a speeding car averaging 68 mph. When you try to start your motorcycle to follow the car, it won't start. You try again and again, and soon you fear that you won't be able to catch the speeding car before it can turn off the highway. Finally, your motorcycle starts and you begin your pursuit 30 seconds after the speeding car has passed you on the roadside.

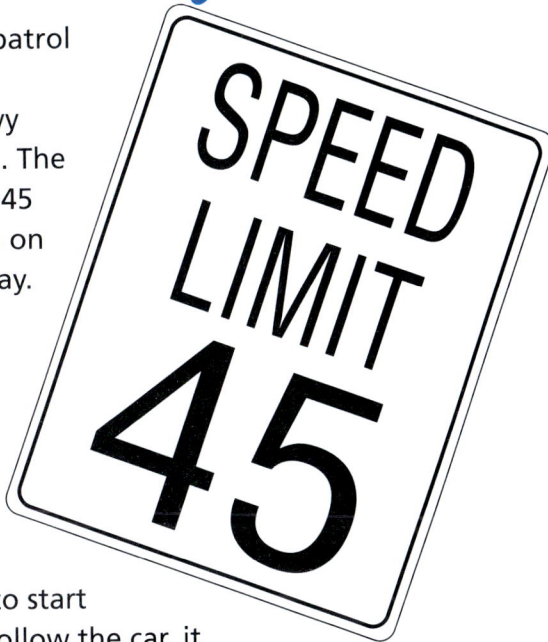

How fast do you need to go to catch up to the speeding car? What is your average speed in pursuit? How fast do you need to accelerate? Is your own speed reasonable and safe? Explain why this is or is not a good location at which to monitor traffic. Illustrate the speed of the speeding car as well as your own motorcycle during this pursuit. Be prepared to share your findings with the class.

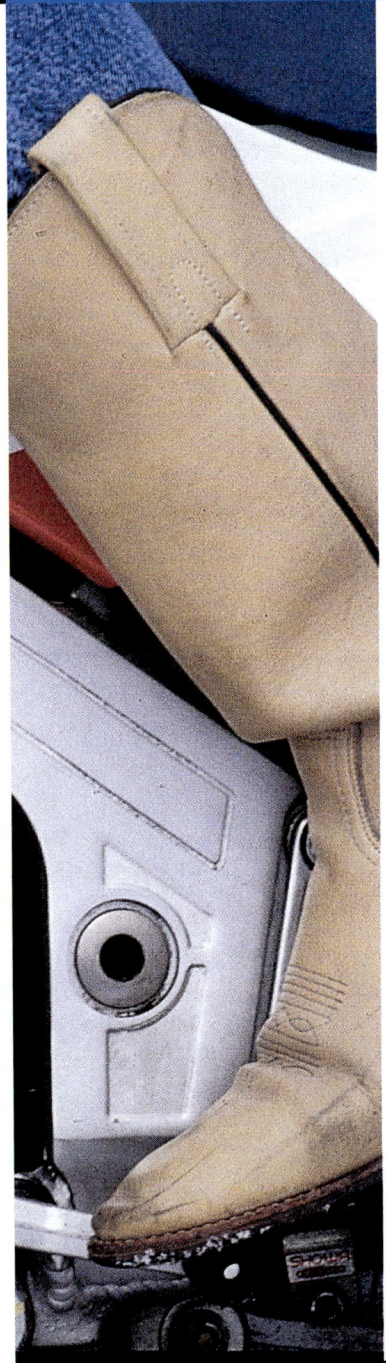

How Far, How Fast?

Speed Racer

Place one end of a board measuring at least 2 meters atop two books, making a ramp. Mark a starting line on the top end of the ramp with masking tape. Let a toy car go at the starting line and clock how long it takes for the car to come to a complete stop. Measure the distance that the car traveled.

Repeat the process, changing the height of the ramp from two books to four books, then six books, and finally, eight books. Sketch two sets of graphs. Compare the distances traveled to the heights of the ramps and compare the average speeds of the cars to the heights of the ramps. Analyze your results and write about your findings

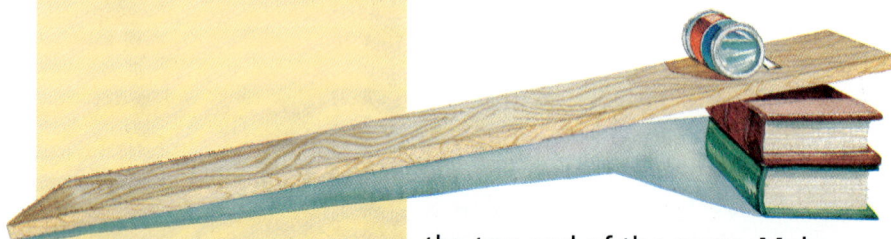

What a Drip!

Place one end of a 2-meter board atop two books, making a ramp with the starting line at the top end of the ramp. Make a small hole in the center of a coffee can and fill it with water. Let the coffee can go at the starting line with the hole at the bottom, touching the board. As the coffee can rolls down the ramp, a spot will appear at each revolution of the coffee can. When the coffee can gets to the bottom of the ramp, let it roll until it comes to a complete stop. Measure the distances of each water spot from the starting line. Make sure that you measure from the top of each dot, as some dots may run.

Repeat the process, changing the height of the ramp from two books to four books, then six books, and finally, eight books. Sketch a set of graphs comparing the distances of each dot from the starting line to the number of books. Analyze your results and write about your findings.

Speed it Up!

Choose a timer and two spotters. Place one end of a 2-meter board atop two books, making a ramp with the starting line at the top end of the ramp. Use masking tape to mark off lines on the board every 50 cm. Also mark off 50-cm intervals on the floor from the end of the board until you have marked 2 meters on the floor. Let a toy car go at the starting line. As the car rolls down the ramp, the timer calls out the seconds ("1, 2, 3,..."). The spotters determine the time that the car crosses each mark as it comes down the ramp.

Repeat the process, changing the height of the ramp from two books to four books, then six books, and finally, eight books. Sketch a set of graphs comparing the time of the car with each of the distances. Analyze your results and write about your findings.

Up and Down

Choose a timer and two spotters. Place one end of a board measuring 2 meters atop four books, making a downward ramp. Then place one end of a board measuring 3 meters against the end of the 2-meter board that is on the floor and place the other end atop four books, making an upward ramp. Mark a starting line on the top end of the 2-meter ramp with masking tape. Then mark off lines on the board every 50 cm down the 2-meter ramp and up the 3-meter ramp. Let a toy car go at the starting line. As the car rolls down the ramp, the timer calls out the seconds ("1, 2, 3,..."). The spotters determine the time that the car crossed each mark as it goes down and up the ramps. Note the point at which the car begins to travel backward down the ramp or note that the car went off the edge of the 3-meter ramp.

Repeat the process, changing the height of the ramps from four books to six books and then eight books. Sketch a set of graphs comparing the time of the car with each of the distances. Analyze your results and write about your findings.

A Thrill a Minute

At amusement parks there are a variety of rides in which visitors experience different types of motion. In this activity, you will read about five different ride situations. Read and analyze each situation. Work in your groups to determine the paths, speeds, times, and distances each of the rides take. Sketch graphs of the movement of the objects in the rides. These graphs may be drawn in relationship to distance and time, speed and time, or speed and distance. Then explain how the graph illustrates the speed of the objects and where the objects accelerate, decelerate, or stay at a constant speed. Be prepared to present your analysis to the class.

The Log Ride

You enter a log on a slowly moving turntable. When all have boarded, the log moves in a slow, steady motion to the base of an incline. The log slows almost to a stop as it starts up the incline. The motion is constant as the log climbs the incline on a conveyor belt. At the top of the incline, the log accelerates slowly, building speed as it proceeds to a waterfall. The log speeds down the waterfall and plunges into a pool below, creating a huge splash and nearly stopping the log's forward momentum. The log slowly flows to the end of the ride. You exit the ride where it began as it moves around the turntable again.

The Bumper Cars

Your bumper car ride begins with the car having no power. At the sound of the bell, your car begins to back up. You quickly turn the steering wheel, which enables the car to change directions and go forward. You are gaining speed when suddenly you are hit from behind. Your car lurches forward and comes to a stop. You notice that it is your friend who has hit you. You decide to chase your friend. You start to accelerate. Your friend zooms off in the opposite direction. Suddenly, you are heading straight for your friend's car. You accelerate. WHAM! You slam head on, bounce backwards, and stop. You are shaken up. Two more cars run into you, pushing you forward, then backward. You start your car and are moving forward, accelerating toward one of the cars that hit you. Suddenly, the power is turned off and you come to an abrupt stop.

The Jet Fighters

The jet fighters are attached to a central post. Each jet fighter has a tiller that controls the up and down motion of the jet. You enter your jet. The jet takes off slowly, building speed. You pull down on the jet's tiller. The jet climbs, gaining speed. The jets circle with increasing speed. You decide to go into a dive, then climb again. The jet reaches its maximum circular speed. The ride continues for three minutes at this pace. You continue to dive and climb throughout this period. The jets begin to slow their circular motion, and all of the jets descend. It takes one minute for the jets to slow to a stop.

The Roller Coaster

The picture below is of the Radical Ride Roller Coaster. You start out on this roller coaster on the left side of the page and travel from left to right. Sketch three graphs of the ride: time versus distance, time versus speed, and speed versus distance. Explain the ride in terms of speed, acceleration, and deceleration. Describe how you drew the graph and how it relates to the roller coaster tracks.

The Ferris Wheel

You get on a Ferris wheel with 12 cars. Each car has 2 seats. The operator starts and stops the Ferris wheel to allow riders to board and exit the ride. After each ride, the operator lets the riders in every other car exit the ride. After 6 cars of riders board the Ferris wheel, the operator starts the ride and it then turns 12 times at a constant speed. Then the operator lets customers exit the ride in the same manner that they boarded. You are in the third car of riders to exit the ride.

And They're Off!

In this activity, you will participate in a race in which you move your vehicle by using information about direction and speed. To start, each player places his or her vehicle on the starting line by drawing a dot on the track. No two vehicles may occupy the same spot at the same time. Then the players roll a number cube to determine who goes first; the player with the highest number begins and play follows in a clockwise direction. Each vehicle begins with a speed of (0, 0). The goal is to be the first player to reach the finish line without going off the track.

To move your vehicle, start by choosing any two coordinates that will keep your vehicle on the track. The first coordinate indicates movement left and right. A positive number indicates movement to the right while a negative number indicates movement to the left. The second coordinate indicates movement up and down. A positive number indicates movement up while a negative number indicates movement down. You may change the speed and/or direction of your vehicle by adding 1 (+1), subtracting 1 (–1), or adding 0 (+0). For example, suppose your vehicle's current speed is (1, 2) and you want to accelerate its movement to the left and decelerate its movement up to negotiate a turn. You would subtract 1 from the first coordinate and subtract 1 from the second coordinate. Then the new speed of the vehicle would be (0, 1). Use the recording sheet to record your speed after each turn.

Mark each new ordered pair by drawing a circle on the track and then drawing a line from the dot to the circle. On your next turn, color in the circle and plot a new point by drawing a circle at the new coordinate.

Keep in mind that no dot can be drawn on or outside the track. If your vehicle goes out of control and leaves the track, you must go back to the starting line and begin again. The first vehicle to cross the finish line wins.

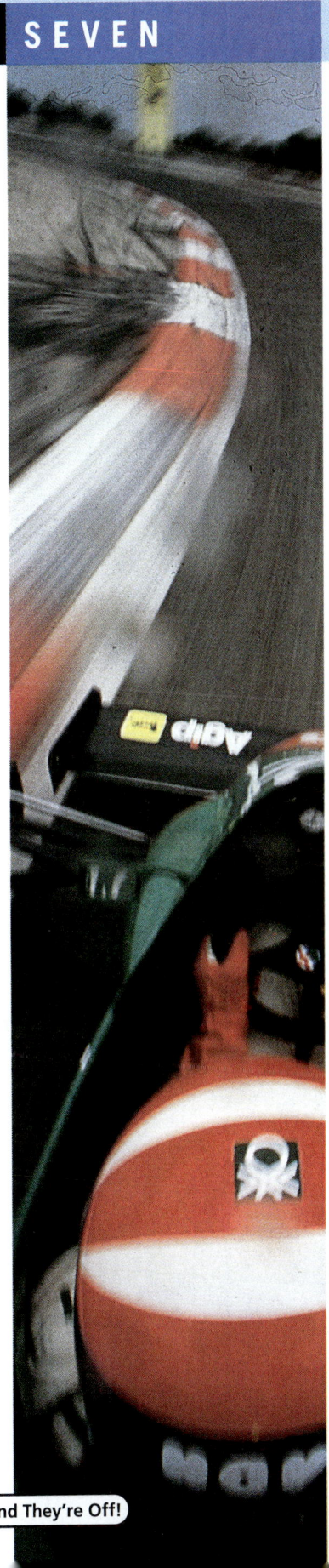

COMPUTER investigation

The Great Race

In this activity, you will use a computer program to run race cars around a track. You may accelerate, decelerate, turn right, or turn left as you drive around the track.

- To accelerate, press the A key.
- To decelerate or slow down, press the S key.
- To turn right, press the K key.
- To turn left, press the J key.
- To quit or stop the race, press the Q key.

Each time the A key is pressed, the car accelerates. Likewise, the car slows down when the S key is pressed and will come to a complete stop if it is pressed enough times. The car turns 30° every time the J key or the K key is pressed. The car will stay at a constant speed and direction if no key is pressed. If a car goes off the track, the race stops. During the race, the current time, speed, and distance appear at the bottom of the screen.

Conduct several races. The computer will record your results. The program compiles data points as you negotiate your way around the race track. The data recorded are the car's current time, speed, and distance traveled.

Analyze your races. Calculate your total time, average speed, and intervals of acceleration. Chart your findings on graphs. Compare your races with other groups and determine how the race would have looked on the same track. Then summarize your findings in writing.

- Describe your race.
- Analyze the speed of your race car.
- When did you accelerate or decelerate?
- Were you able to maintain a constant speed?
- What was easy and what was difficult about driving the car?
- Explain the process you used to study the motion of your car.

Go for the Gold

You are one of the women's track coaches for the United States Olympic team. Your job is to prepare the athletes for the 1,500-meter race. You decide to analyze races from past Olympic games to better inform yourself of race strategy, runners' speeds, and athletic conditioning. You obtain a videotape of the women's 1,500-meter race from the 1992 Olympic Games. After you and your assistant view the videotape, she makes a table of the race data for you to use. This table is shown in the Data Bank. Your task is to analyze the race. Focus in on at least five of the runners. Determine how far the runners run in a period of time. Use that data to create a graph or series of graphs that show their speeds over time. On the graphs, you may track distance against time, time against speed, or distance against speed to illustrate the motion of the runners and the characteristics of the race. Your graphs may focus on more than one runner. Illustrate intervals of acceleration, deceleration, and speed. Note where runners overtake other runners. Calculate the average speed and rates of acceleration of the runners.

YOUR PRESENTATION

Plan and give an oral group presentation. Use chart paper or poster board to display your graphs and analysis. Include a written explanation of your understanding of distance, time, velocity, and acceleration as they pertain to the race. Describe the characteristics of the race and explain how they are illustrated through the graphs that you drew.

Speed Demon

You are a design engineer working for a racing car manufacturer. You have been assigned the task of working with a design crew to build a new race car. Your crew's assignment includes: designing the vehicle, building a prototype, and testing the vehicle for speed, distance, and acceleration capabilities.

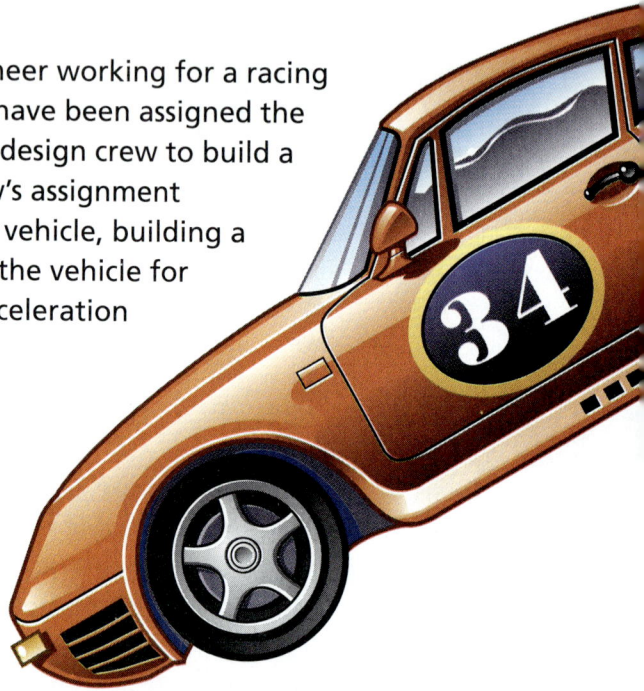

YOUR REPORT

After your crew has designed and tested the vehicle, you must produce an individual report that describes the process. The report must include:

- a scale drawing of the vehicle,
- a description of the design process,
- a justification of the tests conducted,
- the data that were compiled from the tests,
- an analysis of the vehicle's traveling speed and acceleration capabilities,
- graphs of the vehicle's performance, and
- a performance summary to be used for advertising purposes.

SELECTION AND REFLECTION

- The mathematical terms **function, speed, velocity, acceleration,** and **deceleration** were used throughout this unit. What do these terms mean? Explain them in your own words.

- Describe the mathematics that you used in this unit.

- What did you learn while studying this unit? Use examples from several of the activities in the unit in your explanation.

- How did you feel about learning about the mathematics of movement? Did you enjoy the experience?

Sunday Drive

The Problem

The Kanazawa family drove from San Diego, California, to Santa Barbara, California. They traveled at an average speed of 65 miles per hour (mph) for 105 miles, until they reached Anaheim. They slowed down to 35 mph for 45 miles, until they reached Thousand Oaks. Then they sped up to 60 mph until they reached Santa Barbara, 50 miles away. How long did it take them to make the trip?

Anaheim
NEXT 7 EXITS

Thousand Oaks
NEXT 8 EXITS

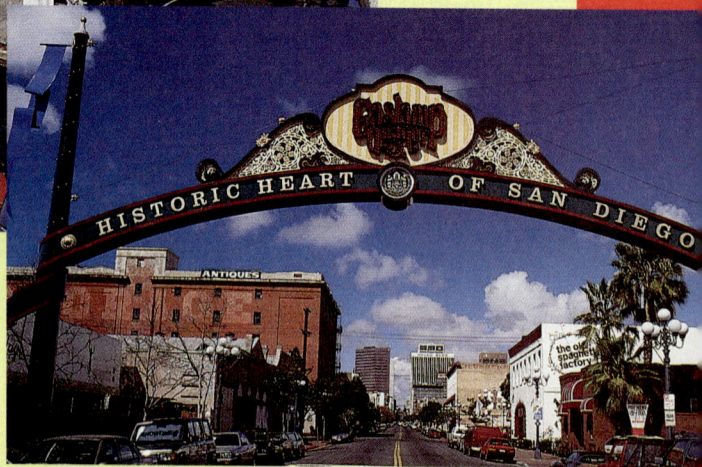

HISTORIC HEART OF SAN DIEGO

Extension What was their average speed for the entire trip, if they did not make any stops?

The Problem

Suppose that every hour of every day, an airplane leaves Los Angeles for New York City and at the same instant, an airplane leaves New York City for Los Angeles. Each flight takes 5 hours. In a single day, how many airplanes originating in New York City will pass airplanes originating in Los Angeles in the air?

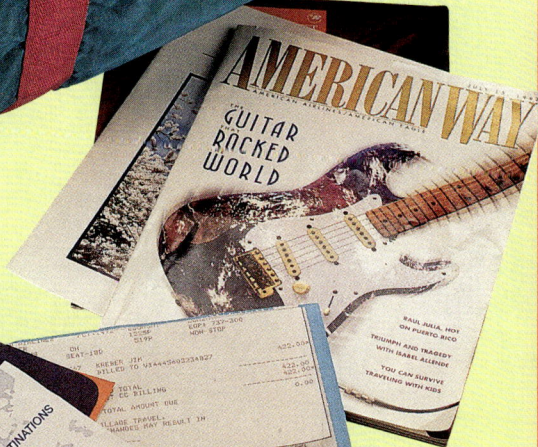

Passing Planes

Space Shuttle Suppers

The Problem

In the early space flights, scientists learned a great deal about the body's response to prolonged weightlessness. Now, space shuttle astronauts have a carefully planned menu to provide the energy and nutrients they need during space flights. Each evening meal consists of one main dish, one vegetable, and two desserts, and an appetizer is included every other day. There are 10 main dishes, 8 vegetable dishes, 13 desserts, and 3 appetizers available. How many different evening meals can be served?

The Problem

You are a police officer investigating an accident. A car has hit a truck and you are wondering whether or not the car was speeding. You measure the skid marks and they are 1,528 feet long. The speed limit for the road is 45 mph. The chart you normally use for determining braking distances is shown below. As you can see, it has an ink stain on it. Without getting another chart, how can you determine whether the car was speeding?

THE POLICE REPORT

Speed (mph)	Braking Distance (feet)
5	15
10	60
15	135
20	240
50	1,500
55	1,815
60	2,160

Extension About how fast was the car going?

All Gassed Up

The Problem

Jorge and Benita traded in their old car, which averaged 22 miles per gallon, for a new car, on which the EPA sticker stated that it should average 37 miles per gallon. If Jorge and Benita drive about 12,000 miles per year and the cost of gasoline averages $1.20 per gallon in their area, how much should they expect to save on gasoline during the first year that they own their new car?

The Problem

Shelly and Keisha spent the day at Tons O' Fun Amusement Park. After lunch, the girls decided to try some games on the midway before taking a few more rides. They stopped at a dart game booth where each person pays $1.00 to play, and is given five darts to throw at a target like the one shown below. The first person to score exactly 21 points wins a prize. Keisha thought about the game for a minute and announced that she did not think it was possible to win the game. Shelly disagreed and played the game three times, but with no success. Is the game fair? Explain.

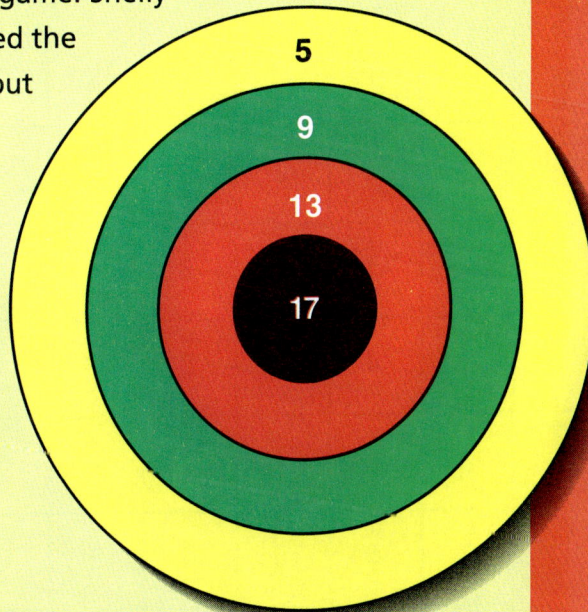

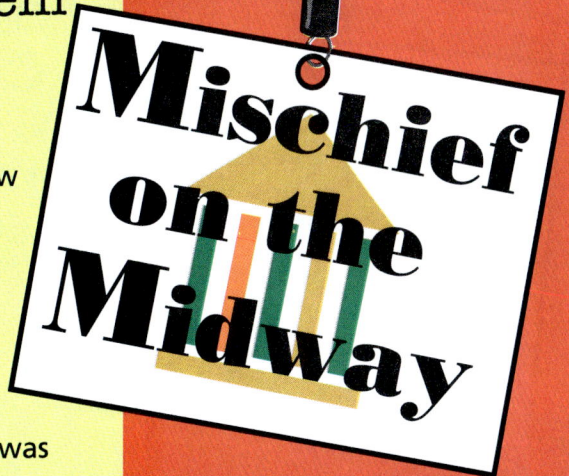

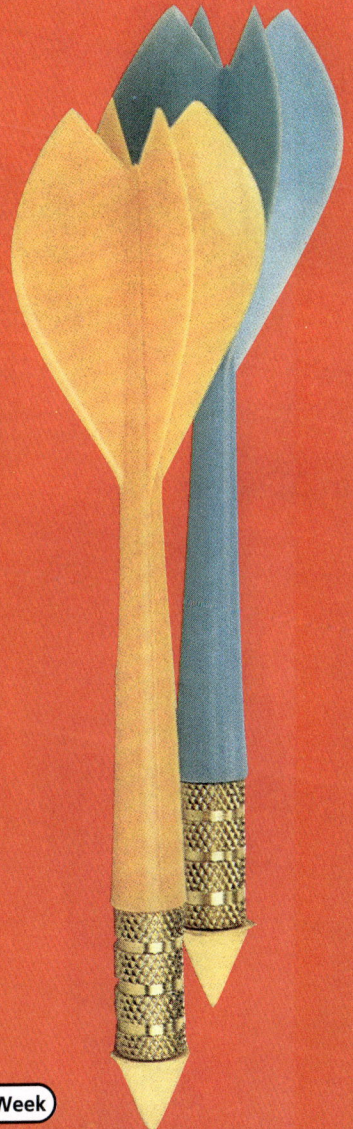

Mischief on the Midway

5
9
13
17

Extension If you determined that the game was fair, write a letter to Keisha explaining why you think so. If you determined that the game was not fair, write a letter to the owner of the amusement park explaining why the game is not fair and how to change the game so that it could be fair.

Blazing a Trail

The Problem

Copy the grid below onto a sheet of paper. Start at the 0 in the top lefthand corner of the grid below and draw a line one square to a 1. Then continue the line two squares to a 2, three squares to a 3, and so on. Make a trail to the 8 in the bottom righthand corner without revisiting any square. You may move horizontally or vertically, but diagonal moves are not allowed.

0	1	3	2	5	3	5	6
1	3	2	4	5	4	6	7
2	3	4	3	4	6	7	5
3	4	5	3	7	7	6	7
4	5	6	5	4	5	7	6
7	6	5	4	5	7	5	7
6	5	4	5	6	4	5	6
7	6	6	7	4	6	7	8

GROWING PAINS

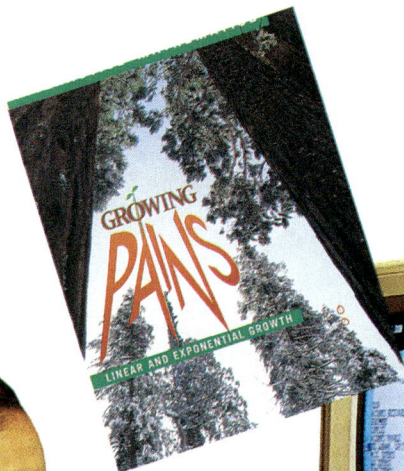

Looking Ahead

In this unit, you will see how mathematics can be used to discover patterns in nature. You will experience:

▶ exploring, defining, measuring, and graphing growth

▶ examining sequences and determining patterns

▶ measuring tall objects indirectly

▶ computing simple and compound interest

▶ exploring population growth

Did You Ever Wonder?

What do mathematics and a large business firm have to do with each other? Turn the page and see how Dee Lakhani of Staten Island, New York, combines the two!

Teens in the News

Featuring: Dee Lakhani
Age: 17
Hometown: Staten Island, New York
Career Goal: Certified public accountant and tax attorney
Interests: Foreign languages, writing

Dee Lakhani was born in India, but grew up in New York City. She loved to visit Manhattan and watch the business people hurrying to work. When she was 17, Dee was chosen for an internship at Smith Barney Shearson, a respected business firm in Manhattan. Dee's dream of being in the exciting world of business came true!

Dee attended the Academy of Finance her junior and senior years of high school. After her junior year, Dee worked for seven weeks as an employment assistant at Smith Barney Shearson. She wrote memos, gave tests to applicants, completed medical paperwork, and got lots of practice with WordPerfect® and Lotus® computer programs. When the regular full-time employment assistant went on vacation, Dee handled her full work load for two weeks.

While at Smith Barney Shearson, Dee learned to compute price-earnings ratios for shares of stock. She also learned how to determine the median ratios for companies in the same industry. Dee put her computer and communications skills to work during her internship at Smith Barney Shearson.

The Academy of Finance awards scholarships to business-oriented colleges. Dee hopes to earn one of those scholarships and attend a business college in New York or Massachusetts. She wants to major in law and accounting. Dee's formula for success is based on good grades, good skills, and good character.

Citicorp dominates market

Citicorp has little competition as an issuer of bank credit cards.

Issuer with number of cards in millions

Issuer	Cards (millions)
Chase Manhattan	8.2
First Chicago	6.5
Bank of America	6
MBNA America Bank	4.8
Citicorp	22

Source: *Credit Card News*

Team Project

Mind Your Own Business!

Dee really enjoyed working with successful people during her internship at Smith Barney Shearson. Any business would be lucky to have Dee on their staff.

You and your group members are forming a small business. Decide what your product will be, what you will charge for it, and to whom you will sell it. Determine the total revenue for your business each month for one year.

Total Revenue = Price × Quantity sold (TR = P × Q)

Make a line graph that shows the *growth* of your business.

Present your graph to the class and convince them that they should invest in your business.

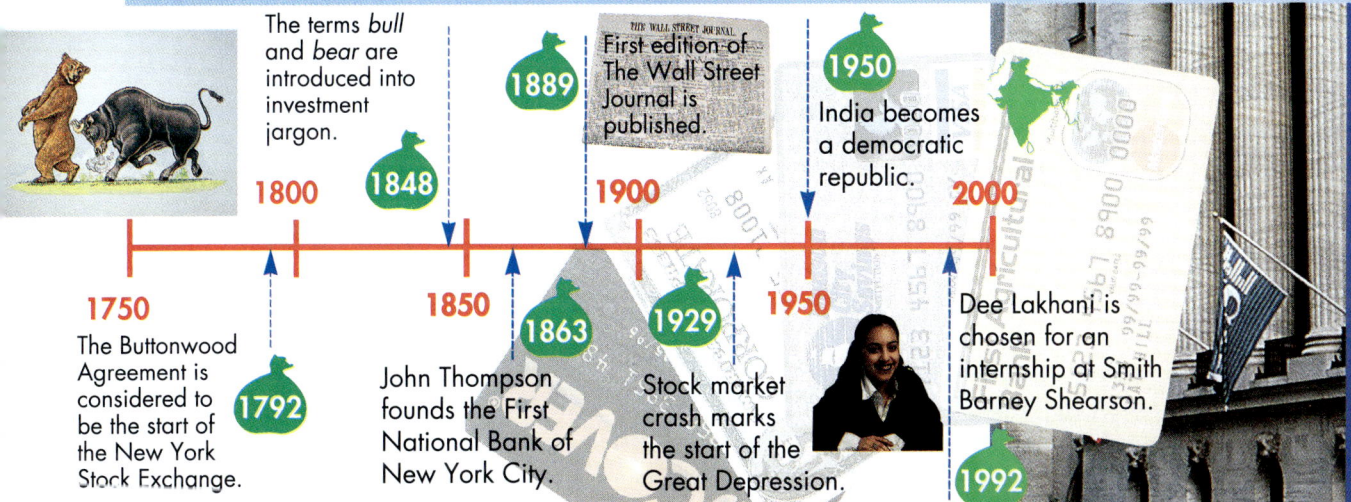

The terms *bull* and *bear* are introduced into investment jargon.

1889 First edition of The Wall Street Journal is published.

1950 India becomes a democratic republic.

1800   **1848**   **1900**   **2000**

1750
1792 The Buttonwood Agreement is considered to be the start of the New York Stock Exchange.

1850
1863 John Thompson founds the First National Bank of New York City.

1929 Stock market crash marks the start of the Great Depression.

1950

Dee Lakhani is chosen for an internship at Smith Barney Shearson.
1992

For more information

If you would like more information about the Academy of Finance, which is a joint venture between Wall Street and the New York City Board of Education, contact:

Academy of Finance
Office of the Director
131 Livingston Street
Brooklyn, New York 11201

You can learn more about the math Dee uses in her finance courses by completing the activities in this unit.

Setting the Scene

MATHEMATICS TOOLKIT

You may remember reading the book The Swiss Family Robinson *by Johann Wyss. It is about a family that was shipwrecked in a violent storm and how they made the island on which they landed their home. In the story, Mrs. Robinson decides that their temporary home, a tent on the beach, is too hot and uncomfortable for her family and looks for a more suitable place for the family to live. She finds a group of trees and suggests to her husband that they build a tree house for the family. Take time to read this toolkit and remember the questions that are asked and answered by the characters.*

Narrator: Ayako, Sam, and Latrisha are students at Walnut Creek High School. They are at Sam's home discussing the book *The Swiss Family Robinson* after reading it for an English assignment.

Ayako: You can tell that this book is really old. There were some really weird words in there.

Sam: I know—some strange creatures, too. But I thought it was kind of interesting. And it kind of sounded like fun, too, living in a tree house.

Latrisha: All I could think about was the animals—I'd be afraid that they could climb into my house!

Mrs. Ruiz: Hi, kids. What's up?

Sam: Hey, Mom. We're talking about *The Swiss Family Robinson.* We've got to write a group book report about it.

Mrs. Ruiz: I remember reading that book a long time ago. I used to wonder what it would be like to live in a tree house thirty feet up.

Ayako: How did you know it was thirty feet up?

Sam: Yeah, Mom—it didn't say that in the story.

Mrs. Ruiz: Oh yes it did! It sounds like you guys need to read the story again. This time, pay attention to the chapter called "Changing Quarters." Sam, I want you to reread that chapter extra carefully. Don't be surprised if I have a few questions for you tomorrow.

Sam: Aw, Mom.

Mrs. Ruiz: I've got to go out now, Sam, but I'd like to see that book report before you turn it in. See you later!

Narrator: Mrs. Ruiz leaves and a huge sigh fills the room.

Sam: I can't believe this. My mom's a teacher—she's really going to lean on me about this book report.

Latrisha: Well, maybe that's good. She can help us make sure that our facts are correct.

Narrator: The students decide to reread the chapter entitled "Changing Quarters" and plan to get together again the next day.

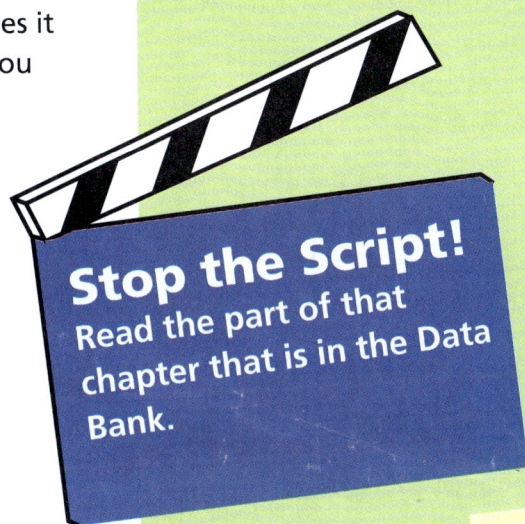

Stop the Script!
Read the part of that chapter that is in the Data Bank.

Narrator: The next day, the students meet again.

Ayako: You know, this time when I read the chapter, I found a lot more math in it.

Latrisha: I know. That whole thing about finding the height of the lowest branch—I guess I wasn't paying attention the first time through.

Listen, you guys—I've got an idea. We've got a group report due in math class this week on "Mathematics and Literature." What do you think about us doing a joint report for both classes?

Ayako: That's a great idea! Let's talk to Mr. Taylor and Ms. Higgins about it.

Sam: Sounds good to me. What kinds of things should we talk about in the report?

Narrator: The students work for several hours, making an outline of their report and writing a general description of *The Swiss Family Robinson*.

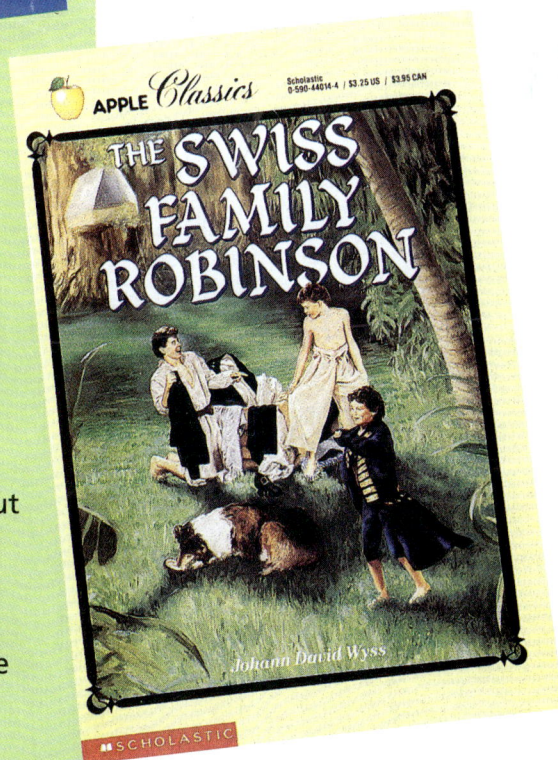

APPLE *Classics*
Scholastic
0-590-44014-4 / $3.25 US / $3.95 CAN

THE SWISS FAMILY ROBINSON

Johann David Wyss

SCHOLASTIC

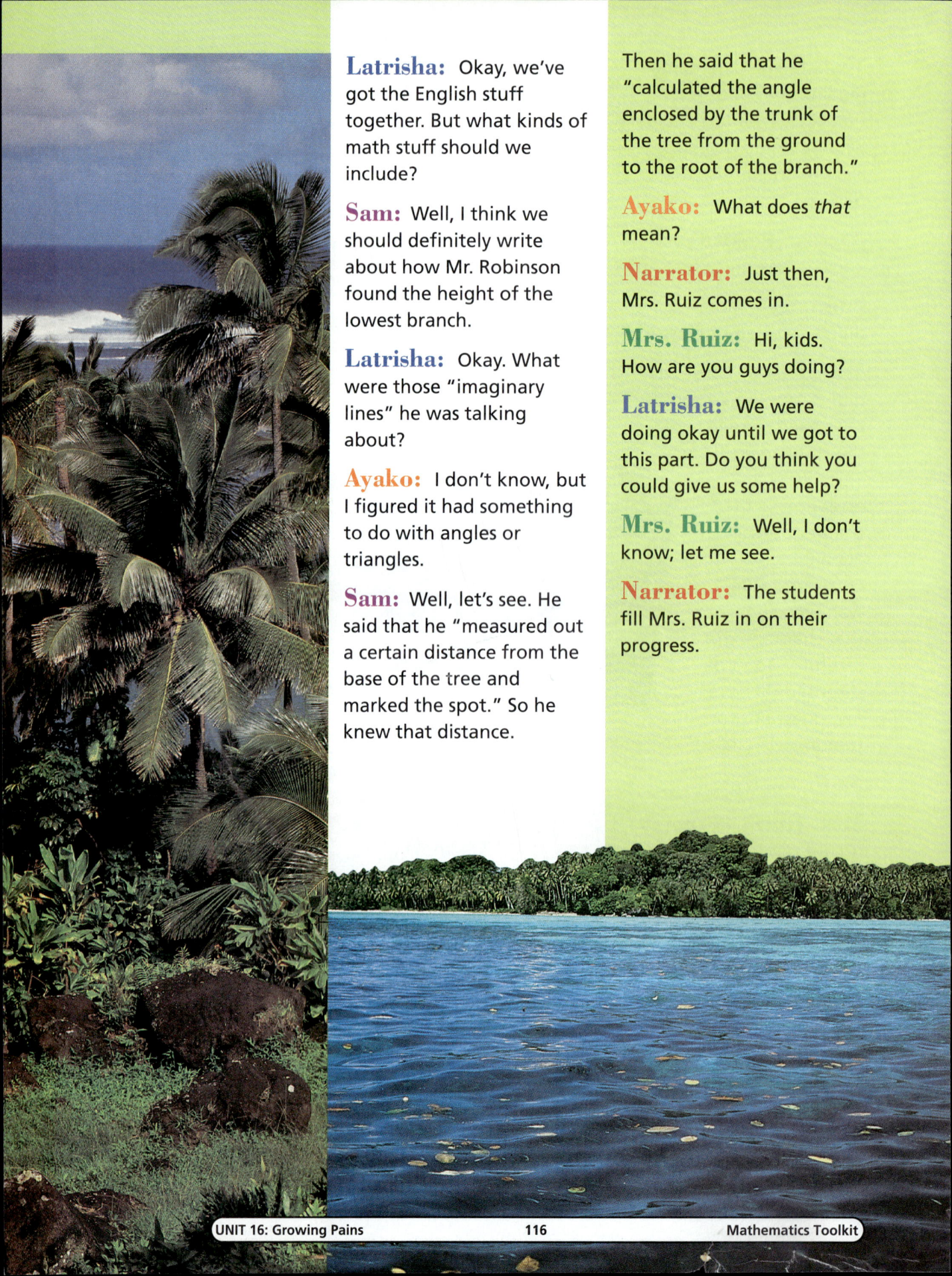

Latrisha: Okay, we've got the English stuff together. But what kinds of math stuff should we include?

Sam: Well, I think we should definitely write about how Mr. Robinson found the height of the lowest branch.

Latrisha: Okay. What were those "imaginary lines" he was talking about?

Ayako: I don't know, but I figured it had something to do with angles or triangles.

Sam: Well, let's see. He said that he "measured out a certain distance from the base of the tree and marked the spot." So he knew that distance.

Then he said that he "calculated the angle enclosed by the trunk of the tree from the ground to the root of the branch."

Ayako: What does *that* mean?

Narrator: Just then, Mrs. Ruiz comes in.

Mrs. Ruiz: Hi, kids. How are you guys doing?

Latrisha: We were doing okay until we got to this part. Do you think you could give us some help?

Mrs. Ruiz: Well, I don't know; let me see.

Narrator: The students fill Mrs. Ruiz in on their progress.

Ayako: I think we're dealing with a **right triangle**. The tree makes one side of the triangle. The "certain distance" he talked about makes another side. There's a **right angle** where the tree meets the ground. And the **hypotenuse** is the "imaginary line" from the spot he marked to the place where the tree branch is connected to the tree...like this.

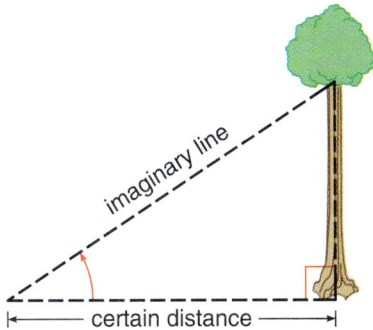

Sam: So how did he find the height of the branch?

Latrisha: Remember what we learned about **trigonometry** last year? If you can find a right triangle, you can calculate the height of something by using a ratio:

tangent x = measure of opposite side ÷ measure of adjacent side.

Sam: Oh, yeah, I remember that stuff. But what is x, which is the opposite side, and which is the adjacent side?

Latrisha: Let's set it up and label the drawing that Ayako made.

$$\tan x = \frac{\text{measure of opposite side}}{\text{measure of adjacent side}}$$

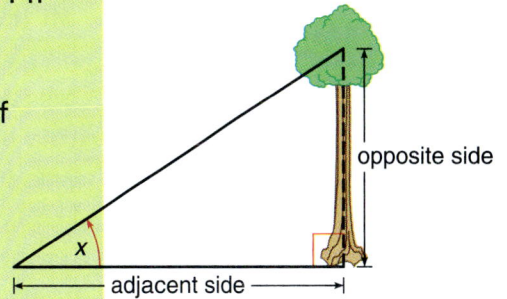

Sam: We need to find the measure of the opposite side. That's the height of the tree branch, isn't it?

Latrisha: Right. Let's say that we knew the angle measured 60° and that Mr. Robinson marked off 50 feet. Then the equation would look like this.

$$\tan 60° = \frac{\text{measure of opposite side}}{50}$$

Ayako: How do we solve that?

Mrs. Ruiz: Well,

$$\tan 60° = \frac{\text{measure of opposite side}}{50}$$

is the same as 50 × tan 60° = measure of the opposite side. Now you can use your calculator to solve that.

Latrisha: Okay, let me plug that in.

50 × 60 tan =

I get 86.60254.

Sam: So that means if Mr. Robinson's measurements were 60° and 50 feet, he would have found the tree branch to be about 87 feet off the ground. We don't know what his measurements were that told him the tree branch was 30 feet off the ground, but I guess we can describe his method in our report.

Mrs. Ruiz: That's right. I'm really proud of you guys. You stuck to it and figured it out. I'm really anxious to read this book report.

This concludes the Mathematics Toolkit. It included many mathematical tools for you to use throughout this unit. As you work through the unit, you should use these tools to help you solve problems. You may want to explain how to use these mathematical tools in your journal. Or you may want to create a toolkit notebook to add mathematical tools you discover throughout this unit.

A Tree Grows In...

GRADUATION TREES

There is a tradition at Sequoia Middle School. In each of the last four years, the eighth grade graduating class has purchased a coastal redwood seedling and planted it in front of the school.

You are the eighth grade class president and want to continue the tradition this year. But before your class can be given approval to plant a new seedling, the principal wants you to write a report that will describe what the front of the school building will look like in five years. Specifically, the principal is interested in the heights of the trees. The heights of the four trees that are currently planted are as follows: 8.3 meters, 6.5 meters, 4.4 meters, and 2.6 meters.

Prepare a presentation for the principal. In your presentation, describe the current heights of the trees and what the front of the school building will look like in five years, given the current tradition. You may want to include a diagram.

As Old as Dirt?

Scientists use several methods to determine the ages of trees. One method is to count the rings in the wood. In most parts of the world, trees produce a growth spurt each spring, which appears as a light band, followed by slower growth in the summer, which appears as a dark band. A wide ring shows that the tree grew well in a particular year, while a narrow band usually means that the weather slowed its growth. If a tree grows out in the open, but out of the wind, the rings will be the same width all around. If the tree is in the shade or the wind, the rings will not be as circular and will look wider on the side toward the light, or away from the wind.

Another method of finding the age of a tree is to measure the circumference of its trunk at a height of 5 feet above the ground. The measure of the circumference in inches is about the same as the number of years in its age. Most trees in temperate regions add an extra inch to their circumference each year. Some trees, like redwoods, firs, and eucalyptuses grow more than this in a year, while yews, limes, and horse chestnuts grow less. Palm trees tend to grow taller without the trunk's growing any fatter.

- A passage in *The Swiss Family Robinson* reads as follows. "I gave Jack some twine, and, scrambling up one of the curious open-air roots, he succeeded in measuring round the trunk itself, and made it out to be about eighteen yards." Calculate the approximate age of the tree.
- Find the approximate circumference and diameter of trees that were started in: the year you were born, 1900, 1776, and 1492.
- Write an equation that you could use to determine the approximate age of a tree. Let the independent variable represent the tree's diameter, given in feet.
- Use your equation to determine the ages of five trees in your neighborhood. Make a chart that includes the type of tree, its circumference or diameter, and its age.

Tree Facts

Choose one of the following projects for your group to do.

1. There are five basic groups of trees on Earth today: the conifers, broad-leaved trees, tree ferns, the ginkgo, and cycads. Research each of the five basic tree types. Write a report about the types of trees. Include the following information.

   • Describe each type of tree. Use pictures and drawings in your descriptions.

   • Describe the *habitat* of each type of tree, that is, where it normally grows.

   • Explain the physical characteristics of each type of tree, for example, how tall it grows, what its leaves and bark look like, how the roots grow, and so on.

   • Describe some common uses for each type of tree.

   • List at least 10 trees for each type. Include at least one graph in your report.

2. Select a topic for a poster or bulletin board that deals with topics related to trees. Here are some suggestions.

   • Uses for trees
   • The changing forests
   • Logging
   • Trees and weather
   • Parts of trees
   • Types of trees

   Work with your group to make your poster or bulletin board. Include photographs, artwork, graphs, charts, and/or diagrams to make it look colorful and attractive.

3. Research things about trees that are mathematical. Give an oral presentation in which every group member participates to describe your findings. Your presentation should include a written report. Make sure that your report includes at least one graph and other artwork and photographs.

You Don't Know Beans!
LIMA BEANS

1. Fill two plastic pots with equal amounts of potting soil. Moisten the soil by adding equal amounts of water. Label one pot *Experimental Group* and the other *Control Group.*

2. In each pot, plant 10 lima bean seeds. Place both pots in a location out of direct sunlight. Keep the soil moist in both containers by adding 25 mL of water to each pot each day, until the end of the experiment.

3. After the first leaves have grown from each seed, measure (in millimeters) the heights of the plants in each pot. Calculate the average height of the plants in each pot. Record your information in a table.

4. Follow the directions on the package of plant food, and mix the fertilizer in a jar with water. Measure 100 mL of fertilizer solution in a beaker. Water the experimental group with the solution. Measure and add 100 mL of water to the control group.

5. Describe what you think will happen to each group of plants over the next four days. This is called a **hypothesis.**

6. Measure the bean plants in both pots each day and calculate the average heights for each of 5–10 days. Record the plant information in a table.

At the end of the experiment, complete the following.

- Make a graph of your data. Describe the shape of your graph.
- What was the independent variable? What was the dependent variable? Explain.
- What was the purpose of using a control group?
- Did your hypothesis in Step 5 hold true? Explain.

Pole Beans

1. Fill ten small flowerpots with equal amounts of potting soil. Moisten the soil by adding equal amounts of water.
2. In each pot, plant one pole bean seed. Place the pots in a location out of direct sunlight. Keep the soil moist in the containers, but not too wet.
3. A few days after the plant has broken through the soil, the two *cotyledons*, which contain the stored food for the growing plant, will spread away from each other. Between them you will be able to see the stem and the first leaves. The portion of the stem between the cotyledons and the first leaves is called the *first internode* of the plant. In a few more days, you will just barely be able to see the *second internode* above the pair of leaves. Measure (in millimeters) the second internode and record the length in a table.

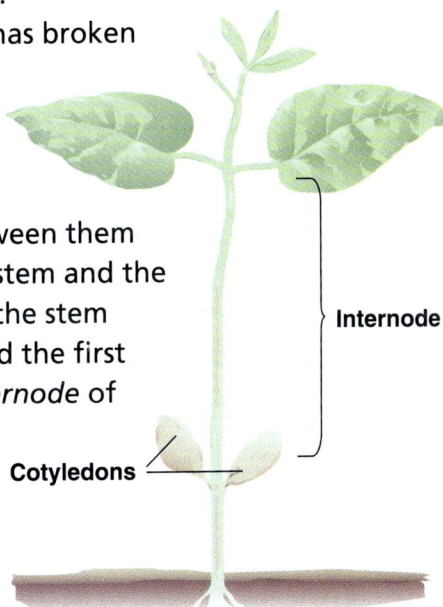

Internode

Cotyledons

4. Continue to measure the second internode until it stops growing. Measure at the same time every day. Record your daily measurements in the table you started in Step 3. Leave an empty spot for the weekend days. Use your growing information to fill in those measurements later.

At the end of the experiment, complete the following.
- Make a graph of your data and describe its shape.
- What was the independent variable? What was the dependent variable? Explain.
- When was the growth fast? When was it slow? Explain.

How Does Your Pattern Grow?

Blocks

In each diagram below, the number of blocks is increasing. Use the following ideas to make sense of the pattern.

- Draw the next two figures in each sequence.
- Explain in words how the pattern is increasing.
- Make a table to record the information.
- Continue each table to include the nth term.
- Make a graph of your data.

A.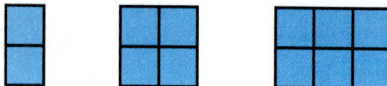

B.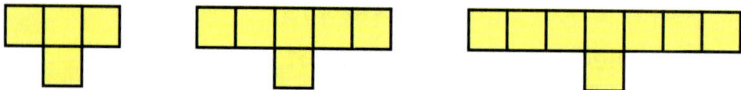

C.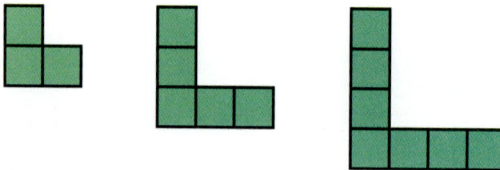

Perimeters

Calculate the perimeters of each figure above and the figures you drew to extend each sequence. Assume that the length of a side of each square is 1 unit. Use the following ideas to make sense of the pattern.

- Explain in words how the pattern is increasing.
- Make a table to record the information.
- Continue each table to include the nth term.
- Make a graph of your data. Connect each pair of points.
- Compare and contrast the two graphs.

Shapes

In each diagram below, the number of shapes is increasing. Use the following ideas to make sense of the pattern.

- Draw the next two figures in each sequence.
- Explain in words how the pattern is increasing.
- Make a table to record the information.
- Continue each table to include the nth term.
- Make a graph of your data.

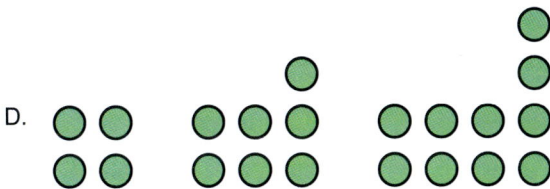

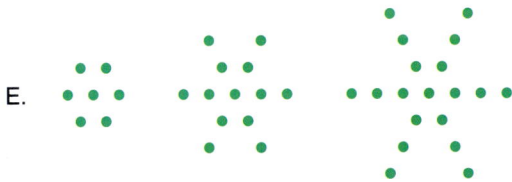

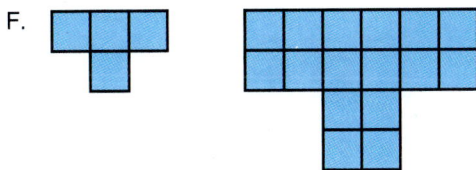

D.

E.

F.

Draw some conclusions based on your work with blocks, perimeters, and shapes. Then write a short report that describes what you found.

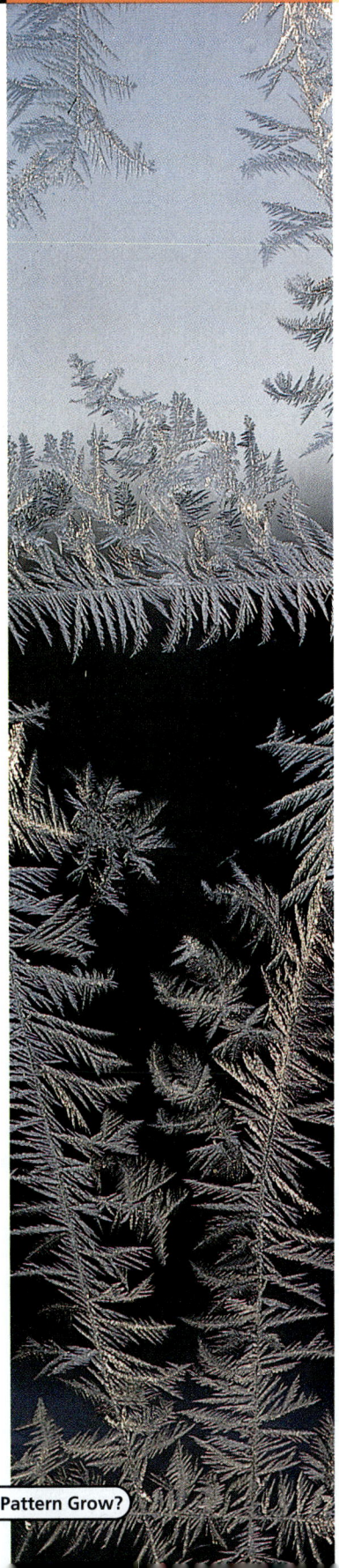

MENU station A

It Keeps On Growing and Growing and...

Office Gossip?

Sarita Webb's department has a system to let people know when they will have a meeting. Ms. Webb calls three people, then those three people each call three other people, and so on, until the whole department is notified. It takes ten minutes for a person to call three people and all calls are completed within 30 minutes.

1 **H**ow many people will be notified in the last round? How many people can be notified within 30 minutes?

2 **M**ake a table to represent the number of people who can be notified in each round.

3 **G**raph the ordered pairs (minutes, number of people notified) on a set of axes. Describe the shape of the graph.

4 **W**rite an equation to represent the situation. Let the independent variable be the number of minutes, and let the dependent variable be the number of people that are notified in that round.

5 **S**uppose another department is going to join Ms. Webb's department for the meeting. How many additional people could be notified in the next 10 minutes if each person notified in the last round calls three people?

Norman Rockwell

Big Bamboo

MENU
station
B

One of the grasses native to tropical Ceylon, a bamboo shoot, grows at an average rate of 16 inches per day.

1 How tall will the shoot be in 1 day? 2 days? 5 days?

2 Make a table of ordered pairs. Use the headings *Days* and *Height*.

3 Graph the data. What is the shape of the graph?

4 Write an equation to represent the situation. Let the independent variable be the number of days, and let the dependent variable be the height.

5 Use your equation to answer the following questions. How tall will the shoot be in 13 days? In how many days would the shoot be 144 inches tall?

MENU station C

ITTY BITTY BACTERIA

Bacteria are very tiny, one-celled organisms that live in huge numbers in almost every habitat, including your body. Bacteria reproduce by splitting in two. The *escherichia coli,* or *e. coli,* is one of the fastest growing bacteria. It splits in two every 15 minutes.

1 **I**f you begin with one *e. coli* cell, how many will there be in one hour?

2 **M**ake a table to represent the growth of the bacteria colony. Use the headings *Minutes* and *Number of Cells.*

3 **G**raph the ordered pairs on a set of axes.

4 **D**escribe the shape of the graph.

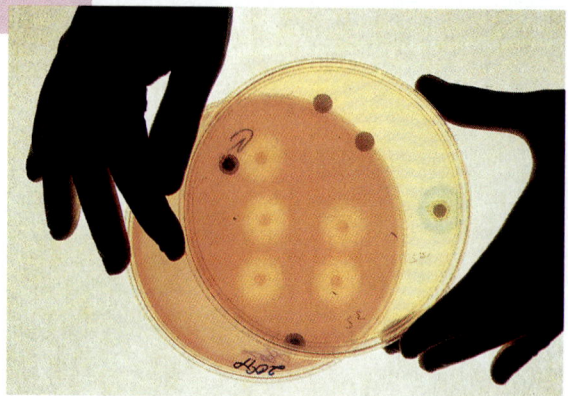

5 **W**rite an equation to represent the situation. Let the independent variable be the number of minutes, and let the dependent variable be the number of cells.

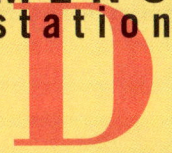

I'd Depreciate That!

The opposite of growth is decay. When people buy new automobiles, the values of the cars begin to decay, or depreciate, as soon as they leave the car lot. The depreciation is the difference between the original cost of the car and the amount received for it when it is traded or sold. The table at the right shows some suggested depreciation percentages for a particular brand of car.

Value of a New Car	
End of Year	% of Original Cost
1	70
2	55
3	42
4	33
5	25

1 **S**uppose you bought the luxury model of this brand of car for $15,000. How much money would you most likely get for the car in 5 years?

2 **W**hat would be the average annual depreciation over the 5 years?

3 **M**ake a table to represent the decay in the value of the car. Use the headings *Year* and *Current Value of Car.*

4 **G**raph the ordered pairs on a set of axes. Describe the shape of the graph.

5 **W**hen does the value of the car seem to take its greatest drop in value? Why do you think this is?

MENU station E

Get Half a Life!

The opposite of growth is decay. Scientists use a unit called **half-life** to indicate the length of time it takes for a substance to decay, or disintegrate, to half of its mass. Radium has a half-life of 1,620 years. This means that if you had a 100-gram sample of radium, in 1,620 years, you would have only a 50-gram sample.

1 **A**fter 2(1,620) or 3,240 years, how much of the radium would remain? after 3(1,620) years?

2 **M**ake a table to represent the disintegration of the radium sample for the first 5 half-lives. Use the headings *Half-Lives* and *Percent Remaining.*

3 **G**raph the ordered pairs on a set of axes.

4 **D**escribe the shape of the graph.

5 **W**rite an equation to represent the situation. Let the independent variable be the number of half-lives and let the dependent variable be the percent of radium remaining.

In Your Best Interest

Money may not grow on trees, but it does grow. When you invest money, the amount of money that is added to your original investment is called **interest**. You can use the formula $I = prt$ to calculate *simple interest*. In the formula, I represents the interest, p represents the principal or the amount you invested, r represents the annual interest rate, and t represents the time or the number of years that the money has been invested. Suppose you invested $1,500 for 5 years at 6% annual interest.

- How much interest would you earn each year?
- What would be the value of your investment at the end of the five years?
- Make a table to show the growth of your money. Use the headings *Year, Interest,* and *Total Investment.* Continue the table to include the nth term.
- Graph the ordered pairs (years, total investment) on a set of axes.

Normally, a bank will not send you a check for the amount of interest your investment has earned. Instead, the money is added to the principal, where it becomes part of the amount used to compute the interest earned in the next period. This is called *compound interest,* since you are being paid interest on the interest as well as on the principal. Suppose you invested $1,500 for 5 years at 6% annual interest compounded annually.

- How much interest would you earn in the first year? What would be the value of your investment at that time?
- How much interest would you earn in the second year?
- Make a table to show the growth of your money. Use the headings *Year, Interest,* and *Total Investment.*
- Graph the ordered pairs (years, total investment) on the same axes as above. Use a different color for these data. Describe the differences in the two sets of values.
- Which type of interest, simple or compound, would cause your investment to grow more quickly? Why?

COMPUTER investigation

Computer Activity

You can use a computer program written in BASIC to find the compound interest for an investment. Type in the program below, or use the software provided by your teacher. Be sure to input the interest rate as a decimal. For example, you would input 6% as 0.06.

```
10   INPUT "PRINCIPAL: ";P
20   INPUT "INTEREST RATE: ";R
30   INPUT "NUMBER OF TIMES COMPOUNDED EACH
     YEAR: ";N
40   INPUT "NUMBER OF YEARS: ";T
50   PRINT "YEAR", "TOTAL INVESTMENT"
60   PRINT "0", P
70   FOR Y = 1 TO T
80   LET A = P * (1 + R/N) ^ (N * Y)
90   PRINT Y, A
100  NEXT Y
110  END
```

- Use the program to verify the amount you calculated on the previous page. Let $N = 1$.
- Find the total investment if you were to invest $12,000 for 3 years at 5% annual interest compounded annually.

Usually banks credit your account with the interest earned more than once a year. This is called *compounding*. Banks commonly compound interest annually, semiannually, and monthly.

- Use the program to find the total investment if you were to invest $1,500 for 5 years at 6% annual interest compounded (a) semiannually and (b) monthly. How does the total investment compare with the total investment when interest is compounded annually? Explain.
- Find the total investment if you were to invest $12,000 for 3 years at 5% annual interest compounded (a) semiannually and (b) monthly. How does the total investment compare with the total investment when interest is compounded annually? Explain.

Height and Growth
Using Trigonometry

In order to determine how an object is growing, you will need to determine the height of the object. You can use **trigonometry**, or the study of triangles, to find the height of an object. The **tangent** function is a trigonometric function that you will use to find heights. It is abbreviated *tan.* Look at the example below.

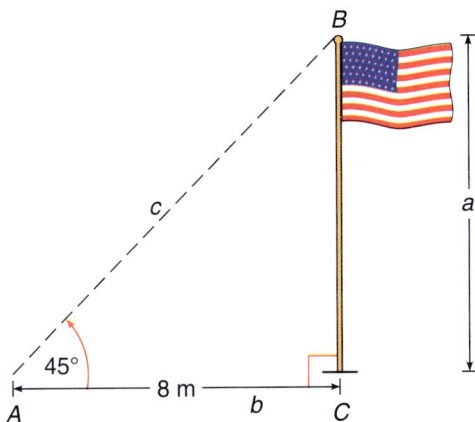

To determine the height of the flagpole, set up a triangle with one side being the height of the flagpole (*a*), another side being a distance from the flagpole to a point on the ground (*b*), and the third side being the distance from that point to the top of the flagpole (*c*). Assume that the flagpole meets the ground in a right angle.

Use the following ratio to find the height of the flagpole.

$$\tan A = \frac{measure\ of\ opposite\ side}{measure\ of\ adjacent\ side}$$

$\tan 45° = \frac{a}{8}$ Substitute 45° for the measure of the angle (*A*) and 8 m for the measure of the adjacent side.

$8 \times \tan 45° = a$ Multiply each side by 8.

$8 \times 1 = a$ Use your calculator to find tan 45°. The tangent of 45° is 1.

$8 = a$ The flagpole is 8 meters high.

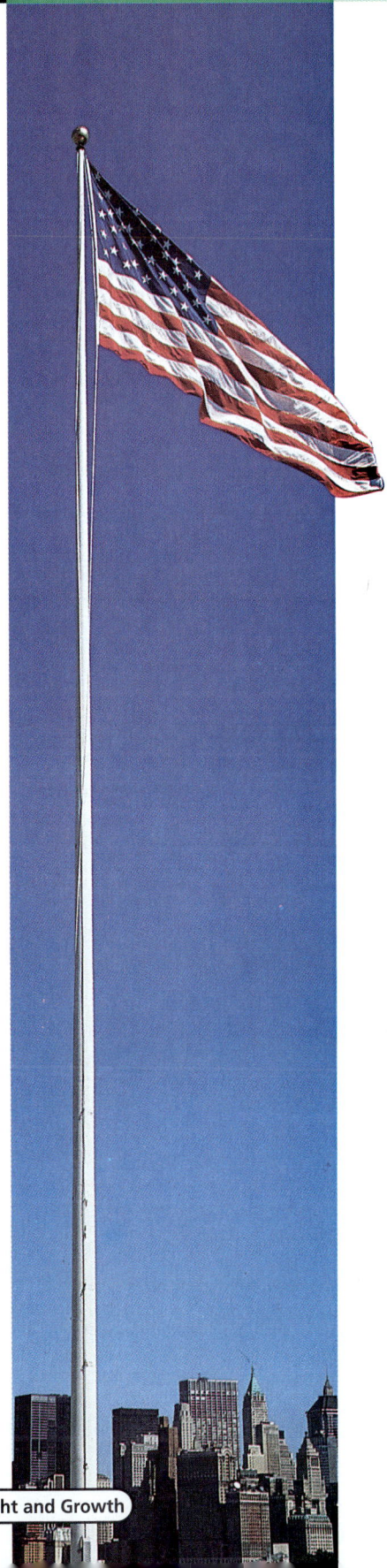

Using a Hypsometer

A hypsometer is an instrument you can use to find the height of very tall objects. To make a hypsometer, you will need a straw, some string, a paper clip, and an index card or protractor. If you do not have a protractor, glue the semicircle on the bottom of the page that your teacher has provided to the index card and cut it out. The semicircle will act as a protractor to help you measure the angles. Attach the straw to the semicircle, with the middle of the straw at the dot labeled A. Attach a piece of string 6 inches long to the center of the straw. Attach a paper clip to the other end of the string. Make sure that the paper clip hangs freely.

Hold the hypsometer up and look through the straw at the top of a tall object. The imaginary line that goes from your eye to the top of the object is called the line of sight. Once you have found your line of sight, look at the point at which the string crosses the semicircle. This is the measure of the angle formed by your line of sight and an imaginary horizontal line.

The girl in the drawing at the right is using a hypsometer.

- How is this example different from the one on the previous page?
- How will that affect the answer?
- What will you have to do to compensate for this difference?
- Will your answer be the same?

Work with a partner to determine the height of the flagpole given these new measurements.

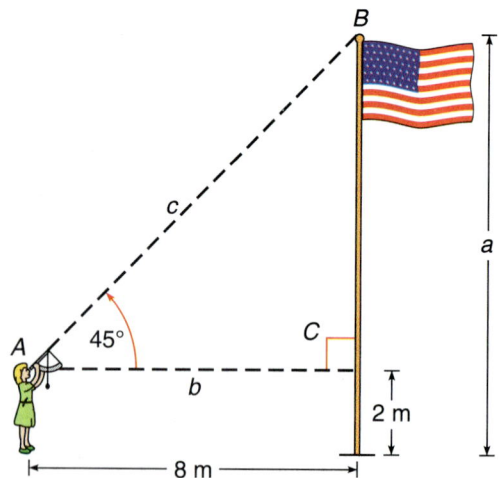

Using a Classmate's Height

Besides using trigonometry, another way to measure the height of an object involves comparing the height of someone you can measure with the height of the object.

1. Have a classmate stand at the base of a tall object, like a tree, a flagpole, a utility pole, and so on.
2. With a meterstick in hand, walk about 30 paces away from your classmate.
3. Hold the meterstick out vertically at arm's length and line up the top of the meterstick with the top of your friend's head in your line of vision. Move your thumb down until it lines up with your classmate's feet. Measure this distance on your meterstick.

4. Still standing at the same spot, move the meterstick upward so that the top of the meterstick lines up with the top of the object in your line of vision. Move your thumb down until it lines up with the bottom of the object. Measure this distance on your meterstick.

5. Examine the two distances. How many times larger is the object than your classmate?
6. Measure the height of your classmate. Then use a **proportion,** which is a mathematical sentence that states that two *ratios* are equal, to determine the actual height of the object.
7. Walk another 20 paces away from your classmate and repeat the calculations.
8. Use the hypsometer and trigonometry to find the height of the object. Then compare the three answers. Explain your conclusions.

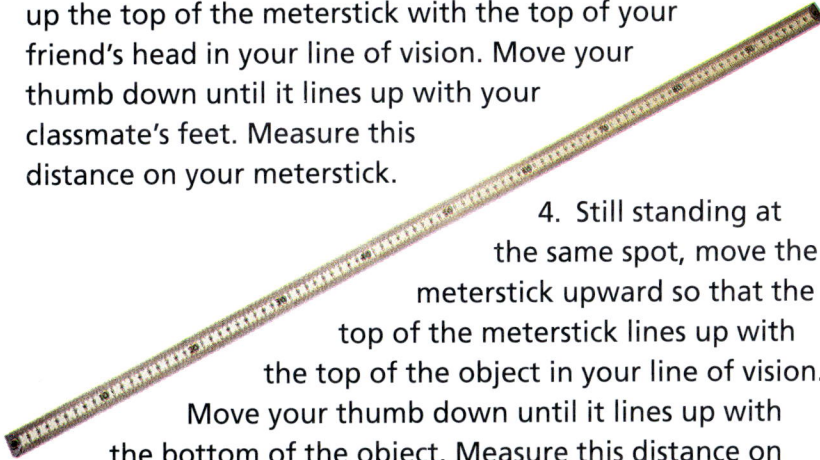

POPULATION TRENDS
Earth's Population

The table at the right illustrates Earth's population since 1500, in millions of people.

- In which century was growth the fastest? Why do you think this is so?
- Graph the ordered pairs (year, population) on a set of axes.
- Is the shape of the graph a straight line? If not, describe the shape of the graph.

Year	Population (millions)
1500	460
1600	579
1700	679
1800	954
1900	1,633
2000 (projected)	6,251

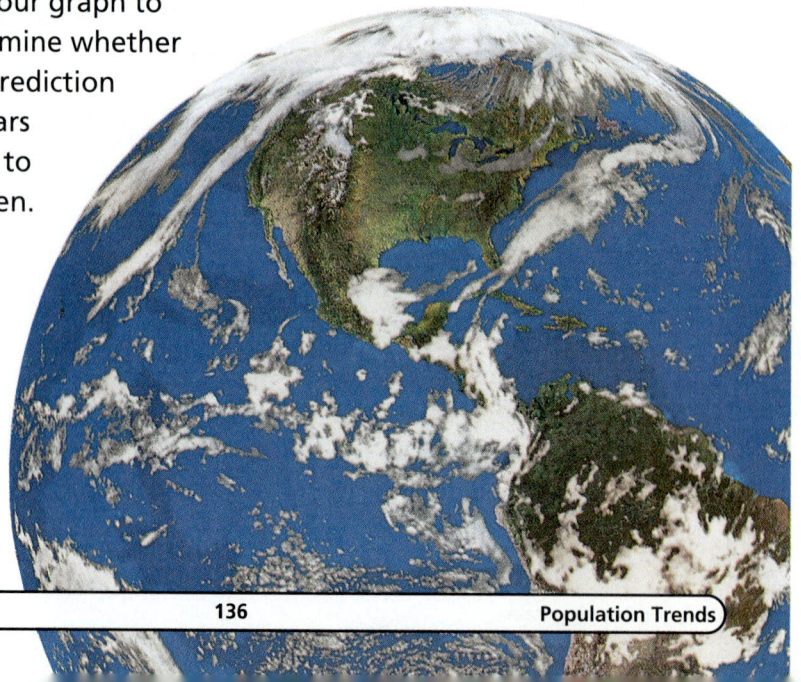

- Use the graph to estimate Earth's population in 1400, today, and in the year 2100.
- According to United Nations estimates, the population of Earth was about 4 billion in 1975, and at that time it was expected to double in 35 years. Use your graph to determine whether this prediction appears likely to happen.

City Population

The population of Manhattan Island in New York City, rounded to the nearest thousand, is shown at the right.
- Graph the data.
- Describe the shape of the graph. Why do you think it is shaped in this way?
- In which 10-year span(s) did Manhattan Island lose population? What factors might explain this loss?
- Use the graph to predict the population of Manhattan Island in the year 2000.
- Find population data from your city or hometown. Graph the data and describe the shape of the curve.

Year	Population
1790	33,000
1800	61,000
1810	96,000
1820	124,000
1830	203,000
1840	313,000
1850	516,000
1860	814,000
1870	942,000
1880	1,165,000
1890	1,441,000
1900	1,850,000
1910	2,332,000
1920	2,284,000
1930	1,867,000
1940	1,890,000
1950	1,960,000
1960	1,698,000
1970	1,539,000
1980	1,428,000
1990	1,488,000

Animal Population

Year	Population
1900	9
1910	10
1920	11
1930	13
1940	9
1950	18
1960	59
1970	81
1980	95
1990	97

The table at the left shows the growth of a population of deer studied in an area designated a wildlife preserve in 1948.

- Graph the data.
- Describe the shape of the graph. Why do you think it is shaped in this way?

This graph is called an **S-curve**. It shows how the size of a population changes over time. There are three phases in the shape of an S-curve. There is an early phase called the *lag phase,* where the graph is quite flat and climbs slowly. The *exponential growth phase* follows, during which the population increases rapidly. In the *stationary phase,* the last of the three stages, the growth of the population slows down and the size of the population remains relatively constant.

- Look at your graph. During what interval of time was the lag phase? What might explain this type of population growth?
- During what interval of time was the exponential growth phase? What might explain this type of population growth?
- During what interval of time was the stationary phase? What might explain this type of population growth?
- Use the graph to predict the population of deer in the wildlife preserve in the year 2000.

YOUR REPORT

Write a report that explains the different types of population growth you have explored in this activity. Include your graphs and analyses of the three types of populations and explain why these populations grow in different ways.

Human Growth

"We do not grow at a constant rate.... After birth, two spurts of growth, in the first two years and again at puberty, are separated by a slower, more steady rate, where height increases by two to three inches a year and weight increases by five to six pounds. By their first birthdays, babies usually weigh three times their birth weight and have grown in height by 50 percent. Parents of small children can estimate the final height of their offspring. By the time a boy is two and a girl eighteen months, they will have reached about half their mature height."

— *The Incredible Machine,* The National Geographic Society

- Make a table to chart the growth of two human beings, a male and a female. Use the data above and your own research to chart how people grow from birth to age 20. Use the headings *Age, Height-Males,* and *Height-Females.* Assume that girls reach their full height by the time they are 18, while boys continue growing until they are almost 21.
- Graph the data. Use one color for males and another for females. Then describe the shape of the graph.

The diagram below illustrates the proportions of the human body from birth to age 25.

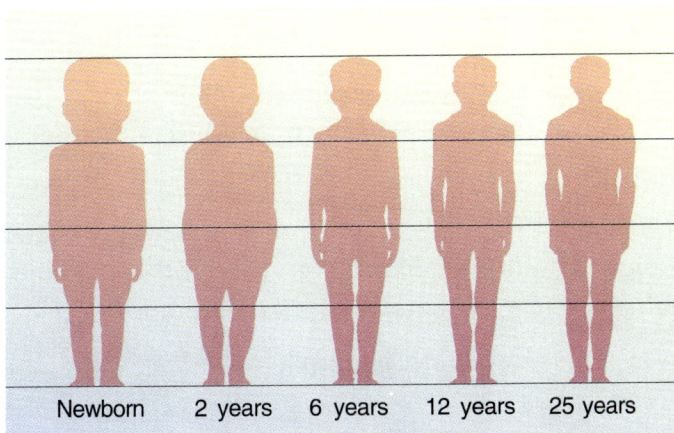

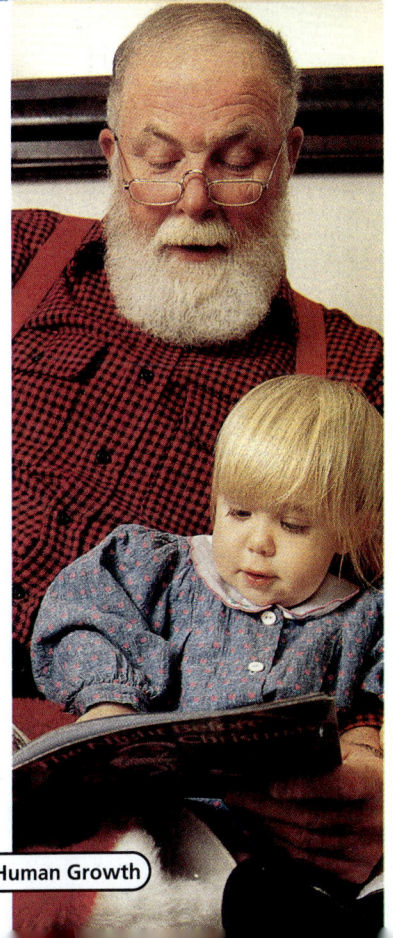

| Newborn | 2 years | 6 years | 12 years | 25 years |

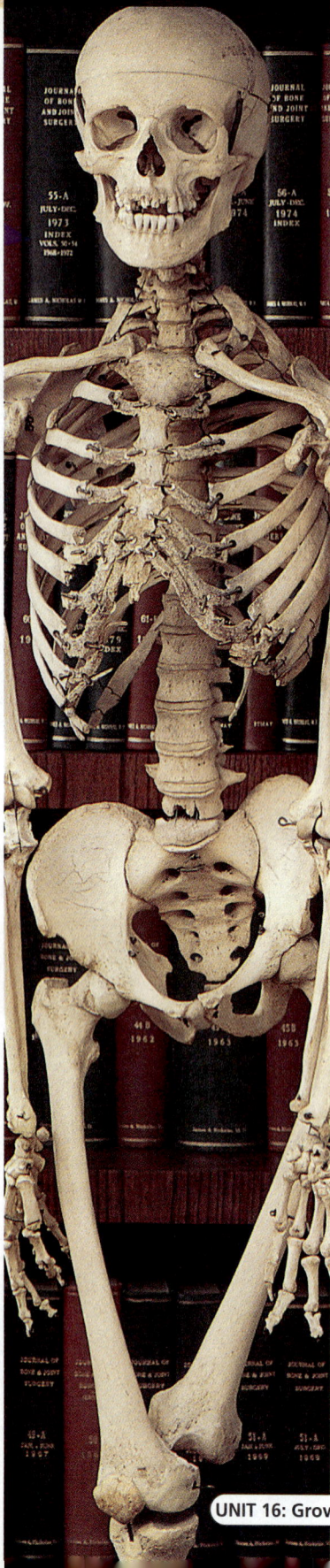

- Make a table to represent the growth of the human head from birth to age 25. Use the headings *Age* and *Percent of Body Length.*
- Graph the data and describe the shape of the graph.

"After about age 25 a person's height can go only one way—and that is down. A man or woman might lose an eighth of an inch between ages 25 and 40 as the spongy disks between the vertebrae in the spine shrink, causing the bones to move closer together. The back begins to bend forward after age 40. From age 20 to age 70, a woman may shrink about 2 inches, while a man might lose about an inch."

— T*he Incredible Machine,* The National Geographic Society

- Extend the table you made on the previous page to include the period from age 20 to age 70.
- Extend the graph as well. Then describe the new shape of the graph.

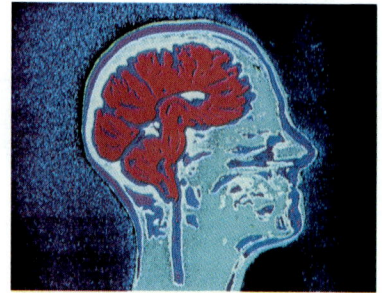

YOUR REPORT

Write a report about the mathematics of human growth. Include your graphs and the analysis that you have already completed. Here are some questions you may want to research and answer in your report.

- What are some of the things that can affect human growth?

- Are human beings generally taller than their ancestors or shorter? Why? On average, how much taller or shorter are we?

- It is said that in nine months, a fetus increases its weight about 2.4 billion times. How is this possible? What are the sizes at conception and at birth?

- Why does a newborn generally have 350 bones, but an adult has 206?

Selection and Reflection

- Describe the mathematics that you used in this unit.
- What did you learn about growth while studying this unit? Use examples from several of the activities in the unit in your explanation.
- What was your favorite activity in this unit? What was your least favorite? Explain what both activities were about and why you liked or disliked them.
- How did you feel about learning about the mathematics of growth? Did you enjoy the experience?

The General Sherman

The Problem

The largest living thing on Earth is a sequoia tree named the General Sherman, standing 274.9 feet tall, in the Sequoia National Park in California. In 1989, the circumference of the tree was 82.3 feet at 4.5 feet above the ground. A sequoia tree seed weighs only $\frac{1}{6,000}$ of an ounce. If a mature sequoia tree weighs 1,300,000,000,000 times as much, how much does the average mature sequoia weigh?

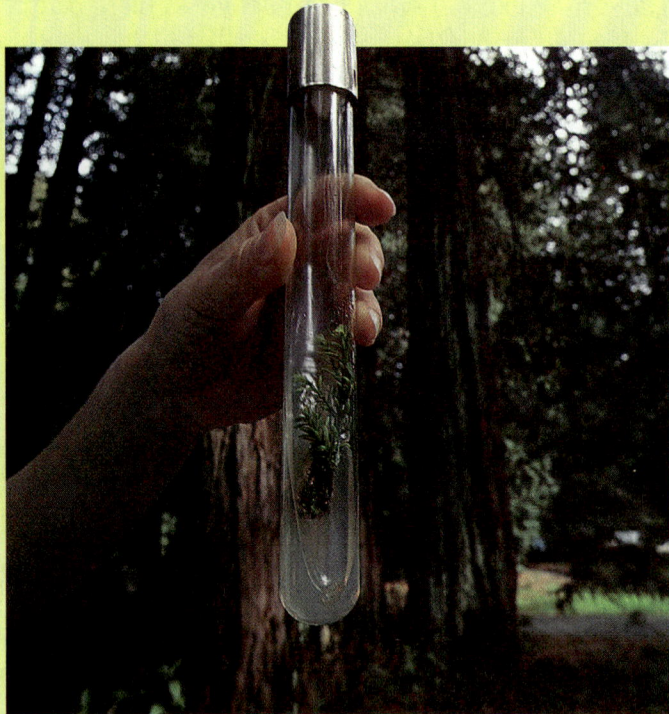

Extension How old would you predict that the General Sherman is?

The Problem

The **Fibonacci Sequence** was discovered at the beginning of the thirteenth century by Italian mathematician Leonardo of Pisa, who was called Fibonacci. The Fibonacci sequence is interesting because it is often found in nature. A seedling tree often displays the sequence in the distances between the buds. Pineapples, sunflowers, and pine cones also display the sequence.

The first eight terms in the sequence are shown below.

1, 1, 2, 3, 5, 8, 13, 21

How is a term in the sequence found?

Fibonacci's Foliage

Extension What is the ninth term in the sequence?

High Rise Blocks

The Problem

How many cubes are in the twenty-fifth building in the sequence of block buildings below?

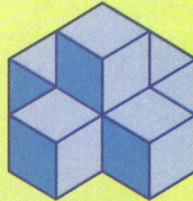

Building 1

Building 2

Building 3

The Problem

Draw the next element in the sequence below.

Follow the Leader!

Plant a Tree

The Problem

The Boy Scouts planted a red fir and a Monterey pine to mark their 1993 camping spot. The red fir was 26 inches tall and the Monterey pine was 8 inches tall. If the rate of growth for the red fir is 20 inches per year, and the rate of growth for the Monterey pine is 2 feet per year, in how many years will the trees be the same height?

The Problem

On his 14th birthday, Reggie received $100 from his grandparents. He decided to use the money to buy a certificate of deposit (CD) to save for a stereo. The County Federal Bank offers a CD that earns 5% simple interest for a term of three years. A CD with 4.7% interest compounded annually is available at Homeguard Savings and Loan. Which CD should Reggie buy?

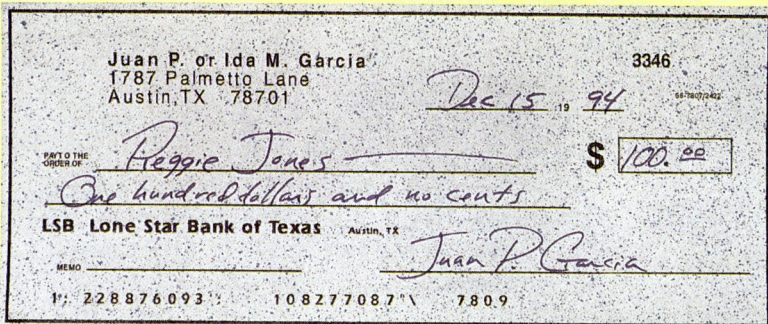

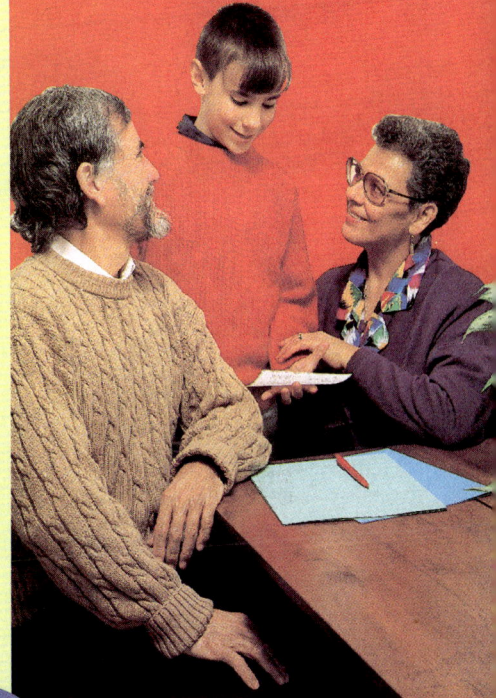

Growing Greenbacks
$ $ $ $$ $

Juan P. or Ida M. Garcia
1787 Palmetto Lane
Austin, TX 78701   3346

Dec 15 19 94

PAY TO THE
ORDER OF Reggie Jones $ 100.00

One hundred dollars and no cents

LSB Lone Star Bank of Texas   Austin, TX

MEMO   Juan P. Garcia

1: 2 2 8 8 7 6 0 9 3 :   1 0 8 2 7 7 0 8 7 \   7 8 0 9

Extension If the terms of the CDs were seven years instead of three, should Reggie's choice be different? Explain.

And a Partridge in a Pear Tree

The Problem

The song "The Twelve Days of Christmas" describes gifts given on the twelve days after Christmas. The number of gifts given grows each day. The first day's gift is a partridge in a pear tree, the second day's gifts are two turtle doves and a partridge in a pear tree, the third day's gifts are three French hens, two turtle doves, and a partridge in a pear tree. How many gifts were given during the twelve days?

"What else did you bring me?"

The Problem

Afforestation is the process of establishing a forest on land that has not previously been forested. The largest afforested area of the world, in northern Russia, measures 2,700,000,000 acres. This region encompasses 25% of the world's forests. In 38% of the acres in this region, Siberian larch trees are growing. On how many acres in this area are Siberian larch trees growing?

Save the Forests

Extension How many acres are there in the world's forests?

An Apple a Day

The Problem

Hatsu works weekends in the produce department at Geyer's Supermart. Today she has to stack the Granny Smith apples that are on special in the bin at the end of the aisle. Her manager suggested using a triangular pyramid arrangement. The top layer is a single apple, the second layer is 3 apples, and the third layer is 6 apples. At this rate, how many apples will be in the tenth layer?

Extension How many apples should Hatsu put on the bottom layer if she has 455 apples to stack?

INFINITE WINDOWS

123456
789 0 123
456 9
123 6
789 3
456 9

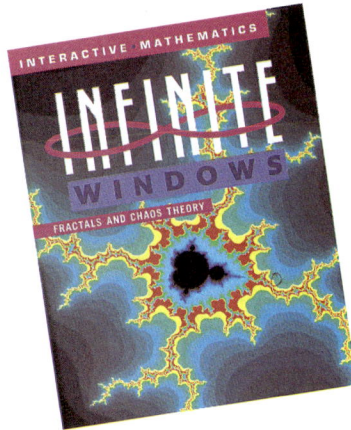

Looking Ahead

In this unit, you will see how mathematics can be used to answer questions about chaos theory and fractal geometry. You will experience:

▶ exploring self-similarity, small numbers, and recursion

▶ creating fractals by folding and cutting paper

▶ plotting random points to create fractals

▶ using computers to investigate chaos theory and fractals

▶ creating posters with self-similar shapes

Did You Ever Wonder?

What do mathematics and learning about health careers have to do with each other? Turn the page and see how Tony Lloyd of San Antonio, Texas, combined the two!

INTERACTIVE MATHEMATICS

INFINITE WINDOWS

FRACTALS AND CHAOS THEORY

Teens in the News

Featuring: Roger Anthony "Tony" Lloyd
Date of Birth: October 24, 1975
Date of Death: August 14, 1993
Hometown: San Antonio, Texas
Life Goal: Medical Doctor
Life Interests: Learning, writing, computers, and medicine

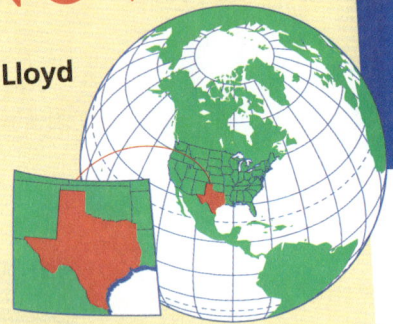

Tony Lloyd was about to enter his senior year of high school when he was killed in an auto accident. However, Tony accomplished a lot in his short life.

Tony attended Health Careers High School in San Antonio, Texas. His dream was to become a doctor. Teachers remember Tony as a super student, a born leader, and a talented writer. Tony's classmates described him as energetic, positive, imaginative, special, and a good dancer. Tony served as Junior Class President, and he had been elected Senior Class President. Tony volunteered for the American Heart Association and Santa Rosa Children's Hospital.

Tony valued education all of his life. He was an electronics and computer whiz and used computer-generated graphics in many of his projects. He really loved mathematics. In an autobiography of his mathematical life, he wrote, "My life in mathematics has been both eventful and fascinating. It is the only subject I take that I truly love, and hope it will be with me forever."

Tony is gone but not forgotten. He wrote many poems, short stories, and autobiographies during his life. Health Careers High School has established a scholarship fund in Tony's name. He lives on through his writing, the scholarship fund, and in the minds of all who knew him.

Ohhh! Leave me alone!

How people want to be treated when they have a cold or flu:

Left alone 77%

Don't know 7%

Waited on hand and foot 16%

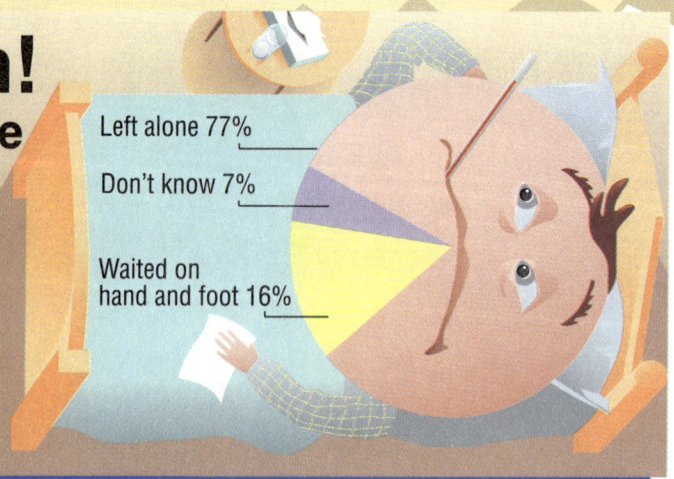

Source: Sterling Health poll of 1,000 people

Team Project

I'm Floored!

Tony had a real gift for mathematics and was highly creative. Many great architects, designers, and artists have this unusual combination of talents.

Create a ceramic tile design. Decide what size and shape your tiles will be and what colors you will use. Suppose you used your tile design to cover the floor of a lobby. Would the large design on the floor look like the design of each small, individual tile? Explain why or why not.

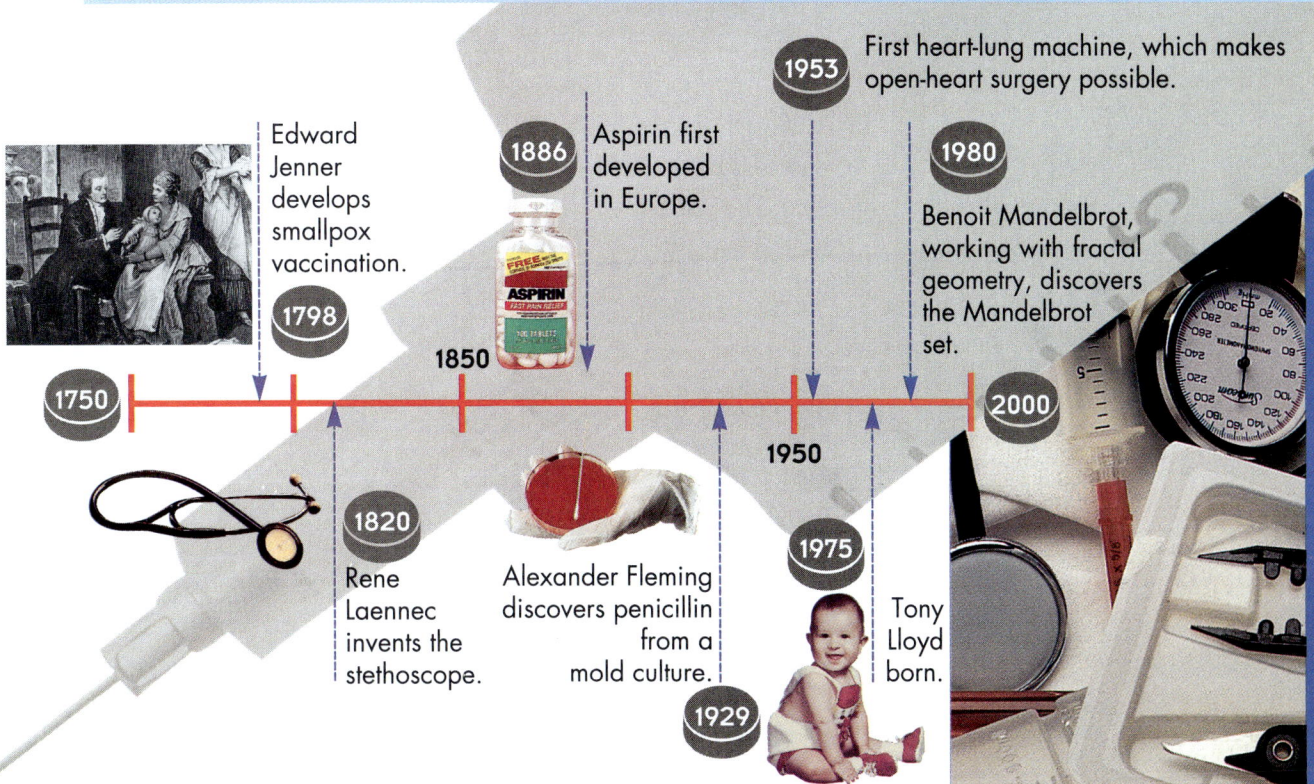

1953 First heart-lung machine, which makes open-heart surgery possible.

Edward Jenner develops smallpox vaccination. **1798**

1886 Aspirin first developed in Europe.

1980 Benoit Mandelbrot, working with fractal geometry, discovers the Mandelbrot set.

1750 — 1850 — 1950 — **2000**

1820 Rene Laennec invents the stethoscope.

Alexander Fleming discovers penicillin from a mold culture. **1929**

1975 Tony Lloyd born.

For more information

If you would like more information about health careers, contact:

**American Medical Association (AMA)
515 North State Street
Chicago, Illinois 60610**

You can learn more about the mathematics Tony used by completing the activities in this unit.

Setting the Scene

MATHEMATICS TOOLKIT

Many professions require the use of tools. This mathematics toolkit includes tools you may find useful as you study this unit. At times you may feel lost or not know where to begin when presented with a problem situation. You should take time to review this toolkit to see how the characters in the script used mathematics to solve their problem.

Narrator: Brandon, Luisa, Kou-Long, Kristi, and Poloma are members of the Students Against Drugs Club at their school. They are having a meeting to decide about the activities they are planning for their club.

Luisa: As you all know, next month is Drug Awareness Month. How are we coming with the plans for the big rally?

Kou-Long: The plans are coming along great. We have the speakers lined up and the refreshments are being ordered. Do we have an estimate for the number of people we're expecting?

Kristi: We think there'll be over 500 people there if it's advertised well. By the way, how are we going to advertise the rally?

Poloma: The national organization has sent us 200 posters to put up at school and at local businesses around town.

Luisa: That's all well and good, but what's our hook? We want to get as many kids as possible to attend. How can we really promote this?

Poloma: Well, the advertising committee has stumbled upon what we think is a great idea. When we went to Mr. Freezie's to ask if they would support us with advertising, the manager said that they would give a 5% discount for a six-month period to any student who attends the Drug Awareness Rally.

Kou-Long: Well, we thought that we could issue a card—sort of like a credit card—to each student who comes to the rally. The card could have an expiration date that is six months from the date of the rally.

Kristi: We'd better make the card look official. I can just see some people trying to use counterfeit cards.

Kou-Long: We thought we'd use the national logo on the cards. It's printed on the advertising posters.

Brandon: Cool! That'll attract a lot of students. Have you talked to any other businesses?

Kou-Long: So far, we've lined up 12 businesses that will give a discount to students attending the rally.

Luisa: That is a *fantastic* idea! But how are they going to know who to give the discount to?

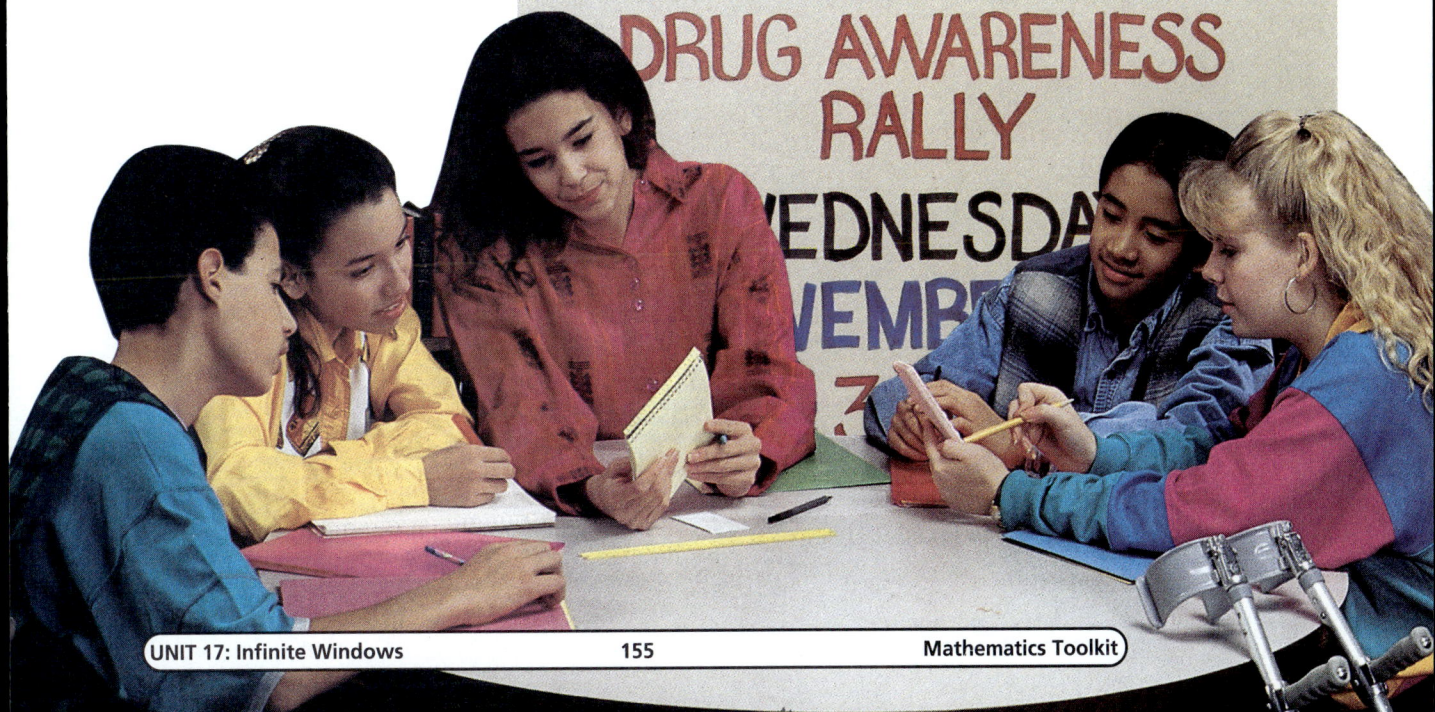

Luisa: Good idea. Poloma and I are office aides and our advisor says that we can use the copy machine for the club's business.

Kristi: Wait a minute. That's a big poster! How are you going to copy the logo?

Poloma: We'll reduce it using the copy machine. It can reduce and enlarge. The reductions can be 57% or 75% and it'll enlarge to 120%.

Brandon: That's going to take a lot of reducing. Can you really use the copier to make it the right size?

Poloma: Well, let's start by measuring the logo on the poster.

Kou-Long: The logo is rectangular and it measures...let me see...$10\frac{1}{2}$ inches by 8 inches.

Kristi: So, how big is a credit card?

Luisa: You know that printing business down the street, We Print It All? Well, they've donated 600 blank business cards. They're 3 inches by $2\frac{1}{4}$ inches.

Brandon: Well, good luck figuring this out. You'd better not waste a lot of time or paper, either—you know how Mr. Johnson's always saying how expensive copying is.

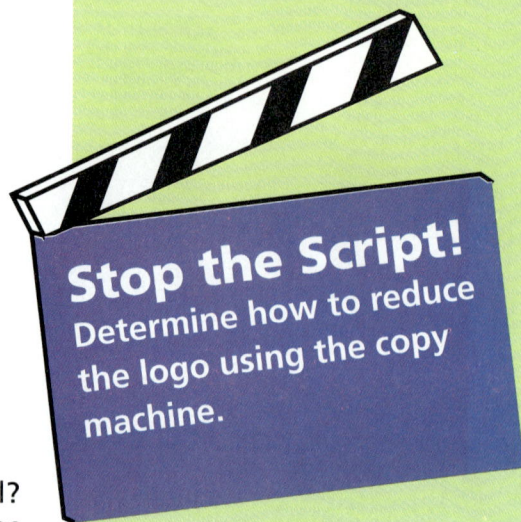

Stop the Script!
Determine how to reduce the logo using the copy machine.

Narrator: The students continue working on the problem.

Luisa: Okay, so where do we start?

Kristi: Let's use a calculator and experiment.

Brandon: How in the world is that going to help? A calculator won't help us see the size of the logo!

Poloma: No, but it will help us see how the size changes when we reduce it. Let's start with the length of the logo. It's $10\frac{1}{2}$ inches now. If we multiply 10.5 by 57%, how long would it be?

Kou-Long: Why would we multiply? I thought we should divide.

Kristi: If we divide 10.5 by 57%, it'll tell us how many times 57% goes into 10.5. We want to know what 57% *of* 10.5 is, so we multiply. I get 5.985.

Kou-Long: That's too long. It's got to be 3 inches long.

Luisa: Well, there's no rule that says we can't do it again!

Poloma: You think we should multiply by 57% a second time?

Luisa: Sure, let's try it.

Kristi: Okay, 5.985 times 57% is 3.41145.

Brandon: That's still too big, but I'm getting the hang of this. How about we try it one more time?

Kristi: Here goes: 3.41145 times 57% is 1.9445265.

Kou-Long: Now it's too small! I guess we can't do it.

Luisa: Don't give up so easily. There are two other buttons we could use. Let's try reducing it three times using the 75% button.

Kristi: Okay, 10.5 times 75% times 75% times 75% equals 4.4296875.

Poloma: Hey, that's way too big. It looks like we're going to have to reduce it by using both reduction buttons.

Kou-Long: Wait— maybe we're doing this backwards. I think we can find out how much we need to reduce it by setting up a ratio. Let's see:
$$\frac{\text{reduction amount}}{100\%} =$$
$\frac{3 \ inches}{10.5 \ inches}$. The reduction amount to the whole is the same as the new size we want to the original size.

Brandon: Okay, I'm with you. So, let's divide 3 by 10.5 to find the reduction amount.

Kristi: That's 0.2857142, or a little less than 29%.

Luisa: So, how is this going to help us?

Poloma: That's our target. We need to use 57% and 75% in some combination to get just under 29%.

Brandon: Man, this is getting complicated. Okay. We know that when we multiply 57% by itself, we get a smaller number than when we multiply 75% by itself. So, let's start from there.

Kristi: If I multiply 0.57 times 0.57, I get 0.3249.

Kou-Long: Okay, now multiply that by 75%.

Luisa: Yeah, that makes sense. Multiplying by 75% will make it even smaller.

Kristi: If I multiply 0.3249 by 0.75, I get 0.243675.

Poloma: Finally! But now I wonder if we could have gotten a little closer to the goal.

Kou-Long: I've got an idea. How about enlarging it by 120%?

Kristi: You guys, my calculator finger is killing me! Okay, 0.243675 times 1.2 equals 0.29241.

Brandon: Isn't that a little too big? Multiply the original length—10.5 inches—by 0.29241.

Kristi: You're right. The length of the logo would be 3.07 inches. That's bigger than the cards!

Poloma: I think we should stick with the reduction we got before. If we used 0.243675, how big would the logo be?

Kristi: It would be 2.56 inches long.

Poloma: Then let's put a border around the logo; that would make it look really professional. And we could put a list of the businesses that are participating on the back of the card.

Luisa: I like it! In fact, we can go print them right now. You guys can finish the meeting without us.

This concludes the Mathematics Toolkit. It included many mathematical tools for you to use throughout the unit. As you work through this unit, you should use these tools to help you solve problems. You may want to explain how to use these mathematical tools in your journal. Or you may want to create a toolkit notebook and add the mathematical tools you discover throughout this unit.

Mirror, Mirror On the Wall

Have you ever sat in a hair salon or barber shop and looked through opposite mirrors? You can look down an endless tunnel of images that are all the same. What you see is the front of your head and the back of your head in a series of identical pictures, appearing smaller and smaller, forever. Likewise, if you look at a picture of a girl holding a mirror while looking in a mirror, you experience the same thing.

Examine the picture of the girl that your teacher will show you. You and your group will write about your reactions to this picture. Be sure that you answer the following questions.

- How do the heights of the girl in the smaller pictures compare to the height of the girl in the original picture?
- If you had a microscope and could zoom in on the tenth picture of the girl, what would be the actual height of the girl in that picture?
- Suppose you could use a microscope to see something 0.0001 millimeter tall. How many pictures of the girl would you be able to see then?

Be prepared to present your group's findings to the class.

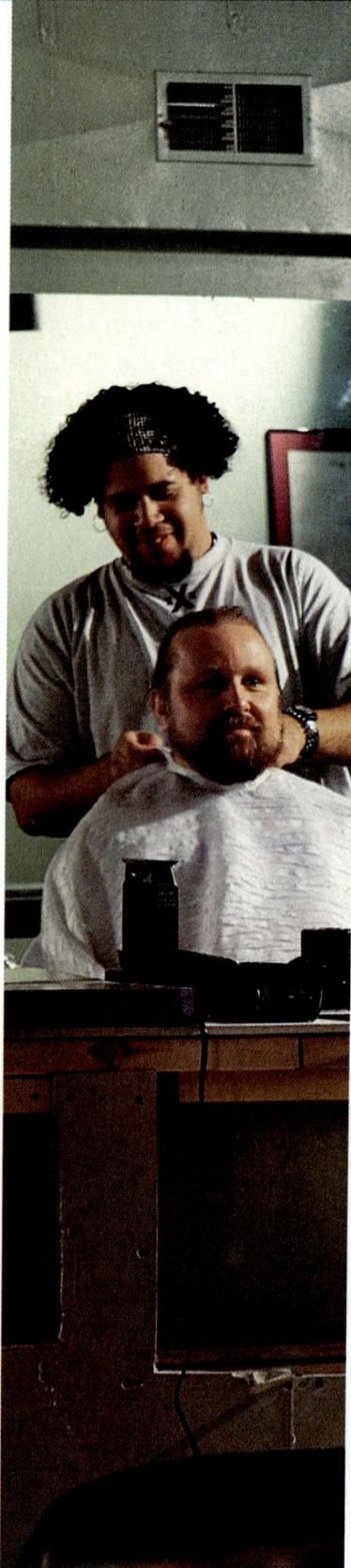

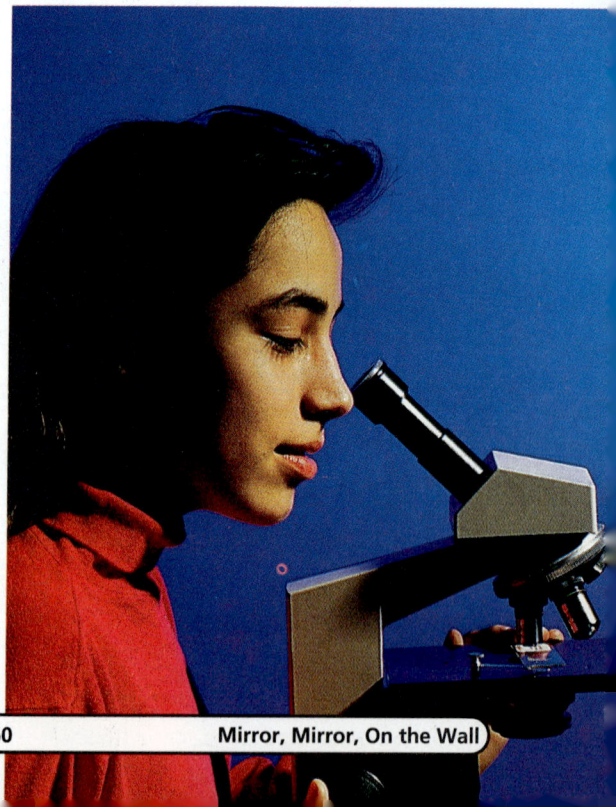

Over and Over and Over...

Folding Something into Nothing

Take an ordinary piece of paper measuring $8\frac{1}{2}$ inches by 11 inches.

1 If you folded it in half with the short sides meeting, what would be the length, width, and height of the folded paper? Fold it and record your measurements.

2 If you folded it in half again, this time with the long sides meeting, what would be the length, width, and height of the folded paper? Fold it again and record your measurements.

3 Continue this process, folding the paper first widthwise and then lengthwise. What would be the length, width, and height of the folded paper if you could fold it 100 times?

4 How many times would you have to fold it in order for the longest side to be less than $\frac{1}{100}$ inch long?

5 Imagine that you could continue folding the paper forever. How many times would you have to fold it in order for the folded paper to be as tall as you are?

MENU
station

B

Double Vision

Set up two mirrors so that they are opposite each other.

1 **P**lace a small object between the mirrors.

2 **L**ook into the mirrors. What are the images that you see?

3 **H**ow far apart are the mirrors? How does the distance between the mirrors affect what you see?

4 **L**ook carefully into the mirrors. How many copies of the object do you see? Sketch a drawing of what you see.

5 **E**stimate how much smaller the first reflection is than the original object. Estimate the size of the smallest object that you can see.

The Tortoise and the Hare

MENU
station
C

Tommy Tortoise and Harry Hare stood at the starting line of the race. Mr. Hare could run twice as fast as Mr. Tortoise. So Mr. Hare, being gracious, gave Mr. Tortoise a head start. The raceway announcer explained the running of the race in the following way. Who do you think won the race? Explain.

1 "That Harry Hare is quite a guy, isn't he folks? He's giving Mr. Tortoise quite a head start! But wait— Tommy Tortoise has just reached the halfway mark and here comes Harry Hare!"

2 "So far, folks, this race has been a real snoozer. Tommy Tortoise has just reached the three-quarter mark and as expected, Harry Hare is gaining on him. Mr. Hare has just passed the halfway point!"

3 "Harry Hare is turning on the speed, isn't he folks? He's just reached the three-quarter mark and Tommy Tortoise is now at the seven-eighths mark. It's anybody's race now!"

FINISH

MENU station D

The Big Countdown

Pick a fraction between 0 and 1.

1 Use a calculator to multiply your number by itself over and over and over. You may need to convert the number to a decimal. After you enter the number, try pressing the multiplication sign and entering the number a second time. Then press the equals sign over and over. Each time you press the equals sign, the number that appears on the display is the new multiple. This method will save you time, since you won't have to enter the number every time you multiply.

2 Record your work. Keep count of the number of times that you multiply your number.

3 How fast does it take for your number to get really small?

4 When does it reach 0?

5 Try at least five different fractions. Describe what you have found and predict what would occur if you tried another number.

Follow the Bouncing Ball

A rubber ball is dropped from a 100-foot building and lands on the concrete street below.

1 **H**ow high would you estimate each bounce to be?

2 **W**hat can you predict about the behavior of the bouncing ball?

3 **W**hat might you need to know about the ball?

4 **H**ow many times do you think the ball would bounce before it comes to a complete stop? Does the ball ever really stop bouncing?

5 **H**ow high are the smallest bounces?

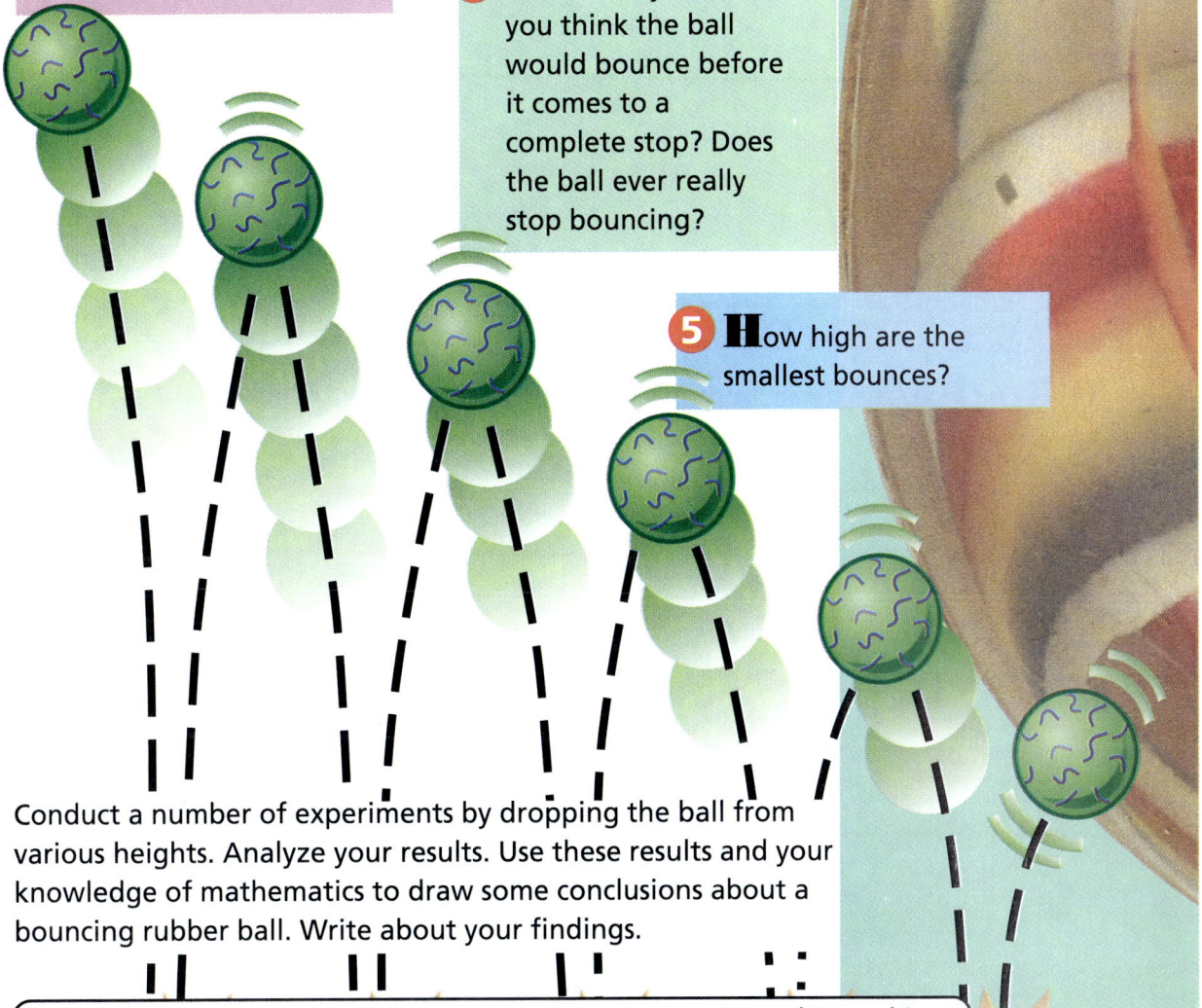

Conduct a number of experiments by dropping the ball from various heights. Analyze your results. Use these results and your knowledge of mathematics to draw some conclusions about a bouncing rubber ball. Write about your findings.

MENU station F

Squares!

Explore the following procedures that are written in LOGO on the computer.

1 Type the following procedure on a computer.

To Square :x
If :x < 0.1 [Stop]
Repeat 4 [FD :x RT 90]
Square :x * 0.5
End

2 Carry out the procedure by typing Square 100.

3 Experiment with the size of the square by changing the number that follows the word Square.

4 Alter the procedure by changing any of the numbers, such as 4, 90, or 0.5.

5 Explain what you have discovered about the procedure.

BREAKING UP

A **fractal** is an image that has self-similarity. In this activity, create a fractal. Start with a square sheet of tissue paper 4 inches on each side.

Level One

Fold the paper by bringing the right side over to the left. Then bring the top down to the bottom. If you were to open the paper up, it would be divided into 4 squares, each measuring 2 inches on a side. Now imagine cutting a square measuring $\frac{1}{2}$ inch on a side out of the upper right corner of the folded paper.

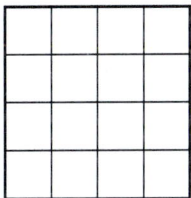

What do you think the paper will look like when it is opened up? Draw a picture to represent the paper after the square has been cut out. Then cut the square out of the upper right corner of the folded paper and open the paper up. What does it look like? How does your prediction compare to the actual result?

Level Two

Take the folded sheet and fold it again by bringing the right side over to the left and the top down to the bottom. If you were to open the paper up, it would be divided into 16 squares. Now imagine cutting another square measuring $\frac{1}{4}$ inch on a side out of the upper right corner of the folded paper. What do you think the paper will look like when it is opened up this time? Draw a picture to represent the paper after the square has been cut out. Then cut the square out of the upper right corner of the folded paper and open the paper up. What does it look like now? How does your prediction compare this time?

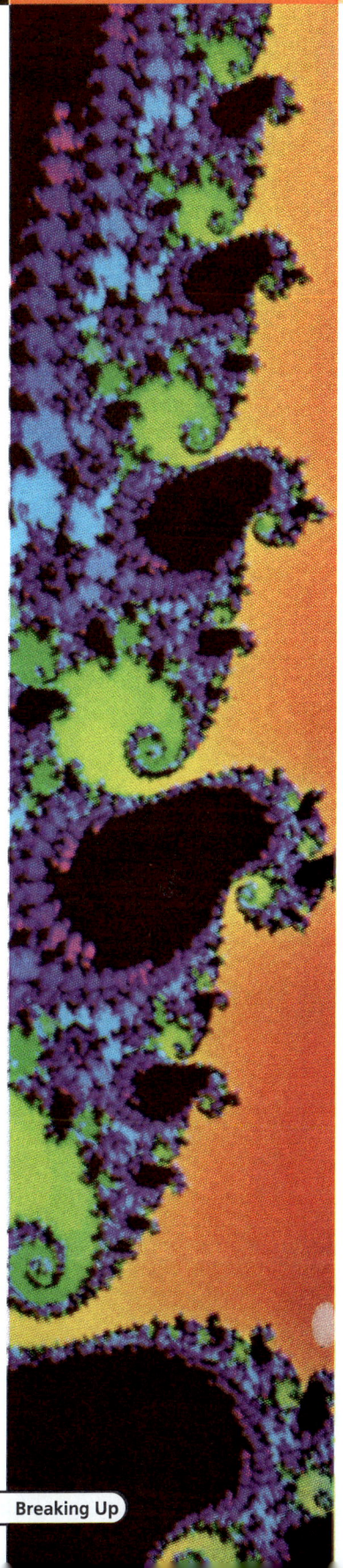

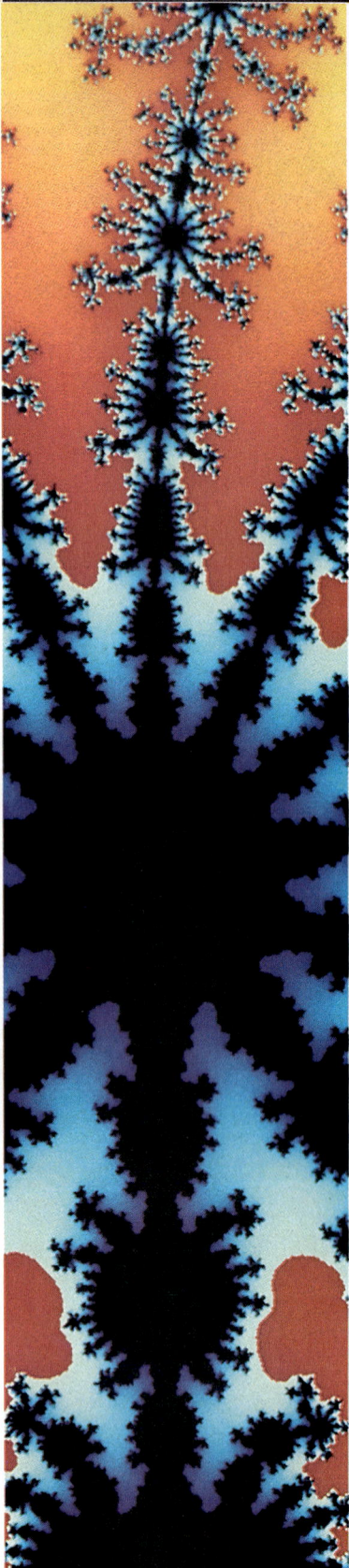

Level Three

Imagine that you could fold the folded sheet again so that if you were to open the paper up, it would be divided into 64 squares. Now imagine cutting an even smaller square out of the upper right corner of the folded paper. What do you think the paper will look like when it is opened up? Draw a picture to represent the paper after the square has been cut out.

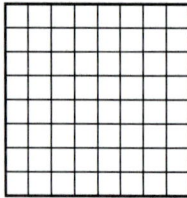

Analysis

Draw a picture of the fractal created when the process is repeated to the fourth and fifth levels.

- How do each of the folded squares compare to the folded square from the previous level?
- How big was the first hole that you cut?
- How big was the second hole that you cut? Why?
- How big would the fifth hole that you cut be? Why?
- Explain what you have learned about this fractal.

Sierpinski's Triangle

Create another fractal called **Sierpinski's Triangle**. Using dot paper, choose three points to be the vertices of an equilateral triangle. Your triangle should be as large as possible. This triangle is Level Zero of this fractal.

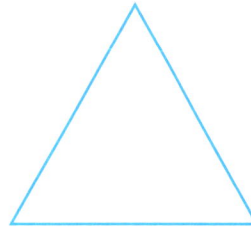

Level Zero

Level One

Locate and mark the midpoints of each side of the triangle. Connect those three points to make a smaller, upside-down triangle in the center of the large one.

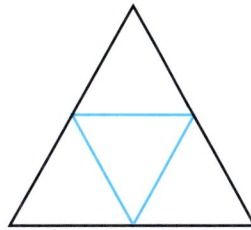

Level One

Level Two

Locate and mark the midpoints of each side of the triangle in the lower left corner. Connect those three points to make an even smaller triangle in the center of the lower left triangle. Do the same thing for the smaller triangle in the lower right corner and the triangle on the top. Leave the center triangle open.

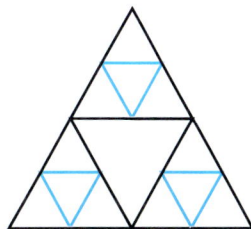

Level Two

Continue creating the fractal by repeating the process of drawing smaller triangles around each of the larger triangles. Do this for Level Three, Level Four, and so on until you cannot draw any more triangles. How many levels can you draw?

Connect the Dots

Work with a partner to complete this activity. One of you should measure and plot points. The other person will roll a number cube to determine which points to use.

Your teacher will give you a sheet of paper with three labeled points on it. Copy the points onto a blank transparency and label them. Consider the points the vertices of a triangle. Plot a fourth point anywhere on the paper to begin. We will call this point the *moving point*. Then follow the process below.

1. Roll the number cube. If you roll 1 or 4, use point 1. If you roll 2 or 5, use point 2. If you roll 3 or 6, use point 3.

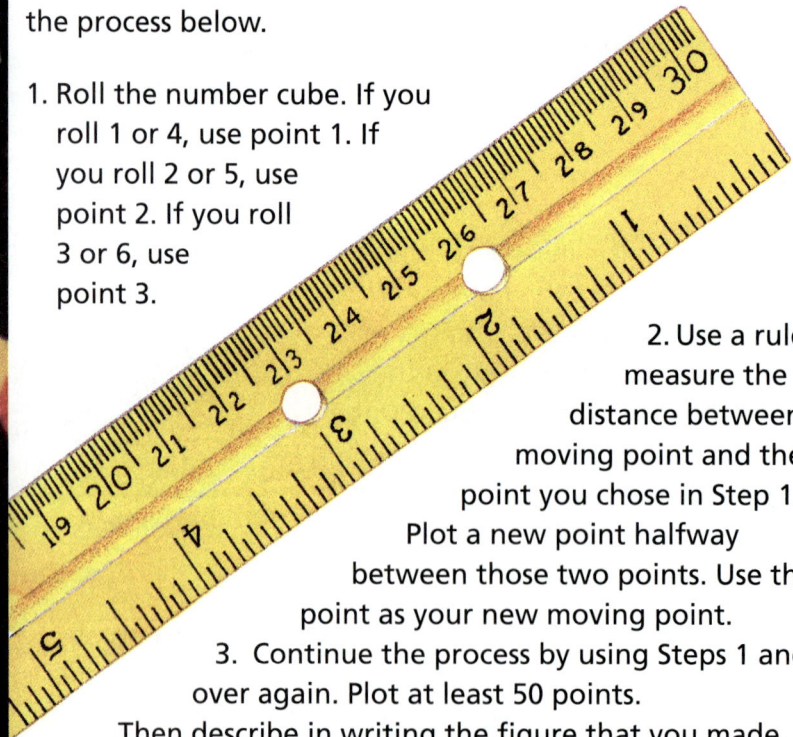

2. Use a ruler to measure the distance between the moving point and the point you chose in Step 1. Plot a new point halfway between those two points. Use this point as your new moving point.

3. Continue the process by using Steps 1 and 2 over again. Plot at least 50 points.

Then describe in writing the figure that you made. Also describe what you think the figure would look like if you plotted 500 points.

Use the technique that you followed on the previous page to create two more fractals.

Your teacher will give you a sheet of paper with four labeled points on it. Copy the points onto a blank transparency and label them. Plot a moving point anywhere on the page.

1. Roll an eight-sided number cube. If you roll 1 or 5, use point 1. If you roll 2 or 6, use point 2. If you roll 3 or 7, use point 3. If you roll 4 or 8, use point 4.
2. Use a ruler to measure the distance between the moving point and the point you chose in Step 1. Plot a new point $\frac{2}{3}$ of the way between the moving point and the point you chose in Step 1. Use this point as your new moving point.
3. Continue the process by using Steps 1 and 2 over again. Plot at least 100 points.

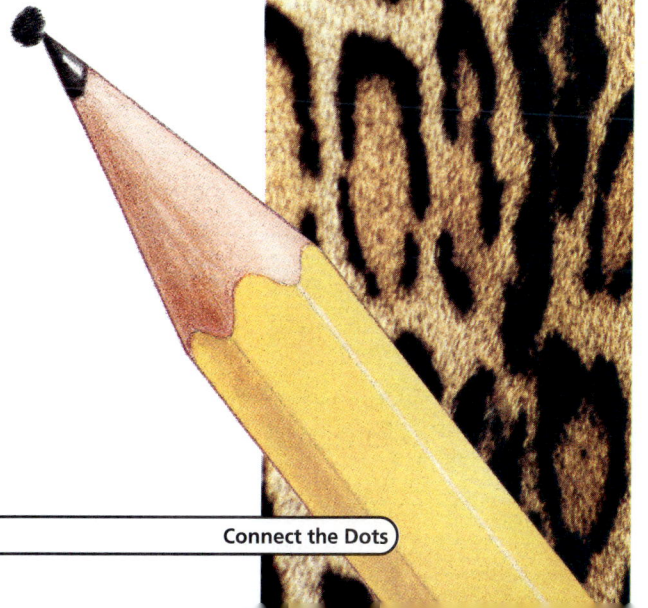

Your teacher will give you a sheet of paper with eight labeled points on it. Copy the points onto a blank transparency and label them. Plot a moving point anywhere on the page.

1. Roll an eight-sided number cube.
2. Use a ruler to measure the distance between the moving point and the point you rolled in Step 1. Plot a new point $\frac{2}{3}$ of the way between the moving point and the point you rolled in Step 1. Use this point as your new moving point.
3. Continue the process by using Steps 1 and 2 over again. Plot at least 100 points.

COMPUTER
investigation

It's Chaos!

In this activity, you will use a computer program called Chaos to create a fractal. Load the program by typing **LOAD "CHAOS**. To run the program, type **BEGIN**.

1. The program will prompt you as follows: **Type in the number of coordinate pairs:**. Choose a figure as the basis for your fractal. You can use a triangle, a square, a rectangle, or a hexagon. Enter the number of vertices in your figure; for example, 3 for a triangle, 4 for a square or rectangle, and so on.

2. The program will prompt you again: **Type in coordinate pair number 1:**. The screen is like a coordinate plane. 0 0 is the exact center of the screen. The first number refers to the left or right direction, and the second number refers to the up or down direction. For example, 100 100 is right 100 and up 100; –100 0 is just left 100. Enter the coordinates of the point as two numbers separated by a space. Do *not* use commas or parentheses when entering coordinates.

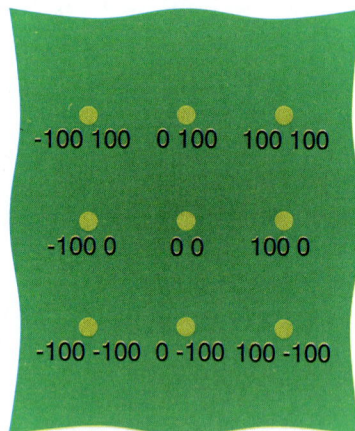

-100 100	0 100	100 100
-100 0	0 0	100 0
-100 -100	0 -100	100 -100

3. The program will prompt you a third time: **Type in coordinate pair number 2:**. Enter the coordinates of the second point as two numbers separated by a space. The program will continue to prompt you until all of the coordinates have been entered. Here are some possible coordinates for the four figures.

triangle: (0 100), (–100 –100), (100 –100)
square: (–100 –100), (100, –100), (100 100), (–100 100)
hexagon: (40 80), (100 0), (40 –80), (–60 –80), (–120 0),
                   (–60 40)
8-point   (–100 –100), (0 –100), (100 –100), (100 0),
rectangle: (100 100), (0 100), (–100 100), (–100 0)

COMPUTER investigation

4. Then, the program will prompt you as follows: **Type in the coordinates of the starting point:**. Experiment with this point; put it anywhere on the screen.
5. To stop the process, press Ctrl-G if you have an Apple II computer, Ctrl-Break if you have an IBM-compatible computer, or Option if you have a Macintosh computer.

Analyze your findings in a one-page report. Here are some things to consider.

- Record your results. Classify the images you created, look for patterns in the images, and sketch drawings of some of the images.
- Record the inputs that you used and determine how they affected the images you created. How did changing the location of the points affect an image?
- How many levels can you see? What is the size of the smallest subsection that you can see?
- Consider how long the program needs to run in order to obtain a clear picture of the image emerging. Be prepared to discuss your findings.
- Summarize your findings. What did you discover about chaos theory?

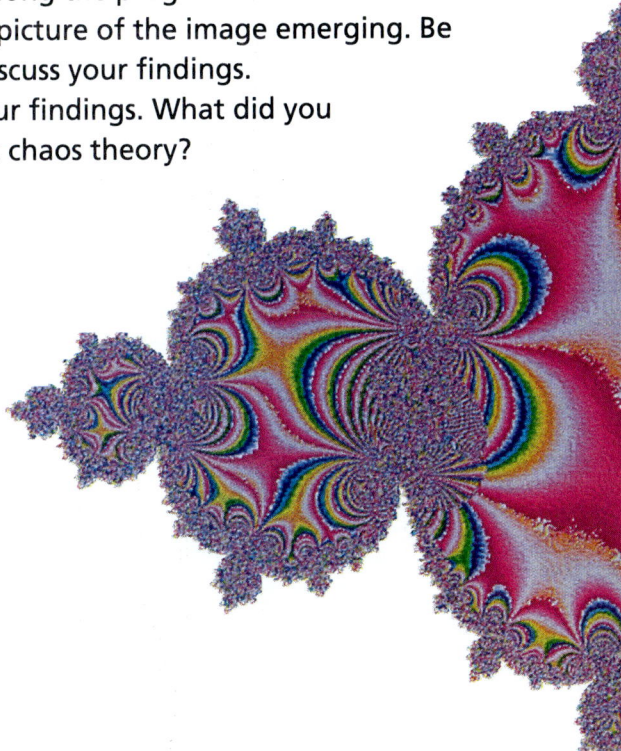

Forest Fire

You and your partner are forest rangers who are concerned about the spread of forest fires in your area. You know that fires spread in a random manner, so you run several chaos games to simulate the burning of the forest in order to make predictions about your area.

To run the simulation, select a probability factor for the spread of the fire. In other words, select a fraction that will predict the likelihood that the fire will spread. Choose from $\frac{1}{6}$, $\frac{2}{6}$ or $\frac{1}{3}$, $\frac{3}{6}$ or $\frac{1}{2}$, $\frac{4}{6}$ or $\frac{2}{3}$, or $\frac{5}{6}$. If you choose $\frac{1}{6}$, that means that the fire will spread only $\frac{1}{6}$ of the time. If you choose $\frac{5}{6}$, the fire will be much more likely to spread.

Each tree in the forest has four neighbors: one to the north, one to the east, one to the south, and one to the west. When a tree is on fire, any one of its neighbors that is not already burned has a chance to catch fire. Each fire lasts one hour. Roll a number cube to determine whether or not a tree catches fire. Depending on your probability factor and the number that you roll, the tree may or may not catch fire. See the table below.

To start the fire, choose a square on your grid paper and label it "1." This means that the tree is burning during the first hour. During this hour, each of its four neighbors will have a chance to catch fire. Roll the number cube to determine if the neighbor to the north will catch fire. If it does, label it "2," because it will be burning during the second hour.

Probability Factor	Catches Fire if You Roll...
$\frac{1}{6}$	1
$\frac{2}{6}$	1, 2
$\frac{3}{6}$	1, 2, 3
$\frac{4}{6}$	1, 2, 3, 4
$\frac{5}{6}$	1, 2, 3, 4, 5

If it does not catch fire, do not label the square. Next, roll the number cube to see if the neighbor to the east will catch fire. If it does, label it "2." Continue with the neighbors to the south and west. If only the neighbors to the east and south caught fire, your grid paper would look like Figure 1.

Figure 1

When all four neighbors have been checked, the first hour is over. During the second hour, each of the trees labeled "2" is on fire, and each of its neighbors that are not already burned must be checked. These neighbors are labeled "*" in Figure 2. You do not need to label the neighbors when you run your simulation.

The tree that is circled will have two chances to catch fire during the second hour, since two of its neighbors are burning. If any of the neighbors catch fire during this hour, label them "3," because they will be burning during the third hour. When all of these neighbors have been checked, the second hour is over. Only the trees labeled "3" are burning, and their neighbors must be checked during the third hour. Continue the simulation and stop when there are no more trees burning or when the fire has burned beyond the boundaries of the forest.

Figure 2

Run several simulations using different probability factors for the spreading of the fire. Try to determine which probability factors will cause the fire to burn out before reaching the boundaries of the forest, and which will cause the fire to spread unchecked. Investigate how the probability affects the shape of the burned area. For those fires that burn out, determine how many trees are consumed by the fire before it dies out.

In your role as forest ranger, write to your supervisor about the likelihood of a fire spreading in your area. Predict how the fires will burn. Discuss what damage will occur when the fire spreading factor changes and what could cause this factor to increase.

The Color Triangle
Multiples

The figure on the sheet your teacher has provided is called **Pascal's Triangle**. Describe any patterns you notice in the first five rows. Then use the pattern to continue the triangle until you have 20 rows.

Each person in your group should roll the number cube. Anyone who rolls a 1 or rolls the same number as another person in the group must roll again. When each of you has your own number, you each should select one color for the multiples of your number and another color for those numbers that are not multiples. For example, if your number is 3, you would have one color for the multiples of 3: 3, 6, 9, 12, and so on, and another for the numbers that are not multiples.

Consider each number in Pascal's Triangle. Is it a multiple of your number? Color each hexagon with the colors you selected. Once everyone in your group has colored their triangle, compare all of the triangles. As a group, make a list of the similarities and differences among your colored triangles.

Make a group poster. Glue each of your triangles, along with your list of similarities and differences, onto the poster.

Remainders

Roll the number cube again to select another number. This time, you will color the triangle based on remainders. For example, if you roll a 3 and you divide a number in the triangle by 3, the possible remainders are 0, 1, and 2. Assign a different color to each of these remainders. Then consider each number in the triangle. Divide each number by 3 and color the entry according to its remainder.

Write about the triangle that you colored. Address the following questions in your remarks.

- What does the triangle look like?
- How does it compare to the triangle that you colored before?
- What do you think would happen if you had rolled a different number?

COMPUTER investigation

Fractured Pictures

In this activity, you will use a computer program called Fractals to create a fractal. Load the program by typing **LOAD "FRACTALS**. To run the program, type **BEGIN**.

1. The program will prompt you as follows: **Type in the number of sides:**. Choose a polygon as the basis for your fractal and enter the number of sides it has. This is the first level of the fractal image.

2. The second prompt will be: **Type in the length of a side:**. Choose a number between 80 and 200. The smaller the number of sides, the larger the length of a side should be.

3. The third prompt will be: **Type in the turning angle:**. This is an angle measurement between 0° and 360°. Divide 360 by the number of sides and enter the result.

4. The fourth prompt will be: **Type in the fractal divisor:**. This number adjusts the size of the subparts of the fractal. For example, 2 will make each part one-half the size of the original, 3 will make each part one-third the size of the original, and so on.

5. The fifth prompt will be: **Type in the number of copies:**. This refers to the number of copies that are made from the original figure. This number should be the same as the number of sides.

6. The sixth prompt will be: **Type in the depth of the fractal:**. This is the number of sublevels that will be drawn. The higher the number, the more dense the fractal. Try numbers between 3 and 6.

7. Finally, **Type in the location of the lower left corner of your figure:**. This location is the point from which the fractal is drawn. The location can be anywhere on the screen.

Look for patterns in the images and sketch drawings of some of the images. Then write a report describing all of the properties of fractals that you have discovered in this unit. Be prepared to share your findings with the class.

Go Fly a Kite

Step 1

In this activity, you will build two kites, each in the shape of a **tetrahedron**. A tetrahedron is a pyramid in which each of the four sides, or *faces*, is in the shape of a triangle. Thus, there are three triangles at each vertex.

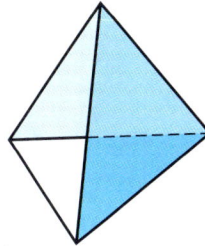

Make each tetrahedron kite with six straws that are the same length. Join the straws together using twist ties and/or tape at four points. Cover two of the faces with tissue paper by wrapping the paper around two of the four faces and securely taping the paper around the straws. Place the kite so that one of the open sides is on the bottom and the other is facing you.

Step 2

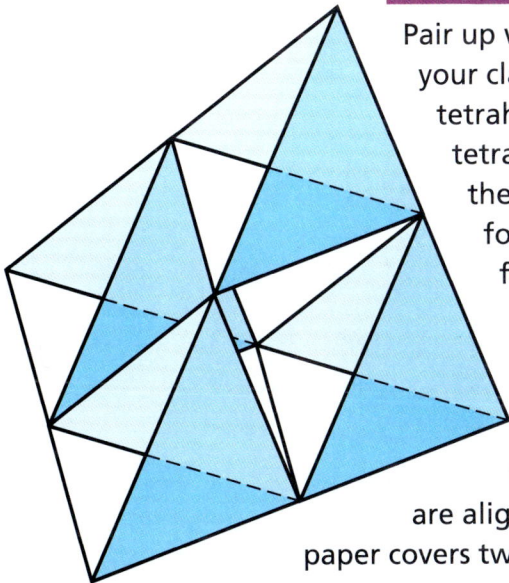

Pair up with another student in your class. Use your four tetrahedra to build a large tetrahedron. Place three of the tetrahedra together to form a base and place the fourth tetrahedron on top. Tape the four smaller kites together at the points where they meet. Make sure that the small kites are aligned so that the tissue paper covers two of the larger faces.

Step 3

Join three other pairs of students in your class. At this point, there should be eight of you and four large tetrahedra. Use these four tetrahedra to build an even larger tetrahedron. Place three of the large tetrahedra together to form a base and place the fourth large tetrahedron on top. Tape the four tetrahedra together at the points where they meet. Once again, make sure that the kites are aligned so that the tissue paper covers two of the large faces.

YOUR REPORT

Write about your kites.

- Analyze the components of your group kite. Describe the self-similar shapes that appear in it.

- Describe the size relationship of the shapes between the levels of the group kite.

- Predict the sizes of the components of the kite if it were to grow larger. For example, what size would the kite be if it were built to level 10?

- Suppose the kite was made up of an infinite number of sublevels; that is, the kite was made of infinitely many smaller kites. What method could you use to find the length of a side of the kite at any level?

I've Got Designs on You

Design a poster that contains a fractal, a self-similar collage, a picture inside a picture, a self-similar geometric design, or another self-similar original creation. It must be an original drawing or design. Your poster may contain photographs, pictures from periodicals, enlargements or reductions from copiers, and/or computer-generated designs. The object can be created by using a chaos technique or a self-similar drawing. You may produce a 3-dimensional model of a fractal. Your design must contain at least four levels of self-similar shapes.

This is an enlargement of the photo of a fractal shown at the right.

YOUR REPORT

Write an individual report that describes the poster and the process that you used to create the design. Be sure to describe the relationship between similar objects in your design. Identify the self-similar shapes or pictures that you used in the poster. Determine the relationship between the sizes of self-similar shapes that you used. Determine a procedure for finding the size of that shape at any given level of the design. Then prepare an oral presentation that includes your poster and written report.

Selection and Reflection

- The mathematical terms **self-similarity, chaos, fractal geometry, infinity,** and **recursion** were used throughout this unit. What do these terms mean? Explain them in your own words and give examples.

- What do these words mean in terms of the work you did in this unit?

- Describe the mathematics that you used in this unit.

- What did you learn while studying this unit? Use examples from several of the activities in the unit in your explanation.

- How did you feel about learning about fractals and chaos theory? Did you enjoy the experience?

The Problem

When books are printed, large sheets of paper are run through the printing presses. These sheets are then folded in half twice to form the pages of the book. Imagine that you are a bookbinder. Take two sheets of paper each measuring $8\frac{1}{2}$ inches by 11 inches. Fold and number the pages in your booklet from 1 to 8. How many sheets of paper would be needed to make a 120-page booklet? What rule or rules can be used to assign numbers to each sheet of paper?

Book Him

The Best Deal

The Problem

Your parents have offered you a choice in the way that you can receive your allowance. You can get $50.00 per month, or you can get 1¢ the first day, 2¢ the second day, 4¢ the third day, 8¢ the fourth day, and so on, doubling the amount each day. Which deal would you agree to? Why?

The Problem

At 8:00 A.M., you told your best friend a deep, dark secret. Then, within 15 minutes, your best friend told two other people. Then, within the next 15 minutes, those two people each told two other people. This continued all day long, with every person telling two other people who hadn't been told every 15 minutes. How many people would know your deep, dark secret by 3:00 P.M.? Write a letter to your best friend explaining what happened to your secret.

The Deep, Dark Secret

The Staircase

The Problem

A certain staircase has 10 steps. Esteban is able to climb up the staircase by either going up the steps one at a time or by going up two steps at a time. How many different ways can he climb the staircase? Keep in mind that taking a single step, then a double step, and then 7 more single steps is a different way to go up the staircase than first taking a double step and then 8 single steps.

Extension In how many ways could Esteban go up and down the stairs if he could take single or double steps each way?

The Problem

Suppose the copier at your school can reduce pictures to 57% and 64% and can enlarge pictures to 120%. You have a picture that you need to reduce to exactly 25% of the original. Determine a method for reducing the original to get the picture as close to 25% of the original as possible.

Copycat!

PASCAL'S TRIANGLE

The Problem

The triangular array of numbers shown at the right is called Pascal's Triangle, for the French mathematician Blaise Pascal. The triangle was published in Europe in 1665, but a Chinese version of the triangle was published in 1303.

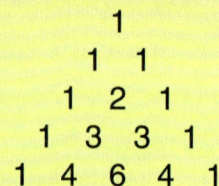

```
          1
         1 1
        1 2 1
       1 3 3 1
      1 4 6 4 1
```

Find the sum of the numbers in each row of the triangle. How is the sum of a row related to the sum of the row just above it?

Extension How is the sum of the numbers in any row of Pascal's Triangle related to the sum of the numbers in all of the rows above the given row?

QUALITY CONTROL

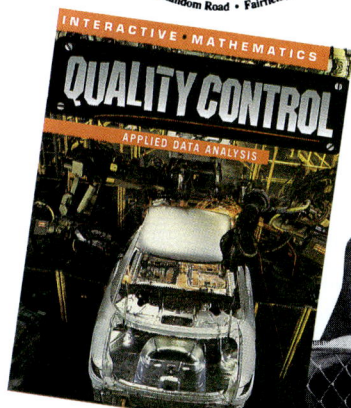

Looking Ahead

In this unit, you will see how mathematics can be used to answer questions about averages and variation. You will experience:

- analyzing data using line plots, box-and-whisker plots, and tables

- working cooperatively to estimate costs

- using or creating data to determine measures of center

- using a calculator to find range, average, and standard deviation

Did You Ever Wonder?

What do mathematics and spicy chocolate cookies have to do with each other? Turn the page and see how Jill Sheiman of Fairfield, Connecticut, combines the two!

INTERACTIVE · MATHEMATICS

QUALITY CONTROL
APPLIED DATA ANALYSIS

Jill's One Smart Cookie Inc. · 128 Random Road · Fairfield, Connecticut 06432 · 203-374-6351

JILL'S COOKIES

Teens in the News

Featuring: Jill Sheiman
Age; 17
Hometown: Fairfield, Connecticut
Career Goal: Sports attorney
Interests: business, sports, community work

Jill Sheiman had volunteered to bake for a homeless shelter when she stumbled on a recipe for a rich, spicy chocolate cookie. Two years later, to her amazement, Jill began distributing "Slightly Hot Chocolate" through her company, Jill's One Smart Cookie, Inc. What's even more amazing is that Jill was only 13 when this all happened!

Jill didn't know how to start a business, so she placed a $15 ad in the newspaper. The ad said that a cookie company was looking for a "concept person." Jill's ad didn't mention her age. Peter Cornish, an executive at a large marketing firm, answered Jill's ad.

Now Peter Cornish helps Jill with the ins and outs of marketing, including focus groups, packaging, and advertising. Jill's father helps with the legal details of owning a business. Her mother is the company's chauffeur and secretary. Jill's sister, 12, is the official taste tester.

Jill says she uses math so much in her business that she just takes it for granted. She does all of the accounting for her company. She also uses math to compute the cost of producing each cookie.

Jill was invited to Switzerland as a consultant to a Swiss cookie company. She has been on many TV shows, and dozens of articles have been written about Jill's company.

Several major food chains have expressed an interest in Jill's cookies. Look for her cookies—they're coming soon to a store near you!

Clamor for Holiday Cookies

More than three-fourths of people who give homemade food as holiday gifts give cookies!

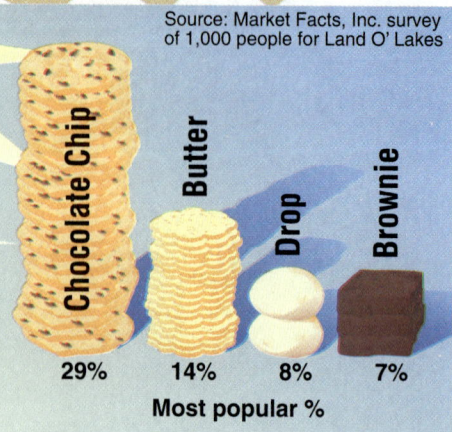

Source: Market Facts, Inc. survey of 1,000 people for Land O' Lakes

Chocolate Chip	Butter	Drop	Brownie
29%	14%	8%	7%

Most popular %

Team Project

Good 'n' Fresh?

Jill's cookies sell for as much as $1.00 apiece. Her customers expect Jill's cookies to be of the highest quality. Help Jill's One Smart Cookie, Inc., keep a check on quality control by listing all of the factors that would affect the quality of the cookies the company produces.

Most of Jill's customers order their cookies by mail. What is the least expensive way to mail cookies? What is the fastest way to mail cookies? What is the best way for Jill's One Smart Cookie, Inc., to mail cookies?

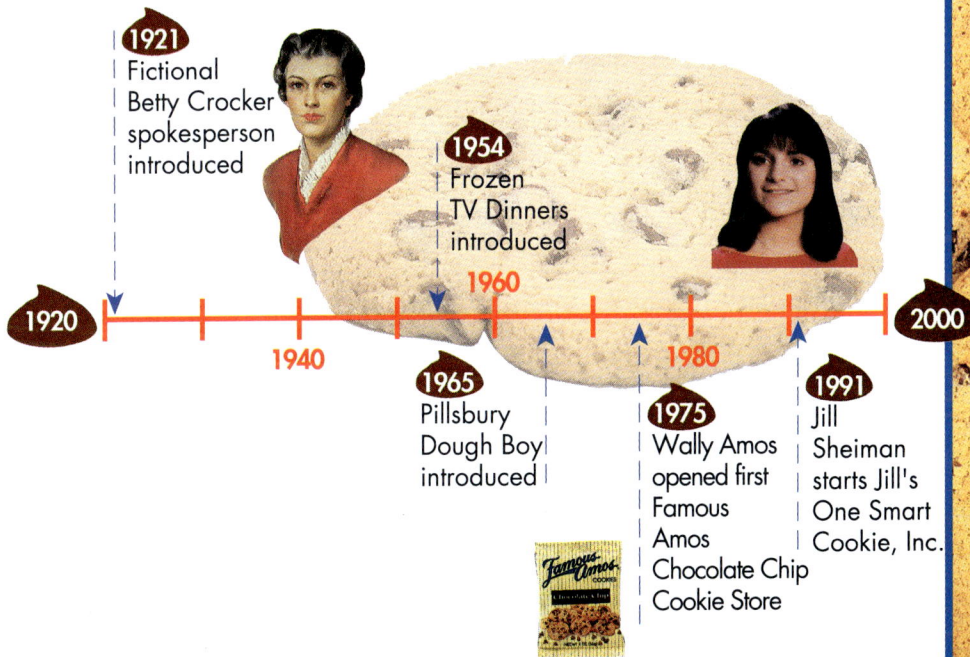

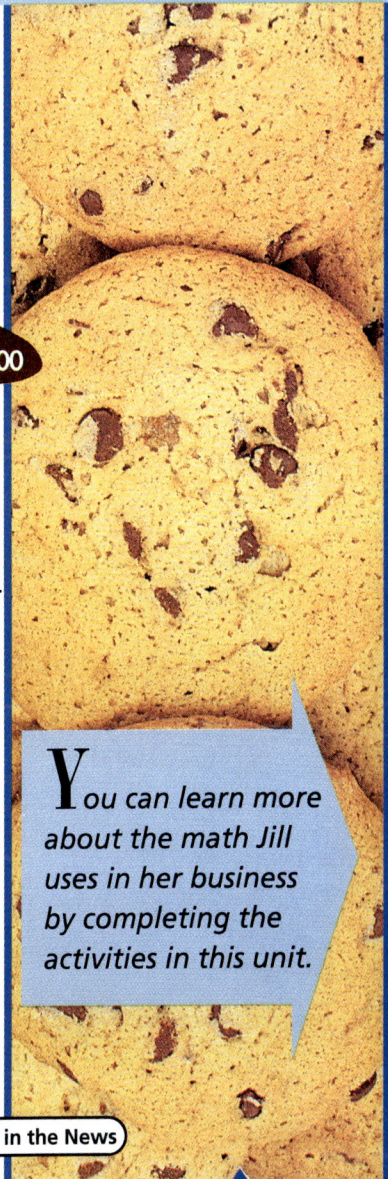

1921
Fictional Betty Crocker spokesperson introduced

1954
Frozen TV Dinners introduced

1920 — 1940 — 1960 — 1980 — 2000

1965
Pillsbury Dough Boy introduced

1975
Wally Amos opened first Famous Amos Chocolate Chip Cookie Store

1991
Jill Sheiman starts Jill's One Smart Cookie, Inc.

For more information

If you would like more information about helping to feed the homeless, contact:

FOOD FOR THE HUNGRY
7729 E. Greenway Road
P.O. Box E
Scottsdale, Arizona 85260

You can learn more about the math Jill uses in her business by completing the activities in this unit.

Setting the Scene

MATHEMATICS TOOLKIT

Many professions require the use of tools. This mathematics toolkit includes tools you may find useful as you study this unit. At times you may feel lost or not know where to begin when presented with a problem situation. You should take time to review this toolkit and remember the different statistical tools and problem-solving strategies the characters in the script used. You don't need to wait until your teacher tells you to make a chart or find the mean. Instead, if it seems like it might help, try it.

Narrator: Enrique, Rick, and Marisela are on the golf team at Marina High School. They are discussing their chipping.

Marisela: I think I could improve my game by five strokes if I could only improve my chipping.

Enrique: I know. I bogeyed eight holes in the last match and half of those I could have parred with a decent chip.

Marisela: We should ask Coach how we can work on our chipping.

Rick: Good idea. I think he's on the practice green.

Narrator: The players find their coach near the practice green.

Marisela: Coach, we need to work on our chipping. Do you have any suggestions?

Coach: I've watched your techniques and they're pretty good. What you need is just a little more practice. Maybe we can devise a friendly little competition to help you concentrate.

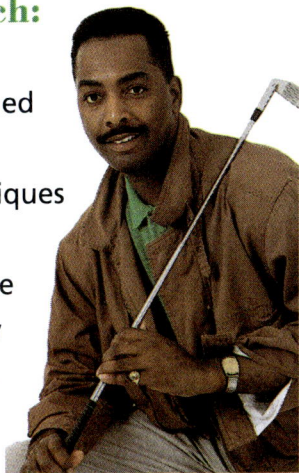

Rick: That sounds great. I know I'll whip these guys.

Enrique: Oh sure, you'll choke, like you always do.

Coach: Now wait—this is a friendly competition. You'll need to encourage each other as you work to improve.

Rick: Okay, cool. What are the rules?

Coach: Pick a certain distance from the green. Each of you choose a different color ball. Marisela you take white, Rick you take light green, and Enrique you take orange. Each of you chip five shots, and the player who is consistently closest to the cup wins.

Marisela: Yeah, that sounds great. Come on guys, let's play.

Narrator: The players each take five shots. When they are done, the practice green is scattered with fifteen balls.

Rick: So, how do we know who wins?

Enrique: Let's measure the distance each ball is from the cup. I'll get the measuring tape. Let's measure in inches.

Marisela: Rick, yours are 40, 60, 100, 152, and 312 inches from the cup. Enrique, yours are 52, 64, 76, 184, and 288 inches from the cup. Mine are 84, 99, 129, 165, and 200 inches from the cup.

Rick: Okay, how can we tell from these numbers who wins? The balls are all spread out. No one was close every time!

Narrator: The players decide to ask their coach how to determine who wins the chipping contest.

Coach: In the game of golf, getting close and being consistent are important. So, you should consider who is closest and most consistent. Don't just consider who had the best shot. You're the math whizzes—I'm sure you can figure it out.

Marisela: I know—let's graph the numbers with a **line plot.**

Rick: All right, let's go into the clubhouse, and I'll plot the numbers.

Narrator: The players go into the clubhouse and Rick makes the following line plots using the distance each ball was from the hole.

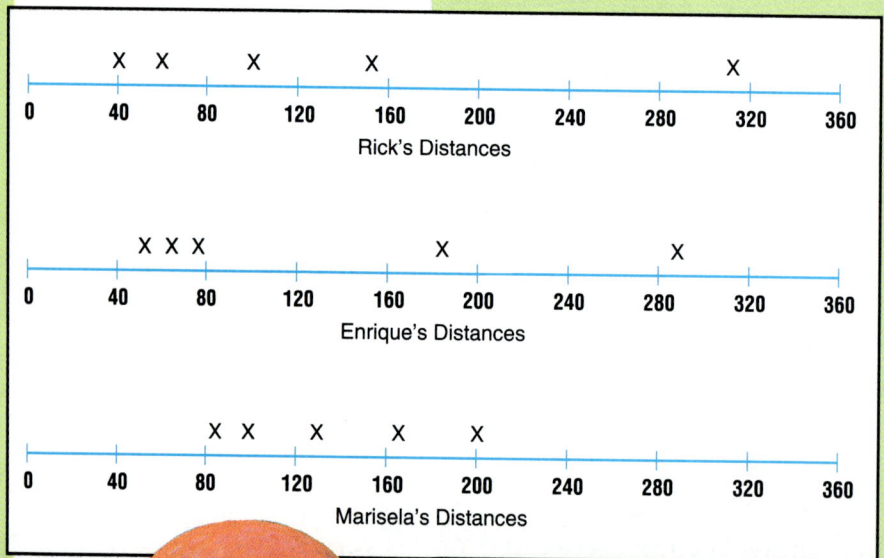

```
         X  X      X        X                              X
   |----+----+----+----+----+----+----+----+----+
   0    40   80  120  160  200  240  280  320  360
                    Rick's Distances

         X X X              X              X
   |----+----+----+----+----+----+----+----+----+
   0    40   80  120  160  200  240  280  320  360
                  Enrique's Distances

            X  X    X     X      X
   |----+----+----+----+----+----+----+----+----+
   0    40   80  120  160  200  240  280  320  360
                  Marisela's Distances
```

Stop the Script!
Determine which player is the best chipper. Defend your answer using mathematical reasoning.

Rick: Wow, I have the best shot.

Marisela: Yeah, but you also have the worst.

Rick: Maybe we should throw out the worst shot. I think I would win hands down.

Enrique: Right, that's really fair! Just like in a game. Can you throw out a shot? Get real!

Marisela: Yeah, besides if you can throw out your worst shot, we should also throw out your best.

Rick: Okay, Okay! Maybe we should add up all the distances. What do you think?

Enrique: I've got my calculator in my bag. I use it to keep my stats. Here, I'll figure them out. Marisela, your distances add up to 677. Rick, yours and mine each add up to 664.

Rick: If we divide those distances by 5 shots, we'll get the average distance from the hole.

Enrique: Okay, Marisela's average distance is 135.4 and Rick's and mine are both 132.8. What do you think, Rick? Did we tie?

Marisela: Wait a minute. Mine are all close together. Look at the graph. Remember, Coach says that consistency really counts and I didn't make any real bad shots.

Enrique: Look at mine. My three best are the closest together and all three are better than your best.

Marisela: If you look at it another way, my five are all better than each of your worst.

Rick: Let's stop arguing! This is getting us nowhere. I know another graph that might help us decide. It's called a **box-and-whisker plot**. The lines show the two extremes and the data are broken into quarters.

Marisela: See, the graph shows that I'm very consistent.

Rick: We already knew that. Can't we find a number or score that we could use?

Enrique: I know. I just learned how to do standard deviation on my calculator. We learned in math class that standard deviation shows how closely a set of numbers are grouped together. Doesn't that mean consistency?

Rick: Do you really remember how to calculate that?

Enrique: Sure, it's easy! You just put a set of distances in the data

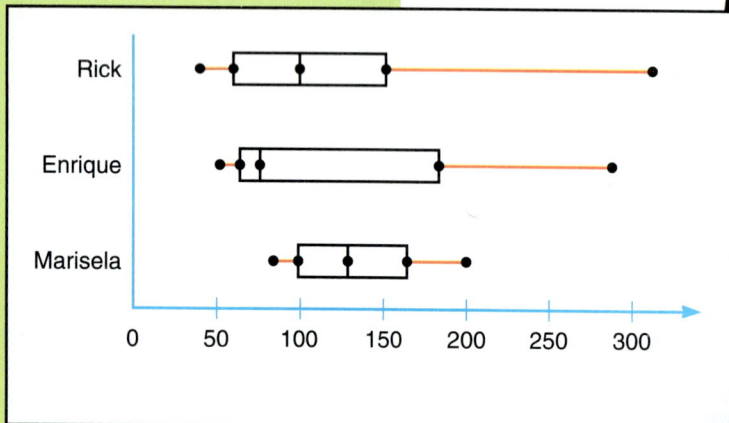

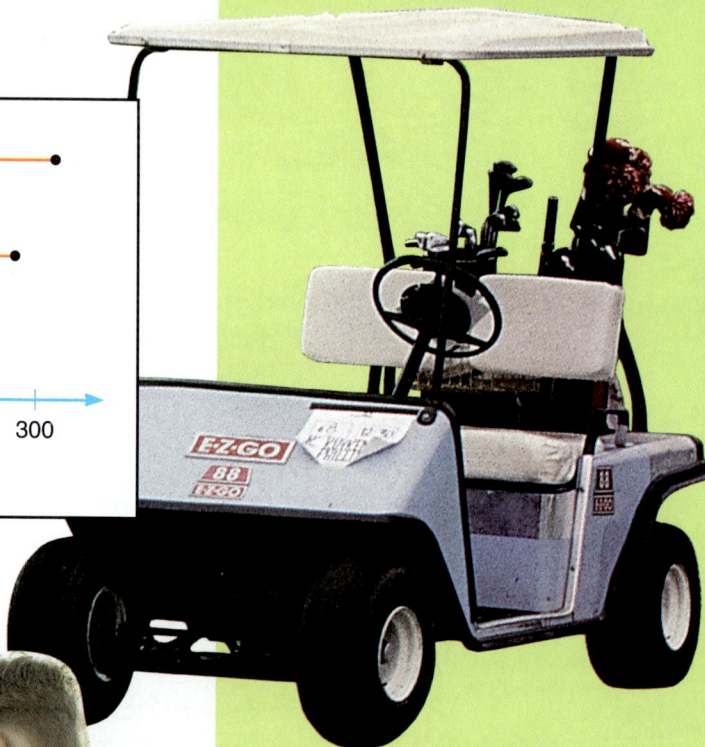

Enrique: Well, we can usually sink putts five feet or less.

Rick: Yeah, and if your ball is between 5 and 15 feet, it's reasonable to expect two putts.

Marisela: Okay, let's agree that if it's within 5 feet it's a one putt. Between 5 feet and 15 feet it's a two putt, and over 15 feet it's a three putt.

Rick: I'll convert these lengths to inches. The 5-foot boundary is 60 inches, and the 15–foot boundary is 180 inches.

Enrique: I get it. Picture the practice green like a bull's-eye. Let's figure where our distances lie.

memory and press the σx key. The calculator does all the work. Here–watch me do it. Rick's standard deviation is 97.4, mine is 90.8, and Marisela's is 42.6.

Marisela: See, mine is so much smaller. That means the numbers are close together like the graphs show and that I'm the most consistent.

Rick: Yeah, the most consistent at missing. I still have the best shot and my average ties for the best.

Enrique: And Rick, you're also the most inconsistent!

Marisela: Wait—let's stop arguing and consider the qualities of the shots. Like how they would play out in a game.

Rick: Yeah, let's figure out which shots would only take a single putt to finish the hole, then which shots would probably take two putts, and which would take three putts.

Marisela: I'll make a table.

Name	1 putt	2 putt	3 putt
Rick	II	II	I
Enrique	I	II	II
Marisela		IIII	I

Rick: What did I tell you? See, this chart shows that I won. I had the most quality chips.

Marisela: I don't know about that. I think we showed we could use different measurements to plead any of our cases. What's most important? Having the closest shot, being the most consistent, or having the best average?

Enrique: I agree, but we have to use something to measure quality and in this case, the most quality chips is as good a standard as any. Besides, it's probably the easiest thing to measure, and I need to practice my chipping.

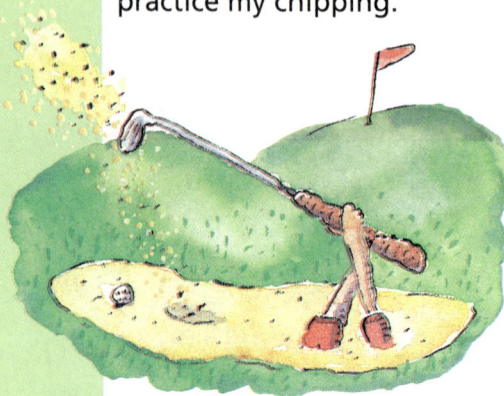

Rick: Yeah, let's play again. I'll show you who the superior chipper is!

Marisela: Right! Listen to Mr. Golf Pro.

This concludes the Mathematics Toolkit. It included many mathematical tools for you to use throughout this unit. As you work through this unit, you should use these tools to help you solve problems. You may want to explain how to use these mathematical tools in your journal. Or you may want to create a toolkit notebook to add mathematical tools you discover throughout this unit.

BRAKE INSPECTION

You are test engineers on a quality control team for a major U.S. automobile manufacturer. Your assignment is to determine the safety of the brakes on a new model car in production.

The brakes of a new model car were tested forty times for their safety. The car was tested by first reaching a speed of 55 mph. At this point, the brakes were applied. The distance that it took the car to come to a complete stop was measured. The test results, measured in meters, are shown below.

It has been determined by U.S. Highway Department standards that a safe driving distance is one car length for every 10 miles per hour a car is traveling. The new model car measures 5 yards in length.

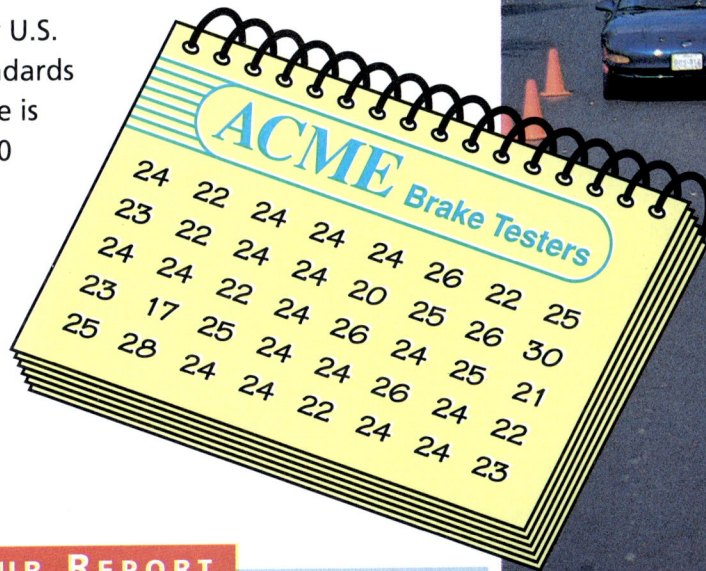

ACME Brake Testers

24 22 24 24 24 24 26 22 25
23 22 24 24 24 20 25 26 30
24 24 22 24 26 24 25 21
23 17 25 24 24 26 24 22
25 28 24 24 24 22 24 24 23

YOUR REPORT

Your test manager needs a detailed report on the braking system. In your report, state whether or not the braking system is safe.

- What factors were considered in your conclusion?
- What mathematical concepts were used in arriving at your conclusion?
- What important elements were considered?
- Under what conditions might you change your overall opinion?

TOWER CONSTRUCTION

You are a member of a contractor group that will supervise the construction of the tower shown at the right. Before you can begin construction, however, you must submit a construction bid. This bid should include a budget. Each contractor group estimates the amount of construction time, determines the amount of raw materials needed, and totals its cost estimates. Assume that labor costs will be $1,000.00 per minute. Raw material costs will be $100.00 per beam and $7.50 each per nut and bolt.

Once a contractor group submits a bid, the requested raw materials will be delivered. Verify that all requested materials have been delivered. If additional materials need to be purchased during construction, an additional delivery fee of $500.00 will be charged. No excess materials may be sold back after construction begins. Each contractor group should wait for the signal before beginning construction. Record the time when construction is completed.

Each tower will be inspected. The inspector will guarantee that the tower is constructed in accordance with the company blueprint. All joints must be securely fastened. In case a tower does not meet the standard, a five-minute delay will be charged and the tower must be adjusted. The total time accumulates while revisions are made.

Tower Diagram

Debriefing Guide

Write a full-page narrative on your tower construction. Consider the questions below when writing your narrative.

- What methods of construction were considered?
- How did your group arrive at your bid estimate?
- How did you control your time?
- How was quality checked and accuracy insured?
- What actions helped the group in doing this task?
- Were people's individual skills taken into consideration?
- Was anyone left out?
- Were anyone's ideas ignored?
- What would you do the next time to improve the construction process and insure quality?

The narratives will be discussed in class.

CONSUMERS FIGHT BACK
Chip Off the Old Block

You are a member of a consumer advocate group. Recently, it has come to your attention that the chips in potato chip bags are getting smaller and smaller. Since the only measure that appears on the bag's label is the weight, there is no way of knowing the size of the typical chip in the bag. It has been suggested that a typical chip size should also be listed on the bag along with the weights and ingredients.

Experiment by sorting, measuring, and classifying the chips in a bag of potato chips and determine which statistical measures should be used to determine the typical size of a chip in the bag.

Write a letter to the editor of *Consumer Findings* stating your concerns, findings, and a recommendation for the listing of a typical chip size on the package of the potato chips. State in the letter exactly how the typical chip should be determined and why you believe your typical chip size is a valid number.

CDs for Sale

The following prices for similar CD players were taken from a survey of stores in the Atlanta area. Describe to a friend the range of the prices. Using the data, describe the typical price and what you think a fair or competitive price would be.

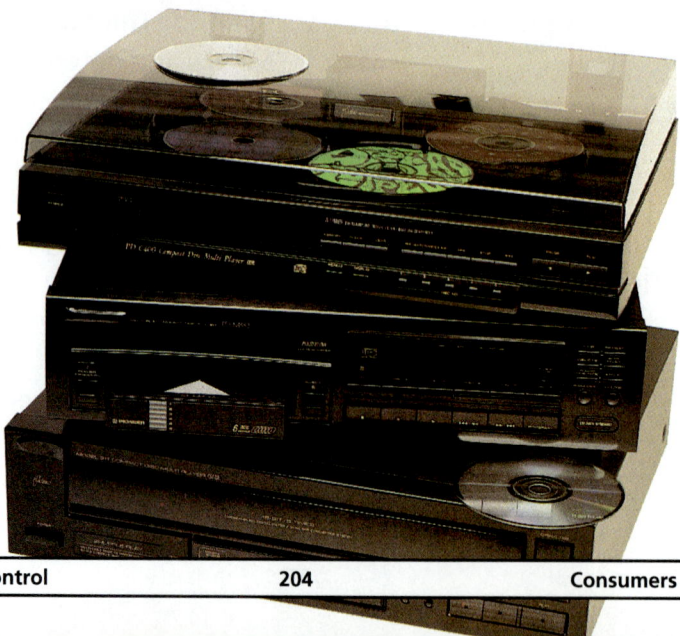

		$190	$300
$195	$299	$200	$299
$300	$220	$225	$275
$265	$250		$285
$299	$275	$285	
$220	$190	$225	$285
$325	$250	$195	$195

The Ultimate Deli

COMPUTER investigation

You work for The Ultimate Deli. The Ultimate Deli sells different foods throughout the day. In the mornings, bagels, donuts, and sweet rolls are sold. At lunch, people usually order sandwiches. In the afternoon, drinks, cookies, and other desserts are sold.

You are the manager and your job is to determine how many servers should be scheduled during the day, taking into account peak hours. Customers form a single line and are waited on when the next server is available. If you don't have enough servers, the customers will be subject to long periods of waiting, which may result in customer loss. If you have more servers than the demand requires, servers will be standing around waiting, costing the company money. You have access to a computer program that simulates or mimics the store's operations. Using this technology, you can gather experimental data. Then you will use statistics and graphing techniques to present these data to the company in an optimum management proposal.

During each simulation, you will be prompted as follows.
a. Type in the number of minutes for this simulation:
b. Type the average arrival time between customers:
c. Type the average service time for each order:
d. How many servers?

COMPUTER investigation

The computer program will run the simulation according to your specifications. Keep in mind that the store does not have room to have more than 10 servers working at any one time. The store can handle no more than 25 customers in line. If a line ever gets so long that the customers overflow into the street, the simulation will automatically end and a message will appear.

Since this simulates what may happen in the real world, the outcomes may differ every time you run the simulation even though you may use the same specifications. At the end of the simulation, the program will provide the following information regarding that simulation:

a. server utilization time (the time the workers were actually serving),

b. average length of the customer line,

c. average amount of time a customer waited in line,

d. number of customers left in line at the end of the operation, and

e. total number of customers who entered the store.

Your store opens at 10:00 A.M. and closes at 4:00 P.M. The peak hours are around lunch time. Your store supervisor studied the flow of customers into your store and how fast your servers work. The Efficiency Analysis Study shown at the left is taken from her report.

Efficiency Analysis Study

... At ten A.M. when the store opened, business was slow. Customers arrived on the average of every three minutes and the orders were small, mostly drinks and sweets. Your staff could serve the average customer in two minutes. At 11:00 A.M., business picked up. Customers were arriving every two minutes and orders were more demanding. The service time increased to five minutes. By 11:30 A.M., the store was reaching its peak. Customers were arriving at a rate of one per minute and it took the servers about six minutes to complete the order. This peak period lasted until 1:30 P.M. From 1:30 P.M. until 2:30 P.M., business was slower. Customers were arriving about every three minutes and the service time took about four minutes and the for drinks and sweets increased between 2:30 P.M. and 3:00 P.M. with people arriving every two minutes but an order only took three minutes to complete. The last hour of operation was very slow. Customers were arriving about every four minutes and most of the orders took about four minutes to complete.

COMPUTER investigation

Using this information, the computer simulations, and your knowledge of statistics, determine the number of servers required to staff your store. Keep in mind that your recommendation should balance the utilization of your workers with the waiting time of customers.

Run a number of computer simulations using both the same and different specifications. Record all of the information. Analyze the information and draw some conclusions. Design a schedule for the employees of the store based on your conclusions. Make sure the workers have reasonable working hours and breaks.

YOUR REPORT

Write a report to your immediate supervisor detailing your recommendations. State how you reached your conclusions and final recommendation. Specifically, your report should include:

- an employee schedule for a week,

- a justification of your findings and conclusions, written to your immediate supervisor,

- a report on your study that includes an estimation of the total number of customers served per day, the total number of employees used, the number of hours each employee worked per day, the average waiting time of the customers, and the average time the employees were actually serving customers,

- a description of the process used in writing this report, and

- charts or graphs that may help explain the report.

Rat Race

Maria Sanchez and Tran Nguyen are in the same life science course. They both own pet rats. There is a maze in their science classroom. They want to determine which of their rats travels faster through the maze.

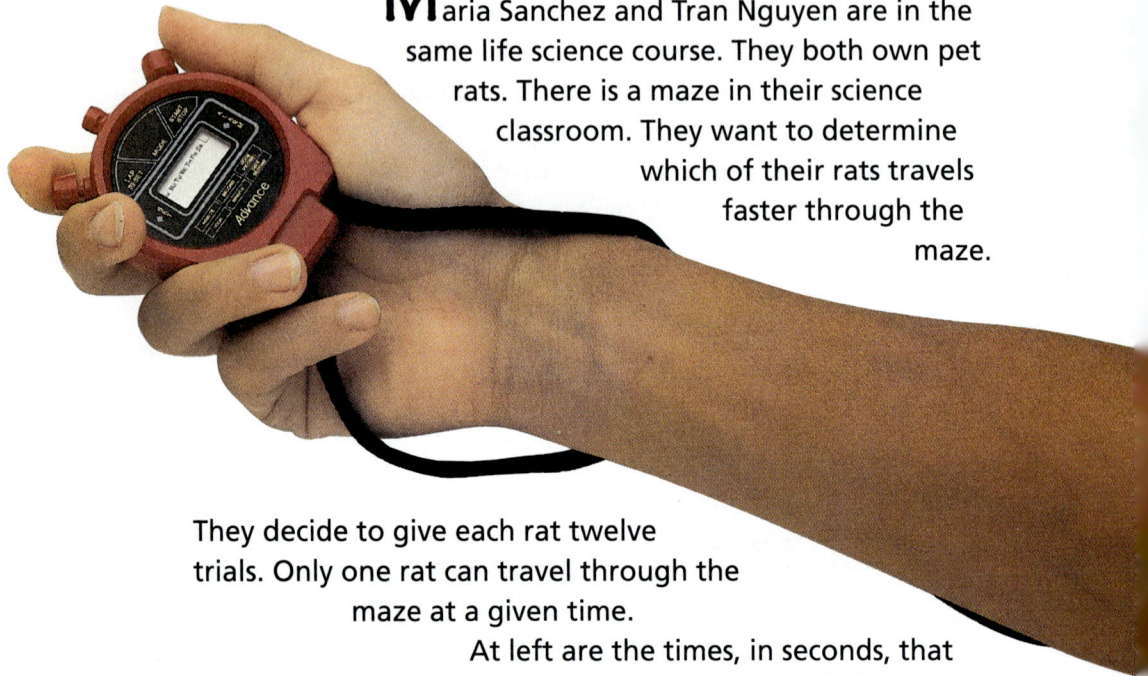

They decide to give each rat twelve trials. Only one rat can travel through the maze at a given time.

At left are the times, in seconds, that it took each rat to travel through the maze. From the data, determine which rat is faster and/or smarter at traveling through the maze. Make a persuasive argument using statistics to justify your judgment.

Trial	Maria's Rat	Tran's Rat
1	33	49
2	75	45
3	38	51
4	42	49
5	47	63
6	68	56
7	51	51
8	51	48
9	58	52
10	31	42
11	51	51
12	64	52

STRAWBERRIES!

The following data are the masses in grams of strawberry boxes that have been shipped from a processing and distribution plant.

76	78	85	78	80	82	80	82	85	87
82	83	86	83	87	82	80	84	85	82
84	85	85	83	87	78	82	85	84	89
86	85	84	84	88	81	81	85	84	82
90	86	88	84	88	81	87	89	88	85

As a newly-hired manufacturing engineer, it is your job to determine the average mass of a strawberry box and decide the margin of error to maintain quality control.

Use statistical measures and graphs to analyze the data. Determine if any masses are significantly different and how they affect the averages.

- What measure should be the standard mass for a box of strawberries?
- What is the margin of error that should be allowed per box in order to maintain a quality standard?

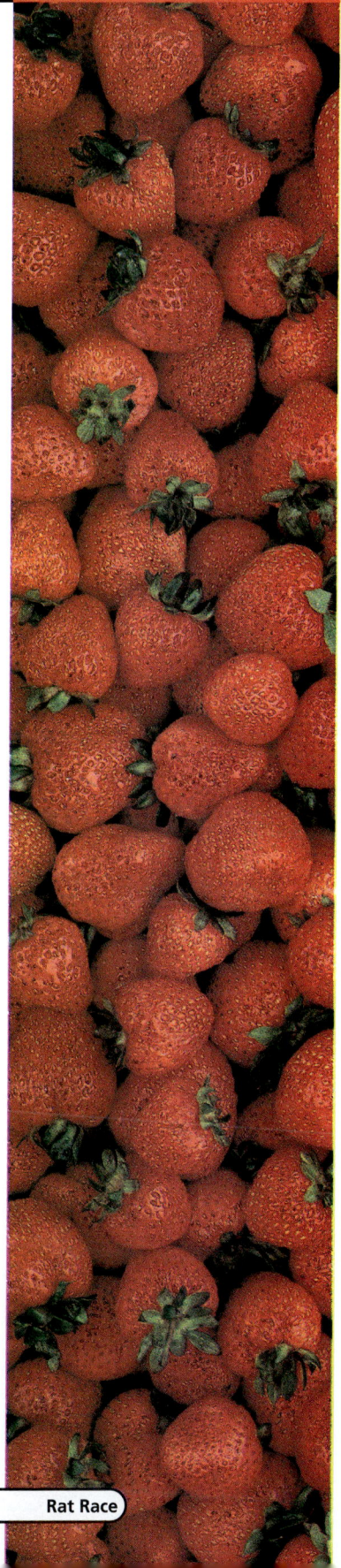

MENU
station
A

BELL-SHAPED CURVE
Bull's-eye

Throw ball darts at a bull's-eye that has a vertical line dividing it into two halves.

1 **M**easure the distance the ball lands from the bull's-eye. Also record whether the ball landed on the left or right side of the center line. Do this at least 30 times.

2 **D**isplay your results in graphic form. The center of the bull's-eye should be located at the middle of your graph. Plot each distance on the graph, depending on whether the ball landed on the left or the right of the bull's-eye.

3 **F**ind the range, average distance, and standard deviation by using a calculator.

4 **W**rite a concluding statement.

Leaves, Leaves

1 Measure the lengths of the leaves in the bag.

2 Display your results in graphic form.

3 Find the range, average length, and standard deviation by using a calculator.

4 Write a concluding statement.

MENU station C

Noses

Measure the length of your nose. Be careful to remember where you start and end your measurement.

1 **M**easure the lengths of 20 of your classmates' noses who are willing to let you.

2 **D**isplay your results in graphic form.

3 **F**ind the range, average length, and standard deviation by using a calculator. What was the average or most typical nose length? Explain.

4 **W**rite a concluding statement.

MENU
station
D

Raisins

Scoop a cup of cereal from a large bowl. Dump the cup of cereal out onto wax paper.

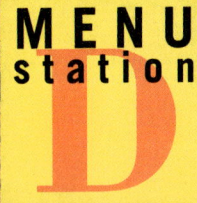

2 Display your results in graphic form.

1 Count the number of raisins in the cereal. Record that amount. Carefully return the cereal to the large bowl. Gently stir or shake the bowl to remix the cereal. Repeat the above process 20 to 30 times.

3 Find the range, average number, and standard deviation by using a calculator.

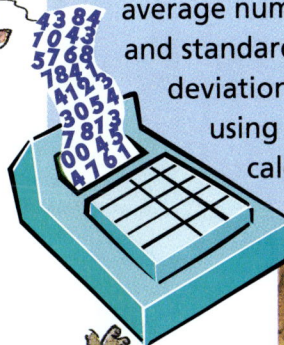

4 Write a concluding statement.

MENU
station
E

How Tall?

1 **M**easure the height of at least 20 of your classmates. Be careful to make accurate measurements. Measure only the classmates who are willing to let you.

2 **D**isplay your results in graphic form.

3 **F**ind the range, average height, and standard deviation by using a calculator. What was the average or most typical height? Explain.

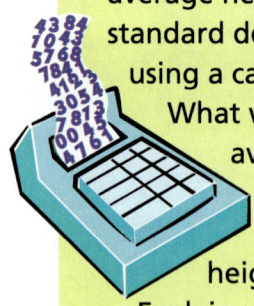

4 **W**rite a concluding statement.

Compare Your Results

Look at the results from *Bull's-eye, Leaves, Leaves, Noses, Raisins,* and *How Tall?*

How are the results alike? How are they different? Explain your comparison.

Think of an extension of what you have learned in this activity. What new questions do you have?

Pursue at least one of your new questions. How could you find a solution?

Stacking Up

In this activity, your group will create a 3-dimensional bar graph using counters and cubes. Place a cube on the hexagon labeled "Start." Then shake nine counters or coins in a paper cup and pour them out. One student calls out the colors of the counters, or whether they show heads or tails, one at a time. Another student moves the cube down the path using the following rules.

1. If the counter is red (or the coin shows a head), move the cube down to the next level to the right.

2. If the counter is yellow (or the coin shows a tail), move the cube down to the next level to the left.

Look at the example at the right.

Continue until the cube reaches a numbered hexagon at the bottom of the page. Leave that cube where it is, and repeat the process with a new cube, beginning again at "Start." If a cube reaches a numbered hexagon that already has a cube on it, stack the cube on top of the existing cube.

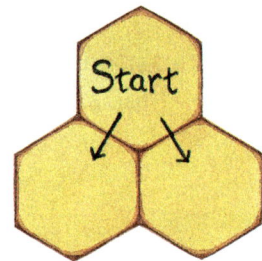

Run the experiment 30 times. Then present an oral report to the class on your experiment. Your report should include the following:

- an explanation of the experiment, in your own words,
- a drawing of the shape of the stacks of cubes,
- a list of the quantity of cubes on each numbered hexagon,
- a list of the measures of central tendency, the range, and the standard deviation of the generated data, and
- an explanation of why the arrangement of cubes occurred in the manner that it did.

The graphs of a number of distributions form bell-shaped curves. The properties of these distributions include the following.

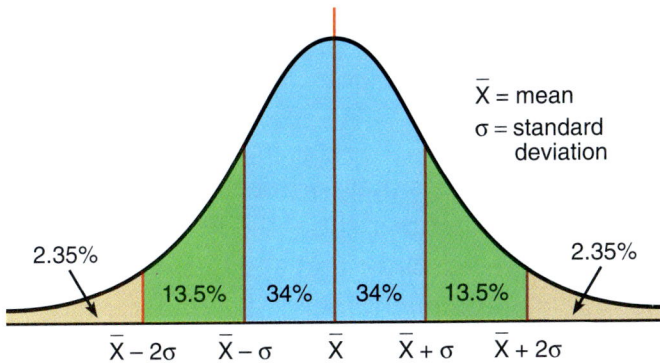

$\overline{X}$ = mean
σ = standard deviation

2.35% 13.5% 34% 34% 13.5% 2.35%

$\overline{X} - 2\sigma$ $\overline{X} - \sigma$ $\overline{X}$ $\overline{X} + \sigma$ $\overline{X} + 2\sigma$

- The mean, median, and mode have the same value and are located at the center of the graph.
- Most of the items in the set of data are close to the mean. The frequency of the items decreases equally in both directions from the mean. The smaller the standard deviation, the closer the data are to the mean.
- If the data are normally distributed, then we might expect that 68% of the data lie between the mean and one standard deviation. This means that more than two-thirds of the data lie between the mean minus the standard deviation and the mean plus the standard deviation. Also, 95% of the data lie within two standard deviations from the mean and 99.7% lie within three standard deviations.

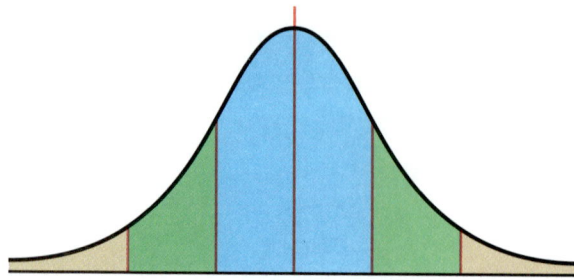

Not all sets of data have graphs that form bell-shaped curves. In each of the following situations, suppose 2,000 random samples have been measured. Draw and describe what you think a representative graph might look like and determine whether or not it is likely to be similar to a bell-shaped curve.

- the height of students at our school
- the number of VCRs sold each year since 1980
- the lengths of bridges in the United States

Test Engineers

You are a member of a test engineering group. The Navy is testing a new landing control device for aircraft landings on aircraft carriers. The length of the flight deck is 750 feet. When an aircraft initially touches down on the flight deck, the tail-hook catches the aircraft 300 feet from one end of the flight deck. The remaining area of the flight deck is the runway stopping distance on the aircraft carrier.

Using a computer simulator, the device was tested 50 times in order to determine the distance it takes the aircraft to come to a complete stop when landing. Below are the recorded distances in feet between the initial touchdown and the location at which the aircraft came to a complete stop for each simulation.

```
305  283  254  210  278  189  222
149  307  211  432  333  451  298
297  300  267  240  365  392  390
301  288  293  198  302  319  402
267  303  278  409  415  176  378
313  300  211  271  303  252  345
287  295  324  296  405  300  296
               300
```

YOUR REPORT

Write a report to your supervisor on the accuracy of this landing device. Make a convincing argument, using your knowledge of statistics, as to whether or not this device is reliable. Be prepared to present and defend your findings to your supervisor.

Hitting the Mark

It is the year 2010. Commercial space flights are a reality. You are an engineer for Out of this World, Inc. The company is about to complete its newest spacecraft. You've been assigned to work on the landing components of the new spacecraft.

One of NASA's functions is to regulate spacecrafts. Before a spacecraft can be licensed, it must meet a number of minimum standards, including standards for landings.

The spacecraft must pass a rigorous test. The goal is to land as close to the center of the Edwards Air Force Base landing strip as possible. The landing procedure is started 30 miles from the landing strip. The distance from that point to where the spacecraft comes to a stop is recorded. Each spacecraft is tested ten times. The ten stopping distances are used in conjunction with the landing strip's dimensions to determine the spacecraft's accuracy.

Design, build, and test your spacecraft to prepare for the NASA licensing test.

It is the year 2010. Commercial space flights are a reality. You are a test engineer for NASA who specializes in the landing of spacecraft, and several new spacecraft designs are ready for testing. Your job is to test the landing of each new spacecraft ten times. These tests are conducted to determine how accurate a spacecraft is when it lands.

Test all of the new spacecraft designs. Decide which statistical measures should be used to determine the landing accuracy of the spacecrafts. Rank the spacecrafts in your class in order of landing accuracy and justify your rankings. Determine a minimum safe standard for the landing of spacecrafts and determine which of the tested spacecrafts meet that standard.

Below is a diagram of the landing strip. Use masking tape and a tape measure to designate the landing strip. Measure 250 centimeters to the start of the landing strip. The actual landing strip should be 120 centimeters long. Make a mark on the landing strip every 10 centimeters. Make the width of the landing strip 100 centimeters wide.

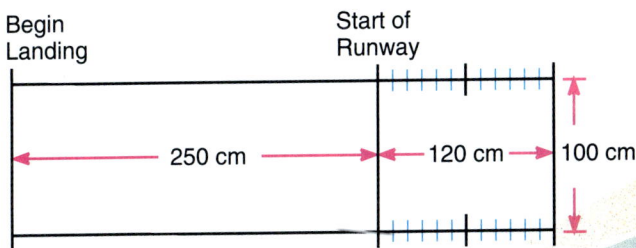

Begin
Landing

Start of
Runway

←— 250 cm —→ ←— 120 cm —→ 100 cm

YOUR REPORT

Write a report to the licensing board summarizing the test and reporting your analysis and your conclusions. Graphs and charts may be helpful in illustrating your findings. Include your recommendation as to which spacecrafts should be licensed and which should be denied a license. Give a complete explanation to prevent companies from taking NASA to court.

Selection and Reflection

Making quality products, ensuring safety standards, and performing efficiently and effectively are important in the workplace and in everyday life.

- What have you learned about quality control while studying this unit?
- What mathematical ideas are helpful in determining quality standards?
- Explain the statistical ideas and tools you have been using. Use the tasks in the unit to illustrate your explanation. In your explanation, you may want to compare the effectiveness of the tools in those situations.

The Problem

One side of the Try-All-Angles Tower is made of three vertical supports, four horizontal supports, and 12 cross braces as shown. How many triangles are formed? Benito says, "I can see 24 triangles." However, you must count more than the small triangles. How many triangles are on the side of the tower?

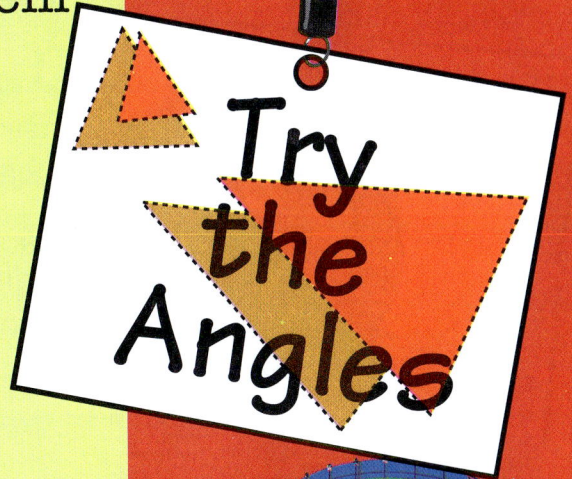

Try the Angles

Bowl Me Over

The Problem

Jana has an average score of 142 for her bowling team's first 8 games. She would like to raise her average to 145. There are 2 games left in the series.

Jana thinks that if she averages 148 for the next two games, she can reach her goal. Do you agree? If not, what should be her average for the next 2 games?

Extension Jana's scores range from 139 to 148. Mike's scores range from 120 to 160. They both have a 142 average for 8 games. Which student do you think has a better chance of raising their average to 145 after two more games? Explain your reasoning.

The Problem

It's a HIT!

During one season, Will Clarke has 486 official at bats and 158 hits, Barry Bonds has 412 official at bats and 131 hits, Darryl Strawberry has 456 official at bats and 140 hits, and Tony Gwynn has 498 official at bats and 161 hits.

Determine each player's batting average and rank them from best to worst. Which player has the best batting average?

Aver-Ages

The Problem

A small-town newspaper reporter is writing an article about two family reunions that were held the previous weekend. He recorded the ages of all the people in attendance and was surprised to find that there were 12 people at each reunion and the average age at each reunion was 26 years. Using the data recorded below, do you think that this information adequately describes the ages of the people at the two reunions? If not, what further information would you include in the article?

Reunion	Ages (in years)
Wang Gamily	$\frac{1}{2}$, 1, 2, 32, 2, 4, 25, 27, 30, 60, 65, 90
Blackburn Family	12, 12, 13, 14, 15, 16, 36, 37, 39, 40, 40, 41

The Problem

The head nurse at San Diego General Hospital is performing a study on the birth weights of babies born at the hospital. She records 19 birth weights in one day and discovers that they form a bell-shaped curve, as shown below.

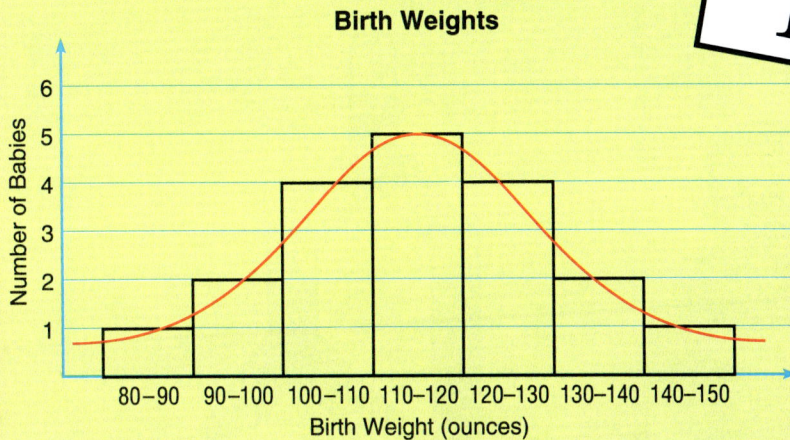

A Weighty Matter

Birth Weights

Number of Babies (y-axis: 1, 2, 3, 4, 5, 6)

Birth Weight (ounces) (x-axis: 80–90, 90–100, 100–110, 110–120, 120–130, 130–140, 140–150)

Later, she discovers that she forgot to include the weight of one baby. This baby's weight was 88 ounces at birth. Can the head nurse still claim that the weights form a bell-shaped curve? Why or why not?

Down the Hatch

The Problem

Suppose you rolled 100 marbles down the trough shown below. At every intersection, there is an equal chance for the marble to travel either left or right. How many marbles do you think would likely end up in each of the 6 lettered spaces at the bottom? Explain.

A   B   C   D   E   F

TABLE OF CONTENTS

There are several stories or legends about the origin of tangrams. One of these stories is about a man named Tan.

Tan lived in China about 4,000 years ago, and he owned a beautiful ceramic tile. He valued his tile and decided to show this special tile to the emperor. Unfortunately, Tan tripped as he was going to see the emperor and dropped the tile. The tile broke into 7 pieces. Of course, Tan was devastated. He spent the rest of his life trying to put his tile back into its original shape of a square.

According to the story, Tan was never able to put the tile back into its original shape, but he did make interesting pictures and designs. Tan shared his broken tile and its many shapes with his friends who visited him. Everyone liked making pictures with the pieces. Tan particularly liked the picture of his cat that he made, as well as the pagoda that resembled the one where he often went to meditate.

The puzzle of the tiles did not die with Tan. Instead, it grew in popularity as it was passed on from one generation to the next and from one country to another. Legend says that Napoleon used tangrams to help calm himself while he was imprisoned on St. Helena.

A famous puzzle expert by the name of Sam Lloyd wrote about tangrams in the early 1900's. Tangrams can be as simple as shapes cut out of paper or as elaborate as a fancy wood-carved set. Whatever you use, tangrams will open a world of creativity. Perhaps you will understand why tangrams can be a special gift to someone with an imagination.

USA School Enrollment (1988-89)

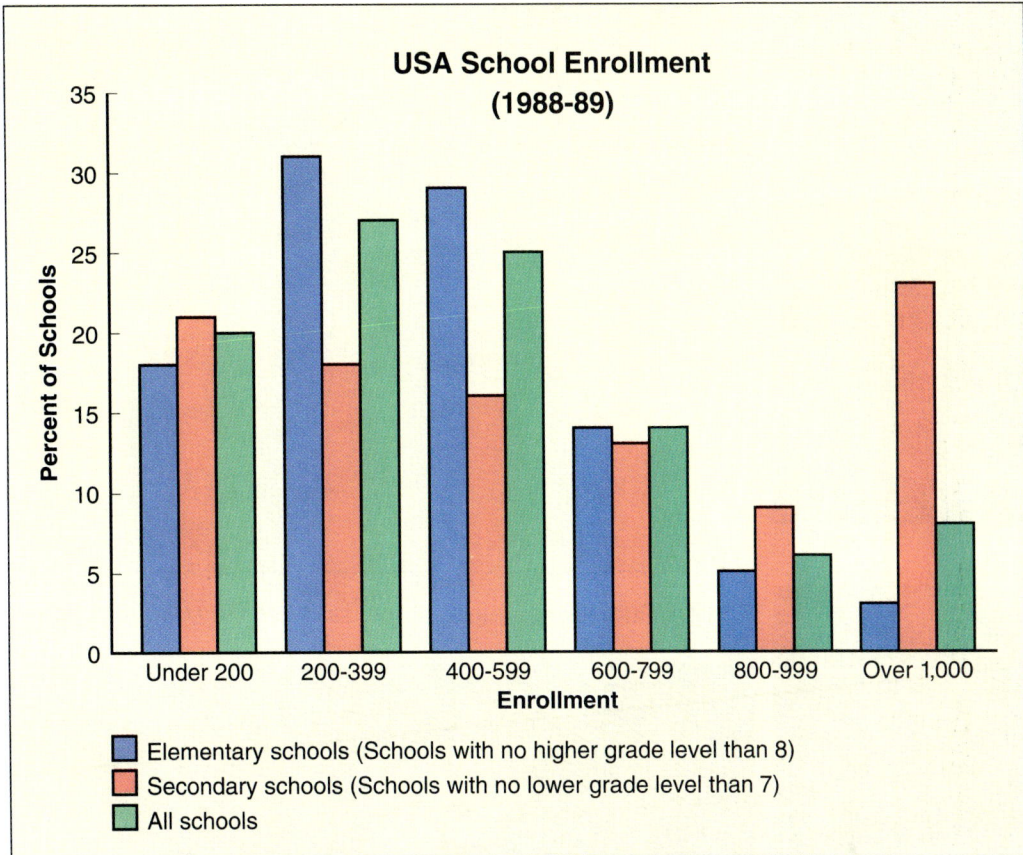

Source: U.S. Department of Commerce, Bureau of the Census

Legend:
- Elementary schools (Schools with no higher grade level than 8)
- Secondary schools (Schools with no lower grade level than 7)
- All schools

DATA BANK FAST FOOD COSTS

City	Price of a Cheeseburger, Soft Drink, and French Fries in U.S. Dollars
Copenhagen, Denmark	$11.25
Paris, France	7.97
Tokyo, Japan	5.39
Los Angeles, California	3.78
U.S. median	3.71
Beijing, China	3.30
Islamabad, Pakistan	2.02

Source: Runzheimer International, as quoted in *USA Today*

Many people like to collect sports items such as posters or cards. Baseball cards are the most popular of these collectibles. The front of a baseball card shows the player, his team, and the maker of the card. The back of the card shows the following.

① ③ ② ④

4 **MIGUEL HERNANDEZ** | Height 6" 2", Weight 205 Bats Right, Throws Right Born 7-2-64, San Pedro, CA Home Huntington Beach, CA | **SS**

COMPLETE MAJOR LEAGUE BATTING RECORD

Yr. Club	Pct.	AB	R	H	2B	3B	HR	RBI	SB	BB	SO
85 Elks	.295	214	41	96	8	6	3	35	12	35	42
85 Loggers	.269	435	49	104	16	8	7	50	4	25	34
86 Retrievers	.240	306	38	54	13	9	14	35	6	42	23
86 Generals	.289	198	60	89	8	0	11	42	8	51	45
87 Angels	.301	209	35	125	19	3	9	25	11	23	27
89 Worms	.357	307	29	95	21	6	16	19	8	43	28
90 Tornadoes	.399	389	65	79	28	7	23	36	9	26	34
91 Tidewtr	.376	432	45	109	15	4	20	55	14	28	38
ML Totals	.219	1218	133	267	128	43	103	138	8	102	167

Set a Major League record in 1989 with 88 errorless games. Also set a club shortstop record for homers in a season and tied the Stars mark for RBIs in a season 5-24-91.

⑤ ⑥

① the series number
② personal information
③ the player's name

④ the position played
⑤ career highlight
⑥ player statistics

Key:

AB = at-bats
 R = runs
 H = hits
2B = doubles
3B = triples

HR = home runs
RBI = runs batted in
 SB = stolen bases
 BB = bases on balls (walks)
 SO = strikeouts

Source: *Universal Press Syndicate*

Landmark	Number of Steps
Wrigley Field, Chicago	67
Louisiana Superdome, New Orleans	80
Lombard Street, San Francisco	305
Statue of Liberty, New York	354
Space Needle, Seattle	832
Washington Monument, Washington	897
Gateway Arch, St. Louis	1,116
Eiffel Tower, Paris	1,652
Sears Tower, Chicago	1,707
World Trade Center, New York	1,760
Mount Katahdin, Maine	9,030
Mauna Kea, Hawaii	23,604
Mt. Kilimanjaro, Tanzania	33,154
Mt. Everest, Nepal	49,762

Note: Each step is approximately 7 inches high.

Source: *The Universal Almanac*

Date	Event
1783	Jean Pilâtre de Rozier made the **first human balloon flight** on Nov. 21, reaching a peak altitude of about 500 feet.
1784	Madame Thible, a French opera singer, was the **first woman to fly**.
1797	André-Jacques Garnerin made the **first parachute jump** in a 23-foot diameter parachute made of white canvas with a basket attached.
1903	Orville Wright made the **first successful airplane flight** on Dec. 17.
1927	Charles Lindbergh made the **first solo, nonstop transatlantic flight** in the *Spirit of St. Louis* on May 20 and 21.
1932	Ruth Rowland Nichols became the **first female airline pilot**. She also was the first woman to hold three international records at the same time—speed, distance, and altitude.
1937	Hanna Reitsch, a German pilot, flew the **first successful helicopter**.
1947	U.S. Air Force captain Charles Yeager made the **first piloted supersonic flight in an airplane**, flying faster than the speed of sound on Oct. 14.
1958	National Airlines inaugurated the **first domestic jet passenger service** between New York and Miami on Dec. 10.
1977	Paul MacCready created and flew the **first successful man-powered aircraft**, *The Gossamer Condor,* on Aug. 23.
1980	Janice Brown made the **first long-distance solar-powered flight** in the *Solar Challenger* on Dec. 3.
1986	Dick Rutan and Jeana Yeager made the **first nonstop flight around the world without refueling** in *Voyager* on December 14–23.
1993	Victoria VanMeter, at 11 years old, became the youngest female pilot ever to fly across the continental United States.

Source: *1993 Information Please Almanac*

Material	Density (g/cm³)
natural gas	0.0006
air	0.001
ethanol	0.79
water	1.00
blood	1.06
glycerol	1.26
rubber	1.34
corn syrup	1.38
table sugar	1.59
table salt	2.16
stainless steel	7.86
copper	8.92
mercury	13.59

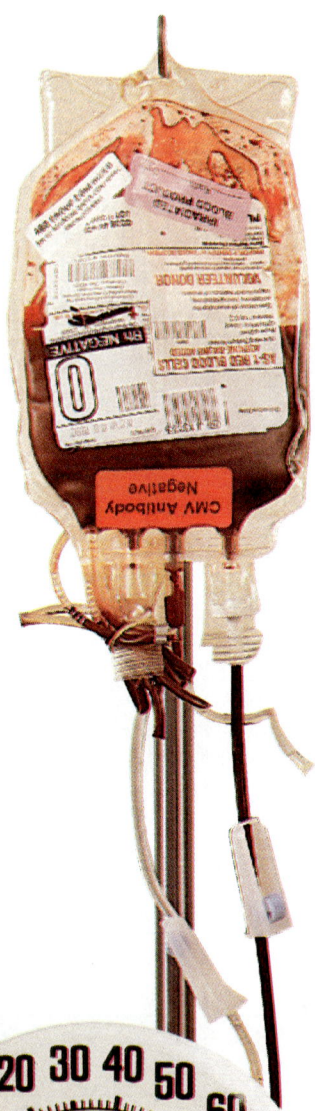

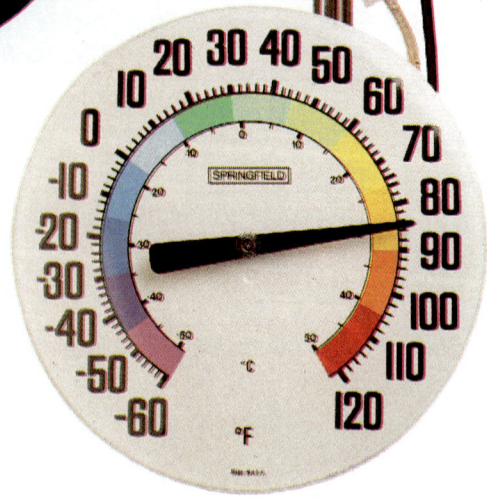

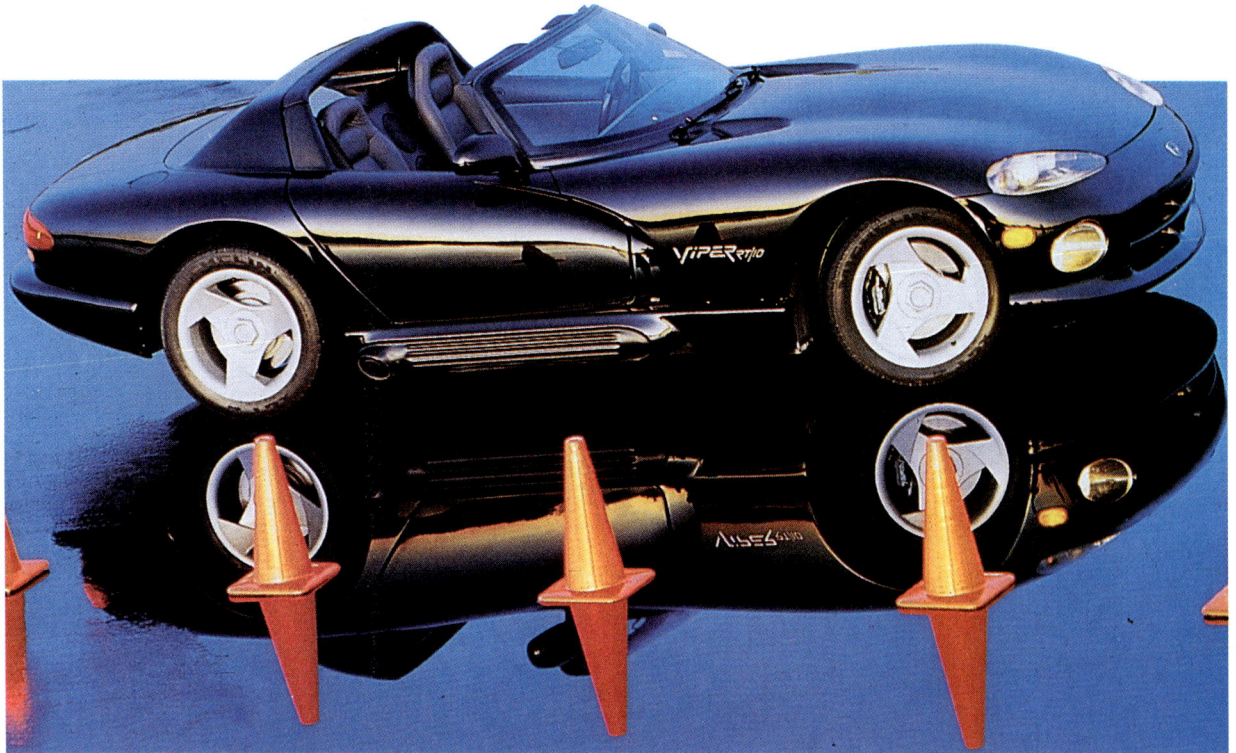

Type of Vehicle	Cars	Motorcycles	Buses	Total
Total travel (in millions of miles)	1,515,370	9,572	5,728	1,530,670
Number of registered vehicles	143,549,627	4,259,462	626,987	148,436,076
Average miles traveled per vehicle	10,556	2,247	9,136	21,939
Fuel consumed (in thousands of gallons)	72,434,884	191,440	900,629	73,526,953
Avg. fuel consumption per vehicle (in gallons)	505	45	1,436	495

Source: *1993 Information Please Almanac*

SPEEDS OF CERTAIN ANIMALS

Animal	Speed (mph)	Animal	Speed (mph)
Cheetah	70	Reindeer	32
Pronghorn antelope	61	Giraffe	32
Wildebeest	50	White-tailed deer	30
Lion	50	Grizzly bear	30
Thompson's gazelle	50	Cat (domestic)	30
Quarter horse	47.5	Human	27.9
Elk	45	Elephant	25
Cape hunting dog	45	Black mamba snake	20
Coyote	43	Six-lined race runner	18
Gray fox	42	Wild turkey	15
Hyena	40	Squirrel	12
Zebra	40	Pig (domestic)	11
Greyhound	39.4	Chicken	9
Whippet	35.5	Spider (Tegenaria atrica)	1.2
Rabbit (domestic)	35	Giant tortoise	0.17
Mule deer	35	Three-toed sloth	0.15
Jackal	35	Garden snail	0.03

Source: *1994 Almanac*

AERODYNAMIC SUMMARY OF SHUTTLE LAUNCH

24.0-second intervals from launch pad at 0.0 seconds through attainment of orbit at 521.20 seconds

Time (s)	Altitude (ft)	Altitude Rate (ft/s)	Velocity (ft/s)
0.00	0	0	0
24.00	5,718	509	554
48.00	23,417	930	1,101
72.00	50,672	1,419	1,789
96.00	92,282	2,005	3,019
120.00	144,771	2,246	4,102
Solid rocket boosters separation at 125.28 seconds			
125.28	156,483	2,188	4,153
144.00	195,611	1,982	4,438
168.00	239,822	1,704	4,908
192.00	277,429	1,433	5,483
216.00	308,675	1,173	6,154
240.00	333,853	927	6,921
264.00	353,288	695	7,781
288.00	367,351	480	8,739
312.00	376,474	285	9,802
336.00	381,196	114	10,982
Altitude Rate changes from positive to negative at 355.12 seconds			
355.12	382,220	0	11,994
360.00	382,138	−29	12,295
384.00	380,076	−135	13,764
408.00	376,009	−193	15,422
432.00	371,315	−186	17,312
456.00	367,679	−102	19,487
Altitude Rate changes from negative to positive at 473.33 seconds			
473.33	366,731	0	21,120
480.00	366,881	47	21,747
504.00	370,199	246	24,017
Main engines cut off at 521.20 seconds (Thrust = 0)			
521.20	375,636	349	24,950

Source: NASA Johnson Space Center, Houston, Texas

External Tank

Solid Rocket Boosters

Orbiter

Space Shuttle Main Engines

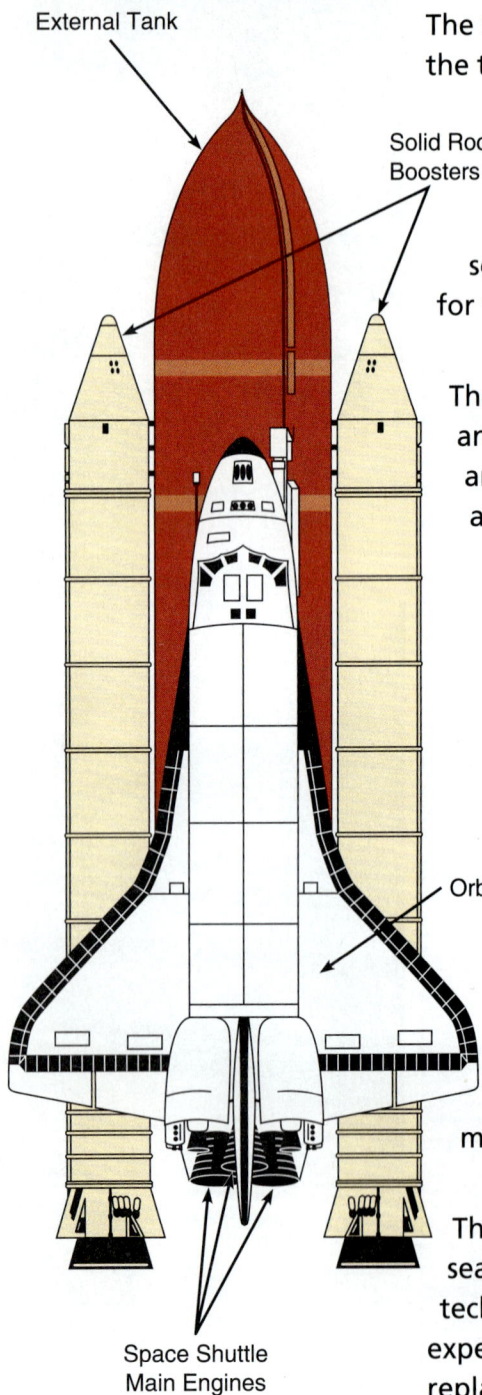

The Shuttle's major components are: the orbiter spacecraft; the three main engines, with a combined thrust of almost 1.2 million pounds; the huge external tank (ET) that feeds the liquid hydrogen fuel and liquid oxygen oxidizer to the three main engines; and the two solid rocket boosters (SRBs), with their combined thrust of some 5.8 million pounds, which provide most of the power for the first two minutes of flight.

The SRBs take the Space Shuttle to an altitude of 28 miles and a speed of 3,094 miles per hour before they separate and fall back into the ocean to be retrieved, refurbished, and prepared for another flight.

After the solid rocket boosters are jettisoned, the orbiter's three main engines, fed by the external tank, continue to provide thrust for another six minutes before they are shut down, at which time the giant tank is jettisoned and falls back to Earth, disintegrating in the atmosphere.

The Space Shuttle Orbiter

The orbiter is both the brains and heart of the Space Transportation System. About the same size and weight as a DC-9 aircraft, the orbiter contains the pressurized crew compartment (which can normally carry up to seven crew members), the huge cargo bay, and the three main engines mounted on its aft end.

The thermal tile system that protects the orbiter during its searing reentry through the atmosphere was a breakthrough technology that proved much more challenging than expected. Designed to be used for 100 missions before replacement is necessary, the Shuttle's 24,000 individual tiles are made primarily of pure-sand silicate fibers, mixed with a ceramic binder. Incredibly lightweight, about the density of balsa wood, they dissipate the heat so quickly that a white-hot tile with a temperature of 2,300 degrees Fahrenheit can be taken from an oven and held in bare hands without injury.

The External Tank
The giant cylinder, higher than a 15-story building, with a length of 154 feet and as wide as a silo with a diameter of 27.5 feet, is the largest single piece of the Space Shuttle. During launch the external tank also acts as a backbone for the orbiter and solid rocket boosters to which it is attached.

Machined from aluminum alloys, the Space Shuttle's external tank is the only part of the launch vehicle that currently is not reused. After its 526,000 gallons of propellants are consumed during the first eight and one-half minutes of flight, it is jettisoned from the orbiter and breaks up in the upper atmosphere, its pieces falling into remote ocean waters.

The Solid Rocket Boosters
The Space Shuttle's two solid-rocket boosters, the first designed for refurbishment and reuse, are also the largest solids ever built and the first to be flown on a manned spacecraft. Together they provide the majority of the thrust for the first two minutes of flight—some 5.8 million pounds.

Source: NASA Fact Sheet

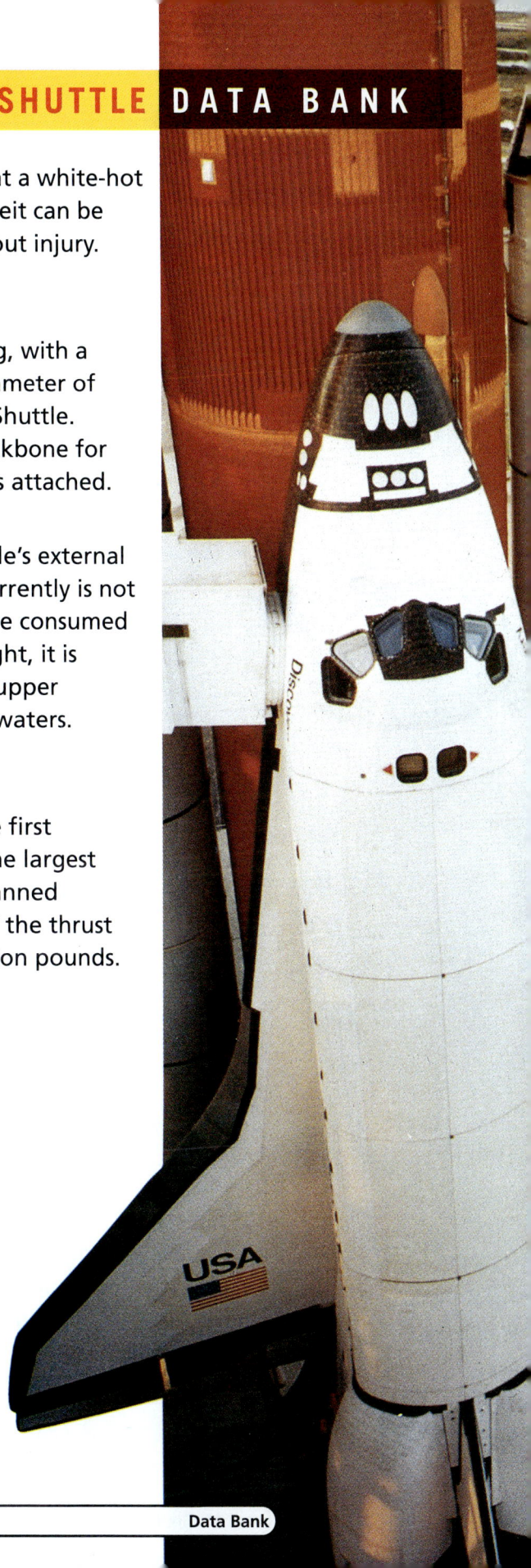

HOW ROLLER COASTERS WORK

Kumba, a state-of-the-art coaster at Busch Gardens in Tampa, is a physics professor's dream. Says David Wright of Tidewater Community College, who teaches basic physics by having his students study coasters: "Instead of just reading about the principles of motion and mechanics, students get inside the experiment and experience them."

Gravity

As a poet once said: "The coaster is basically an ornate means of falling." Potential energy is stored in the cars as they are hauled by chain to the top of the 14-story first hill, then released as kinetic energy when gravity pulls them down at 63 mph. Of course, it's not all downhill. Energy sloshes back and forth between kinetic (motion) energy and potential (height) energy. The roller coaster is a fundamentally simple idea—by ride's end, both the energy and the passengers are spent.

Velocity

Though designers have long dreamed of sending riders upside down, their most difficult trick has been a simple loop. Perfect circles, first tried in 1900, required so much velocity that passengers were whiplashed by high centrifugal force. Success finally came in a teardrop-shaped loop, with slower entry and exit speeds but enough force at the tightly radiused top to keep riders in their seats. Still, beneath Kumba's 108-foot-high loop, one can usually find wallets, keys, and hats.

Inertia

On Kumba's double corkscrew, riders go through two stretched-out loops. The track is steeply banked so that centrifugal force will act perpendicular to the seats of the cars, keeping passengers from slamming into one another like bags of groceries sliding across an auto seat during a sharp turn. The banking also diverts the coaster's inertia, its tendency to keep going in the direction it was headed—straight off the track toward Disney World in Orlando, 60 miles away.

Source: *Life* Magazine, August 1988

Order	Name	Country	Time at 400 m	Time at 800 m	Time at 1,200 m	Time at 1,500 m
1	Boulmerka, Hassiba	Algeria	1:00.65	2:05.61	3:09.92	3:55.30
2	Rogacheva, Lyudmila	Unified Tm.	1:00.55	2:05.02	3:09.88	3:56.91
3	Qu, Yunxia	China	1:01.34	2:06.13	3:10.41	3:57.08
4	Dorovskikh, Tatiana	Unified Tm.	1:01.95	2:06.87	3:11.24	3:57.92
5	Liu, Li	China	1:03.64	2:08.91	3:13.76	4:00.20
6	Zuñiga Dominguez, Maite	Spain	1:04.36	2:09.79	3:14.06	4:00.59
7	Rudz, Malgorzata	Poland	1:05.97	2:10.69	3:15.49	4:01.91
8	Podkopayeva, Yekaterina	Unified Tm.	1:04.26	2:10.48	3:16.01	4:02.03
9	Mutola, Maria de Lurdes	Mozambique	1:06.23	2:12.78	3:16.99	4:02.60
10	Plumer, Patti Sue	USA	1:06.19	2:12.59	3:16.42	4:03.42
11	Fidatov, Elena	Romania	1:07.59	2:13.29	3:17.82	4:06.44

Year	Winner	Speed (mph)
1970	Al Unser	155.749
1971	Al Unser	157.735
1972	Mark Donohue	162.962
1973	Gordon Johncock	159.036
1974	Johnny Rutherford	158.589
1975	Bobby Unser	149.213
1976	Johnny Rutherford	148.725
1977	A.J. Foyt	161.331
1978	Al Unser	161.363
1979	Rick Mears	158.899
1980	Johnny Rutherford	142.862
1981	Bobby Unser	139.085
1982	Gordon Johncock	162.026
1983	Tom Sneva	162.117
1984	Rick Mears	163.621
1985	Danny Sullivan	152.982
1986	Bobby Rahal	170.722
1987	Al Unser	162.175
1988	Rick Mears	144.809
1989	Emerson Fitipaldi	167.581
1990	Arie Luyendyk	185.984

Source: *The 1992 World Almanac*

Women's 1,500-Meter Run		
Year	Winner, Country	Time
1972	Lyudmila Bragina, USSR	4 min 1.4 s
1976	Tatyana Kazankina, USSR	4 min 5.5 s
1980	Tatyana Kazankina, USSR	3 min 56.6 s
1984	Gabriella Dorio, Italy	4 min 3.3 s
1988	Paula Ivan, Romania	3 min 54.0 s
1992	Hassiba Boulmerka, Algeria	3 min 55.3 s

Men's 1,500-Meter Run		
Year	Winner, Country	Time
1972	Pekka Vasala, Finland	3 min 36.3 s
1976	John Walker, New Zealand	3 min 39.2 s
1980	Sebastian Coe, Great Britain	3 min 38.4 s
1984	Sebastian Coe, Great Britain	3 min 32.5 s
1988	Peter Rono, Kenya	3 min 36.0 s
1992	Fermin Cacho Ruiz, Spain	3 min 40.1 s

Source: *1994 Almanac*

The following excerpt is from *The Swiss Family Robinson.*

"Thus chatting, we at length approached my pretty wood. Numbers of birds fluttered and sang among the high branches....We were lost in admiration of the trees of this grove, and I cannot describe to you how wonderful they are, nor can you form the least idea of their enormous size without seeing them yourself. What we had been calling a wood proved to be a group of about a dozen trees only and, what was strange, the roots sustained the massive trunks exalted in the air, forming strong arches, and props and stays all around each individual stem, which was firmly rooted in the center.

"The longer we remained in this enchanting place, the more did it charm my fancy; and if we could but manage to live in some sort of dwelling up among the branches of those grand, noble trees, I should feel perfectly safe and happy.

"Now I hope you approve of the proceedings of your exploring party, and that to-morrow you will do me the favour of packing everything up, and taking us away to live amongst my splendid trees."

* * * * * * *

By this morning's consultation we had settled the weighty question of our change of abode....Our party continued steadily until we came in sight of our future place of residence.

The wonderful appearance of the enormous trees, and the calm beauty of the spot altogether, fully came up to the enthusiastic description which had been give to me.

And my wife gladly heard me say that if an abode could be contrived among the branches, it would be the safest and most charming home in the world.

We examined the different trees, and chose one which seemed most suited to our purpose. The branches spread at a great height above us, and I made the boys try if it were possible to throw sticks and stones over one of these, my intention being to construct a rope ladder if we could once succeed in getting a string across a strong bough.

Ernest at length pointed out a quantity of bamboos half buried in the sand. These were exactly what I wanted, and, stripping them of leaves, I cut them into lengths of about five feet each.

While I was thus employed my sons were endeavouring to ascertain the height of the lowest branch of the tree from the ground. They had fastened together the long reeds I had brought with twine, and were trying to measure the distance, but in vain; they soon found that, were the rods ten times their length, they could not touch the branch.

"Hello, my boys," I said, when I discovered what they were about, "that is not the way to set to work. Geometry will simplify the operation considerably; with its help the altitude of the highest mountains is ascertained. We may, therefore, easily find the height of that branch."

So saying, I measured out a certain distance from the base of the tree and marked the spot. Then by means of a rod whose length I knew, and imaginary lines, I calculated the angle enclosed by the trunk of the tree from the ground to the root of the branch. This done, I was able to discover the height required, and, to the astonishment of the younger children, announced that we should henceforth live thirty feet above the ground. This I wanted to know, that I might construct a ladder of the necessary length.

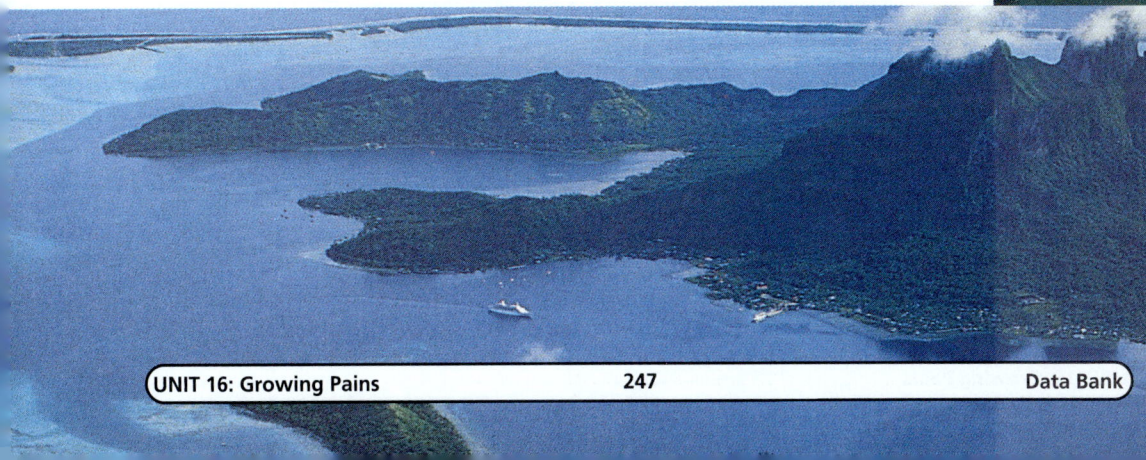

An oak tree and a rosebush grew,
Young and green together,
Talking the talk of growing things—
Wind and water and weather.
And while the rosebush sweetly bloomed
The oak tree grew so high
That now it spoke of newer things—
Eagles, mountain peaks and sky.
"I guess you think you're pretty great,"
The rose was heard to cry,
Screaming as loud as it possibly could
To the treetop in the sky.
"And you have no time for flower talk,
Now that you've grown so tall."
"It's not so much that I've grown," said the tree,
"It's just that you've stayed so small."

by Shel Silverstein (*A Light in the Attic*)

FRANK & ERNEST

THEY SAY THAT SOME OF THESE REDWOOD TREES ARE THOUSANDS OF YEARS OLD!

FRED + WILMA

THAVES 8-6
© 1993 by NEA, Inc.

Actually, Frank and Ernest are a little confused about their trees. Redwoods are related to the giant sequoias, which may live thousands of years. Redwoods do not live as long as sequoias. In fact, few redwoods are more than 1,000 years old.

Redwoods are among the world's tallest living trees, commonly growing 200 to 275 feet tall, with trunks 8 to 12 feet in diameter. The tallest known tree in the world is a redwood in northern California. It is about 368 feet high.

Redwoods grow along the west coast of the United States from southern Oregon to central California. Muir Woods National Monument, near San Francisco, is one place where you can see redwoods. Redwoods generally grow close together and shut out much of the sunlight, making the forest dark and cool. The wood is very resistant to insects, so there are few birds in the forest, making for an almost eerie silence at times. If you ever have the chance, it's a wonderful place to visit.

Source: *World Book Encyclopedia*

The table below shows the amount of interest earned on $1,000 at 10% annual interest, compounded annually, for 10 years.

Year	Amount of Interest Earned	Balance of Account at End of Year
0	$0.00	$1,000.00
1	$100.00	$1,100.00
2	$110.00	$1,210.00
3	$121.00	$1,331.00
4	$133.10	$1,464.10
5	$146.41	$1,610.51
6	$161.05	$1,771.56
7	$177.16	$1,948.72
8	$194.87	$2,143.59
9	$214.36	$2,357.95
10	$235.79	$2,593.74

As a radioactive atom releases radiation from its nucleus, it decays to form an atom of another element. The method of using the decay of radioactive elements to determine the absolute age of things is called *radiometric dating*. The rate of decay has been determined for each radioactive element. The amount of time needed for one-half of the atoms in an element to decay is called the half-life of the element.

Half-Lives of Some Radioactive Elements	
Element	**Half-Life**
polonium-214	0.001 second
radon-222	3.82 days
radium-226	1,600 years
carbon-14	5,730 years
uranium-238	4,500,000,000 years

Carbon-14 is a radioactive element that is present in extremely small amounts in all living matter. It is absorbed by plants from carbon dioxide. Plants, in turn, are eaten by animals. After death, the amount of carbon-14 in an organism is no longer renewed by the life processes and the carbon-14 decays into nitrogen-14.

The approximate time that an organism died is found by comparing the amount of carbon-14 in the fossil remains with the amount of carbon-14 in the same amount of living matter. This type of radiometric dating is called *radiocarbon dating*.

Source: *Merrill Focus on Physical Science* and *Focus on Earth Science*

You can buy a signal mirror for a buck or so at any backcountry or army/navy surplus store. A signal mirror is lightweight and unbreakable, and tucks easily into a pack or pocket. One will also do double duty as a grooming mirror in camp. As a signaling device, it can be life-saving if used properly, sending out a flash visible for up to 10 miles in clear weather.

A survival mirror is glossy on both sides and has a hole drilled near the center. The hole is used as a sight for directing a flash-signal to a precise target. Here's how it works. Sight your target through the center hole, holding the mirror a few inches from your face. Depending on the angle of the sun, this will cause a spot of sunlight to fall either on your face or on your free hand, which should be raised parallel to the mirror. (If the dot lights on your face, you'll see the reflection in the mirror.) Next, tilt the mirror slowly while sighting your target object. When the sun dot aligns with the center hole in the mirror, your flash signal is landing on target.

Send flashes in groups of three: three quick flashes, three slower ones, three more quick ones, which is the standard Morse code SOS call.

Source: Anthony Acerrano, "Signaling for Help," *Sports Afield*, January 1991

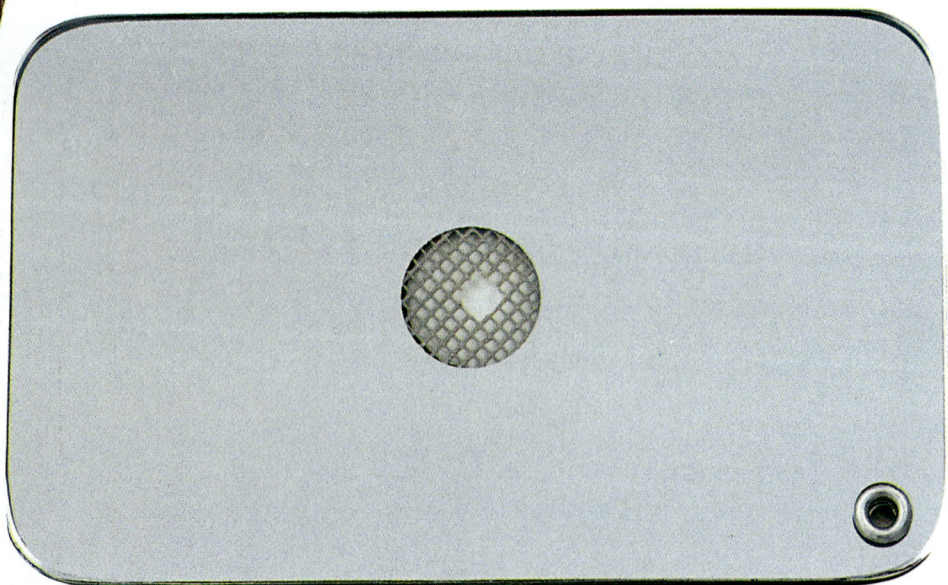

The latter part of the Sung Dynasty, 960–1280 A.D., through the early part of the Yüan Dynasty, 1280–1368 A.D., was the greatest time in ancient Chinese mathematics. Among the many notable Chinese mathematicians of this time were Yang Hui and Chu Shï-kié. The earliest known presentation of Pascal's Triangle was given by Yang Hui. Chu Shï-kié spoke of the triangle as being ancient in his time in a book written in 1303.

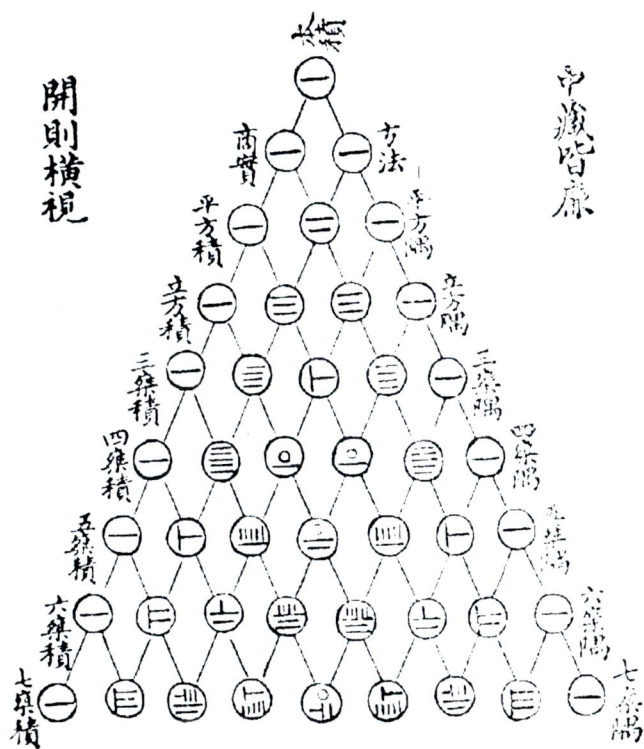

INTRODUCTION TO LOGO

LOGO Command	Description
DRAW	A clear screen appears with the turtle located in the center of the screen.
FD	Move forward. It is followed by the number of units to m.
BK	Move back. It is followed by the number of units to moe.
RT	Turn right (clockwise). It is followed by the number of degrees to turn.
LT	Turn left (counterclockwise). It is followed by the number of degrees to turn.
PU	Pen-Up allows you to move the turtle without drawing.
PD	Pen-Down resumes drawing at that point.
REPEAT	Used with a number and brackets as in REPEAT X[ ]. Repeats the commands inside the brackets X number of times. You must replace X with a number.

The HOME Screen

The turtle is located in the center of the screen. The screen is 278 units from left to right and 238 units from top to bottom.

The HOME screen appears whenever you use DRAW.

Programs

To create a program, type TO and the name you wish to give the program. Press the RETURN key.

A screen appears with your program name at the top. Enter the commands you wish the program to contain. Follow the directions at the bottom of the screen to get back to the DRAW screen.

To run the program, type the name and press the RETURN key.

How Firefighters Battle Wildfires

Firefighters used a three-pronged approach to battling the California wildfires in 1993. Protection of life and property was the first priority.

ENGINES

Engine companies, assigned to streets and homes, protect houses by wetting down brush, hillsides and sometimes roofs. They fight blazes in buildings that catch fire.

HAND CREWS

Teams of 15-16 people use shovels, chain saws and other tools to clear brush and trees, making a clear fire line about 3-6 feet wide. Strong winds usually make it too dangerous to work at the front of the fire. Bulldozers cut wider paths, but can't work on hillsides.

AIRCRAFT

Helicopters drop up to 360 gallons of water at a time directly on the flames. Tanks can be refilled in a minute. Airplane tankers drop a fire-retardant material ahead of the flames. Aircraft will sometimes be used to protect a threatened house.

FIRESTORMS

Whirling masses of hot air called firestorms can wreak havoc:

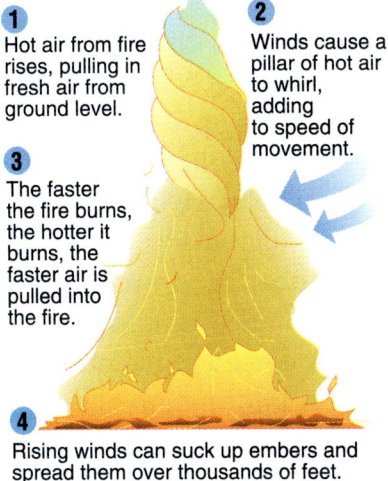

1 Hot air from fire rises, pulling in fresh air from ground level.

2 Winds cause a pillar of hot air to whirl, adding to speed of movement.

3 The faster the fire burns, the hotter it burns, the faster air is pulled into the fire.

4 Rising winds can suck up embers and spread them over thousands of feet.

PROTECTION

Crews are dressed in Nomex, a fire-resistant material, and carry pup-tent like shelters, known as "shake and bakes," for protection if flames are about to overrun them.

FLAMES

Fire usually burns uphill, but can spread whichever way the wind blows, and can jump 8-lane highways.

Winds Fuel Fires

Hot, dry "Santa Ana winds" fueled fires in California. Where they come from:

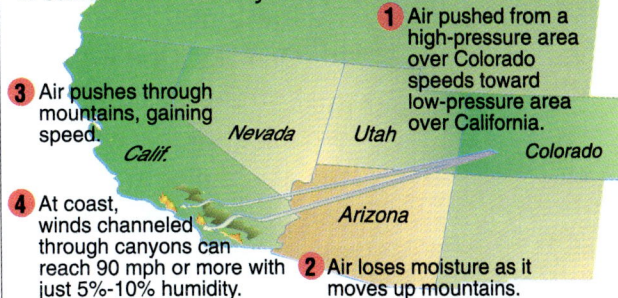

1 Air pushed from a high-pressure area over Colorado speeds toward low-pressure area over California.

2 Air loses moisture as it moves up mountains.

3 Air pushes through mountains, gaining speed.

4 At coast, winds channeled through canyons can reach 90 mph or more with just 5%-10% humidity.

Calif.   *Nevada*   *Utah*   *Colorado*   *Arizona*

Source: Los Angeles County Fire Department; *USA Today* Research, Weather Services Corp.

A universal symbol in art, literature, and folklore, the kite is an efficient and peaceful aircraft. The earliest historic references date to the fourth century B.C., when Kungshu Phan, a Chinese engineer, reportedly sent aloft a "wooden bird." Accounts of kites are also found in the annals of ancient Egypt and Greece.

From Benjamin Franklin's experiments with electricity to the Wright Brothers' first flight, kites have played key roles in scientific discovery and the study of weather. But even for scientists, kite flying can represent a way to relax and have fun. Alexander Graham Bell, the inventor of the telephone, designed a massive six-sided kite that could carry a person into the air.

In the modern world, the venerable kite is experiencing a renaissance that may carry with it a new role as a symbol of global cooperation. The historic 1985 summit meeting of Presidents Ronald Reagan of the United States and Mikhail Gorbachev of the USSR marked a significant step towards peace between the super-powers. The spirit of that meeting inspired American kite designer Jane Parker-Ambrose to create a kite commemorating this new promise of global harmony. The flags of the US and the USSR are joined on the face of the kite. Halley's Comet, which revisited Earth in 1986 for the first time in seventy-six years, is shown as a portent of peace.

On a "people to people" visit to Moscow that year, Jane presented her kite, along with a letter of friendship signed by some 300 kite flyers from the US, Canada, Japan, and the United Kingdom, to the Soviet Women's Peace Committee. This gesture of international goodwill gave birth to the idea for One Sky, One World, an annual global kite-fly held each year on the second Sunday in October. A non-profit organization based in Denver, Colorado, its mission is to focus the entire planet's attention on the need to maintain peace and protect the environment. (For information about now to take part, write to: One Sky, One World, P.O. Box 11149, Denver, CO 80211, USA.)

The first One Sky, One World kite-fly took place in 1986, with more than 10,000 kites and 40,000 participants at ninety locations in fourteen countries. In just six years, the event has grown to include more than 250,000 people in twenty-four countries. In October 1991, One Sky, One World events were held in Moscow, Washington, DC, Bombay, Berlin, Sydney, Beijing, and many other major cities. Kite-flyers from Japan, France, Colombia, Guam, Chile, England, Hungary, Italy, The Netherlands, Scotland, Spain, Hawaii, Alaska, and many other US locations joined in.

Source: Tom Krol, "One Sky, One World," *UNESCO Courier*, July-August 1992

Building	City	Stories	Height	
			ft	m
Sears Tower	Chicago	110	1,454	443
World Trade Center	New York	110	1,377	419
Empire State	New York	102	1,250	381
AMOCO	Chicago	80	1,136	346
John Hancock Center	Chicago	100	1,127	343
Chrysler	New York	77	1,046	319
First Interstate World Center	Los Angeles	73	1,017	310
Nations Plaza	Atlanta	55	1,025	312
Texas	Houston	75	1,002	305
Allied Bank	Houston	71	985	300
311 South Wacker Drive	Chicago	65	969	295
American International	New York	66	952	290
Society Tower	Cleveland	57	948	289
One Liberty Place	Philadelphia	62	945	288
Columbia Seafirst Center	Seattle	76	943	287
Citicorp Center	New York	59	915	279
40 Wall Tower	New York	71	900	274
Two Prudential Center	Chicago	64	900	274
Two Union Square	Seattle	56	886	270
Mellon Bank Center	Philadelphia	56	880	268
NationsBank Corporate Center	Charlotte	60	875	267
Water Tower Place	Chicago	74	859	262
First Interstate Bank	Los Angeles	62	858	261
Transamerica Pyramid	San Francisco	61	853	260
First National Bank	Chicago	60	851	259

Note: Height does not include TV towers and antennas.
Source: *1993 Information Please Almanac*

Snack	Potato Chips	Pretzels	Air-Popped Popcorn	Corn Chips	Salted Peanuts
Calories	152	111	76	153	170
Fat	10 g	1 g	1 g	9 g	14 g
Sodium	160 mg	451 mg	1 mg	218 mg	138 mg

Note: These figures are for a 1-ounce serving.

AGES OF AIRLINE FLEETS

Domestic Airlines	Total Fleet	Age of Aircraft			Average Age of Fleet
		20+ Years	15-20 Years	10-14 Years	
American	576	128	55	57	10.1
America West	108	12	5	19	7.4
Continental	324	83	62	42	13.8
Delta	462	33	91	93	9.2
Northwest	339	154	59	60	16.1
Pan Am	154	79	31	15	16.9
Southwest	106	0	7	41	6.8
TWA	205	97	39	31	17.1
United	467	133	47	129	12.6
USAir	465	82	23	116	9.7

Foreign Airlines	Total Fleet	Age of Aircraft			Average Age of Fleet
		20+ Years	15-20 Years	10-14 Years	
Air Canada	109	28	24	28	13.6
Air France	127	29	24	38	11.2
Alitalia	85	32	2	22	13.8
British Airways	211	36	24	57	10.5
Iberia	100	16	37	22	13.2
Japan Airlines	87	6	14	21	9.3
KLM	60	2	7	11	7.9
Lufthansa	179	0	19	49	6.9
SAS	111	25	23	5	10.5
Swissair	55	0	4	21	7.6

Note: Data as of March, 1991.
Source: *Turbine Airline Fleet Survey,* published by Aviation Information Services, Ltd.

Date	Flight Number	Shuttle Name	Crew Size	Days Duration
3/89	29	*Discovery*	5	5
5/89	30	*Atlantis*	5	4
8/89	28	*Columbia*	5	5
10/89	34	*Atlantis*	5	5
11/89	33	*Discovery*	5	5
1/90	32	*Columbia*	5	10
2/90	36	*Atlantis*	5	5
4/90	31	*Discovery*	5	6
10/90	41	*Discovery*	5	4
11/90	38	*Atlantis*	5	4
12/90	35	*Columbia*	7	9
4/91	37	*Atlantis*	5	6
4/91	39	*Discovery*	7	8
6/91	40	*Columbia*	7	9
8/91	43	*Atlantis*	5	9
11/91	44	*Atlantis*	6	7
1/92	42	*Discovery*	7	7
5/92	45	*Atlantis*	7	8
5/92	49	*Endeavour*	7	7
6/92	50	*Columbia*	7	13
9/92	46	*Atlantis*	7	7
9/92	47	*Endeavour*	7	7
11/92	52	*Columbia*	6	9
12/92	53	*Discovery*	5	4

Source: U.S. National Aeronautics
and Space Administration

GLOSSARY INDEX

A

Acceleration, 75, **92,** 93, 96, 97, 98, 99, 100, 102, 103
   rate of change in speed
   intervals of, 101
   rates of, 101

Accounting, 76

Accuracy, 202

Acute
   angles, 9
   triangle, 45

Adding, 99

Adjacent side, 117, 133

Age, 2, 190, 226, 260

Algebra
   axes, 89, 126, 128, 129, 130, 131, 136
   conversion factor, 50, 51
   coordinate, 99
   coordinates in an ordered pair, 99
   dependent variable, 122, 123, 126, 127, 128, 130
   equation, 120, 126, 127, 128, 130
   grid, 110
   horizontal axis, 85, 86, 87, 89
   independent variable, 120, 122, 123, 126, 127, 128, 130
   intervals, 95
   negative number, 99
   ordered pairs, 126, 128, 129, 130, 131, 136
   ordering, 44
   plot, 69, 87
   positive number, 99
   vertical axis, 85, 86, 87, 88, 89

Amount, 53

Analysis, 46, 168

Analyze, 94, 95, 96, 100, 101, 165, 180
   data, 75

Angles, 8, 9, 116, 117, 133, 134, 223, 247
   acute, 9
   measurement, 178
   obtuse, 9
   right, 9, 117, 133

Apple II, 173

Apple-S, 173

Approximate, 120, 234

Archimedes' principle, 40, 56

Area, 4, 8, 39, 45, 56, 73, 219

Assumptions, 20

Average, 80, 93, 108, 122, 127, 142, 195, 197, 203, 204, 205, 209, 211, 212, 213, 214, 224, 225, 226, 233, 237
   age, 260
   annual depreciation, 129
   distance, 195
   speed, 92, 93, 94, 100, 101, 104

Axes, 87, 88, 89, 126
   set of, 128, 129, 130, 131, 136

B

Base, 67, 96, 116, 179, 180

Basic, 132

Bell-shaped curve, 217, 218, 227

Between, 71, 72, 170, 171

Bivariate data, 52   data that uses two variables

Bottom, 38

Box-and-whisker plot, 196
   a graph in which the lines show the two extremes, and the data is broken into quarters

Braking distance, 77, 107

Budget, 200

C

Calculate, 55, 61, 67, 79, 81, 92, 100, 101, 116, 117, 120, 122, 124, 131, 226

Calculator, 42, 79, 80, 118, 133, 156, 159, 164, 195, 196, 211, 212, 213, 214

Calibrated, 62, 64

Calories, 259

Center, 13, 37, 80, 94, 134, 169, 172, 217
   line, 210

Centimeter ruler, 50, 51

Centimeters, 4, 42, 47, 48, 59, 61, 95, 221

Centrifugal force, 242

Cents, 2, 190

Chance, 174

Change, 75

Chaos, 172, 182

Chaos theory, 182

Charts, 59, 61, 92, 100, 101, 107, 120, 121, 192, 198, 207, 221

Circle, 4, 13, 18, 37, 73, 99, 242

Circumference, 4, 80, 120, 142

Columns, 61, 107

Combinations, 16, 30, 52, 109, 158

Compound interest, 111, **131,** 132, 250   the amount of interest your investment has earned that is added to the principal, where it becomes part of the amount used to compute the interest earned in the next period

Compounding, 132, 250
   earned interest credited to your account more than once a year

infinite, 180
negative, 99
positive, 99
two-digit, 16

O

Obtuse
angles, 9
triangle, 45
Octagon, 7
One square unit, 8
Operation symbols, 30
Operations, 16
Opposite, 24
side, 117, 133
Order, 23
Ordered pairs, 126, 128, 129, 130, 131, 136
Ordering, 44
Ounces, 227, 259
Outcome, 32

P

Paper folding, 161, 168,, 183
Parallelogram, 4, 7, 45
Pascal's Triangle, 176
triangular arrangement of numbers in which each number is the sum of the two numbers to the right and to the left of it in the row above
Pattern, 45, 47, 48, 61, 107, 111, 124, 125, 173, 176, 178
Pentagon, 7
Pentominoes, 11 a polyomino made of five adjacent square tiles
Per beam, 200
Per day, 207

Per minute, 200
Percent, 130, 139, 155, 157, 158, 187, 217
of, 157
Percentage, 22, 62, 76, 129, 233
Perimeter, 4, 124, 125
Perpendicular, 242
Plot, 69, 87, 88, 89, 99, 170, 171, 194, 210
Point, 87, 88, 89, 95, 99, 124, 133, 134, 169, 170, 171, 173, 179, 220
starting, 173
Polygons, 7, 28, 178
Polyominoes, 7, 10, 11
shapes made by placing square tiles side by side (adjacent).Each polyomino can be named by the number of tiles used.
Pounds, 240, 241
Predict, 137, 142, 165
Price-earnings ratios, 112
Price per gallon, 108
Principal, 131
Principle, 40
Prisms, 50
Probability, 22, 32
factor, 174, 175
Problem solving, 12, 18, 22, 43, 78, 81, 154, 198
extended problem, 142, 149
problem of the week, 27-32, 69-74, 104-110, 143-148, 150, 183-188, 223-228
strategies, 192
Properties of distributions, 217
Properties of fractals, 178

Proportion, 135, 139 a mathematical sentence that states that two ratios are equal
Protractor, 134
Pyramid, 4, 179

Q

Quadrilateral, 4, 7
Quantities, 2, 152, 190

R

Radius, 4, 67
Random, 21, 32, 174
samples, 218
Range, 204, 211, 212, 213, 214, 216, 224
Rate, 127, 139, 150, 251
annual interest, 131
interest, 132
Rates of acceleration, 101
Ratios, 117, 133, 135, 158
median, 112
price-earnings, 112
Reasoning, 19
Rectangle, 7, 31, 45, 71, 172
Rectangular, 156
prisms, 44
Recursion, 182
Reduce, 155, 158, 187
Reduction, 158, 159, 181
Relationship, 4, 63, 65
Remainders, 177
Rep-Tiles, 28 polygons that can be fitted together to form the same shape in a larger size
Research, 62, 63, 121, 139
Revenue, 113

COVER: (tl), Gregory Sams/Science Photo Library/Photo Researchers, (tr), Joe Polimeni/Liaison International, (c), Mark Gallup/F-Stock, (bl), Mark Muench/AllStock, (bc), John Kelly/The Image Bank, (br), Jon Eisberg/FPG

iii(l), BLT Productions/Brent Turner, (r), Ron Rovtar; **ix**, Courtesy Carol McCabe; **x**, K S Studio/Bob Mullenix; **xi**, Alex Shoob Photography; **xii**, Doug Martin; **xiii**, Courtesy Stephen Lovett; **xiv**, W. Cody/Westlight; **xv**, Michael Falco; **xvi**, Courtesy Lupe Lloyd; **xvii**, Courtesy Fairfield Citizen-Newsphoto; **xviii**, Jed Shara/Westlight; **1**(l), Courtesy Carol McCabe, (r), Brian Drake/West Stock, (inset), Jon Eisberg/FPG; **2**(t), Courtesy Carol McCabe, (l), Brian Drake/West Stock; **3**(r), Brian Drake/West Stock, (screened), J. Sekowski, (cl), Culver Pictures, (cr), Courtesy Carol McCabe, (bl), Science Photo Library/Photo Researchers, (br), Jim Pickerell/Westlight; **4**, Ross Hickson; **5**, K S Studios/Bob Mullenix; **6**, Aaron Haupt Photography; **10**, Barney/InStock; **11**, Audrey Gibson; **12**, **13**, Doug Martin; **15**, Rick Weber; **16**, **17**(l), K S Studios/Bob Mullenix, (r), Bud Fowle; **18**, Elaine Comer-Shay; **19**, Doug Martin; **20**, Viesti Associates, Inc; **21**(l), file photo, (r), Rick Weber; **22**(l), Scott Cunningham, (r), K S Studios/Bob Mullenix; **23**(r), John Lewis Stage/The Image Bank, (tl)(c), Index Stock, (bl), Telegraph Colour Library/FPG; **25**, Lee Foster/FPG; **26**, Brian Stablyk/AllStock; **27**, Studiohio; **28**(l), Courtesy Professor S. W. Golomb, (r), USC News Service; **29**(l), Mak-1, (r), James W. Kay/Photobank; **30**(l), Studiohio, (r), Todd Yarrington; **31**, LEGO Systems, Inc, Creative Services Department; **32**, K S Studios/Bob Mullenix; **33**(l), Alex Shoob; (r), Don & Pat Valenti/DRK Photo, (inset), Mark Gallup/F-Stock; **34**(t), Alex Shoob, (l), Don & Pat Valenti/DRK Photo; **35**(t), Scott Cunningham, (r), Don & Pat Valenti/DRK Photo, (screened), D. Cavagnaro/DRK Photo, (cl), file photo, (cr), Douglas Engle/Gamma-Liaison, (bl), Michael Nichols/Magnum, (br), Alex Shoob; **36**, **37**(t)(c)(b), Scott Cunningham, (r), K S Studios/Bob Mullenix; **38**, **39**, K S Studios/Bob Mullenix; **40**, Scott Cunningham; **41**(l), K S Studios/Bob Mullenix, (r), Bruce Byers/FPG; **42**, Tom Benoit/AllStock; **43**, **44**, K S Studios/Bob Mullenix; **45**, Charles O'Rear/Westlight; **47**(r), K S Studios/Bob Mullenix, (bl), Joseph A. DiChello, Jr, (br), file photo; **48**(l), Sharon M. Kurgis, (r), Geri Murphy; **49**, Maria Pape/FPG; **50**(l), Tom Bean/AllStock, (r), Crown Studios; **51**(l), Mak-1, (r), K S Studios/Bob Mullenix; **52**, Chuck O'Rear/West Light; **53**, K S Studios/Bob Mullenix; **54**, Mak-1; **56**(l), B. Kurosaki/InStock, (r), Historical Pictures/Stock Montage, (b), Michael Melford/The Image Bank; **57**, K S Studios/Bob Mullenix; **58**, Mak-1; **59**, **60**, **61**, K S Studios/Bob Mullenix; **62**, Kenneth Garrett/West Light; **63**(t), Scott Cunningham, (b), Tony Freeman/PhotoEdit; **64**, Doug Martin; **65**, Andy Caulfield/The Image Bank; **66**, Tony Schanuel/Photographic Resource; **67**, Larry Lefever from Grant Heilman; **68**, Kay McClain; **69**, Grafton M. Smith/The Image Bank; **70**, Scott Cunningham; **71**, Life Images; **72**, Ken Frick; **73**, **74**, Life Images; **75**(l), Courtesy Stephen Lovett, (r), Louis Bencze/AllStock, (inset), John Kelly/The Image Bank; **76**(t), Courtesy Stephen Lovett, (l), Louis Bencze/AllStock; **77**(t), Scott Cunningham, (r), Louis Bencze/All Stock; (screened), Doug Martin, (cl), file photo, (cr), W. D. Kesler/Photo Resources, (bl), Photoworld/FPG, (bc), file photo, (br), Courtesy Stephen Lovett; **78-79**(b), Index Stock Intl, Inc; **78**(t)(c)(b), Scott Cunningham; **81**(t), Elaine Comer-Shay, (b), J. Zimmerman/FPG; **82**(l), Todd Yarrington, (r),

83, K S Studios/Bob Mullenix; **84**(t), Tom Bean/AllStock, (b), G. Robert Bishop/HMS Group/AllStock; **85**(l)(c), K S Studios/Bob Mullenix, (r), Doug Martin; **86**(l), Doug Martin, (r), K S Studios/Bob Mullenix; **87, 88, 89**, Doug Martin; **90**(t), David Ulmer/Stock Boston, (b), Steve Lissau; **91**, Bruce Mathews/Photo Resources; **92**, NASA; **93, 95**, K S Studios/Bob Mullenix; **96**(l), Bob Daemmrich/Stock Boston, (r), Chromosohm/Sohm/AllStock; **97**(l), Aaron Haupt Photography, (r), Jian Chen/Index Stock Intl, Inc, (b), Charles Krebs/AllStock; **98**, Aaron Haupt Photography; **99**, Bernard Asset/Agence Vandystadt/Photo Researchers; **100**, Scott Cunningham; **101**(tl), Bill Gallery/Stock Boston, (bl), Don Graham/AllStock; (r), David Madison/DUOMO; **102**, Stacy Pick/Stock Boston; **103**(tr), James W. Kay/Index Stock Intl, Inc, (cr), Photo Sunstar/F-Stock, (bl), Chris Noble/AllStock, (br), Caroline Wood/F-Stock; **104**(tl), Reed Khestner/Zephyr Pictures, (tr), Tony Freeman/PhotoEdit, (bl), Myrleen Ferguson/PhotoEdit, (br), Reed Khestner/Zephyr Pictures; **105**, K S Studios/Bob Mullenix; **106**, NASA; **107**(l), Ellis Herwig/Stock Boston, (r), K S Studios/Bob Mullenix; **108**, Doug Martin; **109**, Ken Frick; **110**(t), Aaron Haupt Photography, (b), Larry Hamill; **111**(l), Michael Falco, (r), Ted Russell/The Image Bank, (inset), Mark Muench/AllStock; **112**(t), Michael Falco, (l), Ted Russell/The Image Bank; **113**(t), Scott Cunningham, (r), Ted Russell/The Image Bank, (screened), K S Studios/Bob Mullenix, (cl), The Telegraph Colour Library/FPG, (cr), Aaron Haupt Photography; (b), Michael Falco; **114**, Scott Cunningham; **115**, Rick Weber; **116**(l), Tibor Bognar/The Stock Market, (r), Anna Zuckerman/PhotoEdit; **117**, Scott Cunningham; **118**, David Ball/The Stock Market; **119**, Kaz Mori/The Image Bank; **120**(l), Scott Cunningham, (r), Orion Press/Stock Imagery; **121**(t), Richard Stockton/Photobank, (r), Henryk T. Kaiser/Stock Imagery; **122**(l), Elaine Comer-Shay, (r), Scott Cunningham; **123**, Luis Castaneda/The Image Bank; **124**, Joseph DiChello; **125**, Ed Bock/The Stock Market; **126**(t), Rick Weber, (b), Courtesy of The Norman Rockwell Museum at Stockbridge; **127**(l), Viviane Holbrooke/The Stock Market, (r), Gary Crallé/The Image Bank; **128**(l), Howard Sochurek/The Stock Market, (r), Ted Horowitz/The Stock Market; **129**(l), Doug Martin, (r), Jean Miele/The Stock Market; **130**(l), Alexander Tsiaras/Stock Boston, (r), John Coletti/Stock Boston; **131**, Rick Weber; **132**, Paul Conklin/PhotoEdit; **133**, Romilly Lockyer/The Image Bank; **134**, Jeff Spielman/Stockphotos/The Image Bank; **135**(l), Rick Weber, (r), Scott Cunningham; **136**(l), Chromosohm/Sohm/The Stock Market, (r), Tom VanSant/The Geosphere Project/The Stock Market; **137**, Alan Schein/The Stock Market; **138**, Tom Brakefield/The Stock Market; **139**(t), Edgeworth Productions/The Stock Market, (b), Peter Steiner/The Stock Market; **140**(l), Robert Essel/The Stock Market, (r), Howard Sochurek/The Stock Market; **141**(t), Carriere/Photobank, (c), Camera Tokyo/Stock Imagery, (bl), Tim Courlas, (br), Doug Martin, **142**(l), Harald Sund/The Image Bank, (r), M. Richards/PhotoEdit; **143**(t), The Granger Collection, (c), Elaine Comer-Shay, (bl), Cornelius Hogenbirk/Stock Imagery, (br), J. Ramey/The Image Bank; **144**(l), P & G Bowater/The Image Bank, (r), Jonathan Selig/Photo 20-20; **145**, Scott Cunningham; **146**, Craig Hammell/The Stock Market; **147**, Aaron Haupt Photography; **148**(bl), Steve Bentsen/Stock Imagery, (tl), K S Studios/Bob Mullenix, (r), Drawing by Stevenson; ©1974 The New Yorker Magazine, Inc; **149**(l), Don Johnston/Photo-Nats, (r), Jeff Spielman//Stockphotos/The Image Bank; **150**, Aaron Haupt

Photography; **151**(l), Courtesy Lupe Lloyd, (r),KS Studios/Bob Mullenix, (inset), Gregory Sams/Science Photo Library/Photo Researchers; **152**(l), K S Studios/Bob Mullenix, (t), Courtesy Lupe Lloyd; **153**(t), BLT Productions/Brent Turner, (r), (screened), K S Studios/Bob Mullenix, (cl), The Bettmann Archive, (cr), Aaron Haupt Photography, (bl), Steve Niedorf/The Image Bank, (bc), Doug Martin, (br), Courtesy Lupe Lloyd; **154, 155**(t)(b), BLT Productions/Brent Turner, (c), Studiohio; **156, 157**(t), BLT Productions/Brent Turner, (b), K S Studios/Bob Mullenix; **158**, Todd Yarrington; **159**, BLT Productions/Brent Turner; **160**(l), K S Studios/Bob Mullenix, (r), Matt Meadows; **161**(l), Felicia Martinez/PhotoEdit, (r), Studiohio; **162**(l), Janice Sheldon/Photo 20-20, (r), Scott Cunningham; **163**(t), Gene Frazier, (b), William J. Weber; **164**, Jeffrey Sylvester/FPG; **165**, Studiohio; **166**, W. Cody/WestLight; **167**, Homer W. Smith/Peter Arnold, Inc; **168**, Scott Camazine/Photo Researchers/ **169**, Gregory Sams/Science Photo Library/Photo Researchers; **170**, Studiohio; **171**, Steve Bentsen/Stock Imagery/ **172**, Hickson-Bender Photography; **173**(l), Gregory Sams/Science Photo Library/Photo Researchers, (r), Hickson-Bender Photography; **174**, Stan Osolinski/The Stock Market; **175**, David Frazier Photo Library/PhotoBank; **176**(l), Studiohio, (b), Ken Ross/FPG; **177**(l), Masa Uemura/AllStock, (r) Chuck O'Rear/WestLight; **178**, Gregory Sams/Science Photo Library/Photo Researchers; **179**, Gene Stein/WestLight; **180**, Ron Rovtar; **181**, Carlos Ginzburg; **182**(l), Homer W. Smith/Peter Arnold, Inc, (r), Gregory Sams/Science Photo Library/Photo Researchers; **183**, Alvis Upitus/The Image Bank; **184**, K S Studios/Bob Mullenix; **185**, Scott Cunningham; **186**, Doug Martin; **188**, The Bettmann Archive; **189**(l), Courtesy Fairfield Citizen-Newsphoto, (r), K S Studios/Bob Mullenix, (inset), Joe Polimeni/Liason International; **190**(t), Courtesy Jill Sheiman, (l), K S Studios/Bob Mullenix; **191**(t) BLT Productions/Brent Turner, (r)(screened), K S Studios/Bob Mullenix, (cr), Courtesy Jill Sheiman, (cl), Used with the permission of General Mills, Inc, (b), Courtesy Famous Amos Cookies; **192-193**(b), Warren Morgan/Westlight; **192**(t)(c)(b), **193**(l) BLT Productions/Brent Turner, (r), C. Bush/FPG; **194**, BLT Productions/Brent Turner; **195**, Del Sol Productions/The Image Bank; **196**(t), Bob Daemmrich Photography, (b), BLT Productions/Brent Turner; **197, 198**, BLT Productions/Brent Turner; **199**, Doug Martin; **200**(l), Paul Steel/The Stock Market, (r), John Ker/Superstock; **202, 203, 204, 205, 207, 208,** KS Studio/Bob Mullenix; **209**, Paul Chauncey/The Stock Market; **210**, Doug Martin; **211**, Paul Avis/FPG; **212**, Pete Saloutos/The Stock Market; **213**, K S Studios/Bob Mullenix; **214, 215**(l), BLT Productions/Brent Turner, (r), KS Studio/Bob Mullenix; **216**, Brownie Harris/The Stock Market; **217**, Mitch Diamond/Photobank; **218**(l), Mark Downey, (r), Mary Kate Denny/PhotoEdit; **219**, PH2 Dennis D. Taylor/U S Navy/Department of Defense; **220**(l), Kitt Peak National Observatory, (r), **221**, NASA; **222**, Courtesy Saturn Corporation; **223**, David Ball/AllStock; **224**(t), Gianni Cigolini/The Image Bank, (b), Studiohio; **225**, K S Studios/Bob Mullenix; **226**(l), Matt Meadows, (r), Doug Martin; **227**(l), Jeffry Myers/FPG, (tr)(br), Studiohio; **229**, K S Studios/Bob Mullenix; **230**, Jed Shara/Westlight; **231**, Doug Martin; **232**(tl), G. Anderson/The Stock Market, (cl), Dallas & John Heaton/Westlight, (cr), Willie Holdman/Photobank, (bl), Takeshi Takahara/Photo Researchers, (br), John Roberts/The Stock Market; **233**, Brian Stablyk/AllStock; **234**(l), Bill Ross/Westlight, (r), Douglas Peebles/Westlight; **235**, J. Pat Carter/Liason Internation; **236** (l)(c)(tr), Doug Martin, (br),

Tim Courlas; **237**(t), Courtesy Chrysler Corporation, Dodge Division, (bl), Elaine Comer-Shay, (br), Aaron Haupt Photography; **238**(t), Animals Animals/Anup & Manoj Shah, (b), Lynn M. Stone; **239, 241**, NASA; **242**, Paul L. Rueben; **243**, David Madison/DUOMO; **244**, Tom Ebenhoh/Photographic Resources; **245**(l), T. Zimmermann/FPG, (r), Peter Saloutos/Photographic Resources; **246**, Alain Choisnet/The Image Bank; **247**(r), F. Stuart Westmorland/Stock Imagery, (b), Harvey Lloyd/The Stock Market; **248**(l), Grant Faint/The Image Bank, (r), Tom Brakefield/The Stock Market; **249**(l), FRANK & ERNEST reprinted by permission of NEA, Inc, (r), Kaz Mori/The Image Bank; **250**(l), Rick Weber, (r), Garry Gay/The Image Bank; **251**, Steve Satushek/The Image Bank; **252**, Scott Cunningham; **253**, Grant V. Faint/The Image Bank; **254**, Tim Courlas; **256, 257**(b), Aaron Haupt Photography, (r), Axel Voss/One Sky One World; **258**, David Hanson/Tony Stone Images; **259**(tl), Aaron Haupt Photography, (bl)(r), Studiohio; **260**, Joe Towers/The Stock Market; **261**, NASA.

Acknowledgements

28, Herbert Kohl, Mathematical Puzzlements, Schocken Books, New York, 1987, p. 27. **12e,** Blackline Master 13-3A, 1989 Regents, University of California, EQUALS, Lawrence Hall of Science; **12f,** Blackline Master 13-3B, 1989 Regents, University of California, EQUALS, Lawrence Hall of Science; **36-43,** From *James and the Giant Peach* by Roald Dahl. Copyright 1961 by Roald Dahl. Copyright renewed 1989 by Roald Dahl and Alfred A. Knopf, Inc. Reprinted by permission of Alfred A. Knopf, Inc.; **119,** "The Oak and the Rose" from *A Light in the Attic* by Shel Silverstein. Copyright ©1981 by Evil Eye Music, Inc. Reprinted by permission of HarperCollins Publishers. **240–241,** Source: NASA Fact Sheet; **242,** "The Physics of Fear," by George Howe Colt. George Howe Colt, *Life Magazine* ©Time Warner, August 1993, pp. 68–71. Reprinted with permission; **252,** Reprinted from *Sports Afield* magazine, January 1991 Issue. Copyright 1991 The Hearst Corporation. All Rights Reserved; **253,** Joseph Needham, *Science and Civilisation in China,* Volume III, Cambridge: Cambridge University Press, 1959, p. 135; **260-261,** Tom Krol, "One Sky, One World," *UNESCO Courier*, July-August 1992. Reprinted from the UNESCO Courier.